Yoga Chudamani Upanishad

With kind regards, ॐ *and prem*

Swami Niranjan

Yoga Chudamani Upanishad

Crown Jewel of Yoga

Treatise on Kundalini Yoga

Original Sanskrit text with
Transliteration, Translation and Commentary

Swami Satyadharma

Under the Guidance of
Swami Niranjanananda Saraswati

Yoga Publications Trust, Munger, Bihar, India

Published by Yoga Publications Trust
     First edition 2003

ISBN: 81-86336-27-3
Price: Indian rupees one hundred and fifteen only

Publisher and distributor: Yoga Publications Trust, Ganga Darshan, Munger, Bihar, India.

Printed at Thomson Press (India) Limited, New Delhi, 110001

SWAMI SIVANANDA SARASWATI

Swami Sivananda was born at Patta-madai, Tamil Nadu, in 1887. After serving as a medical doctor in Malaya, he renounced his practice, went to Rishikesh and was initiated into Dashnami sannyasa in 1924 by Swami Vishwananda Saraswati. He toured extensively throughout India, inspiring people to practise yoga and lead a divine life. He founded the Divine Life Society at Rishikesh in 1936, the Sivananda Ayurvedic Pharmacy in 1945, the Yoga Vedanta Forest Academy in 1948 and the Sivananda Eye Hospital in 1957. During his lifetime Swami Sivananda guided thousands of disciples and aspirants all over the world and authored over 200 books.

SWAMI SATYANANDA SARASWATI

Swami Satyananda was born at Almora, Uttar Pradesh, in 1923. In 1943 he met Swami Sivananda in Rishikesh and adopted the Dashnami sannyasa way of life. In 1955 he left his guru's ashram to live as a wandering mendicant and later founded the International Yoga Fellowship in 1963 and the Bihar School of Yoga in 1964. Over the next 20 years Swami Satyananda toured internationally and authored over 80 books. In 1987 he founded Sivananda Math, a charitable institution for aiding rural development, and the Yoga Research Foundation. In 1988 he renounced his mission, adopting kshetra sannyasa, and now lives as a paramahamsa sannyasin.

SWAMI NIRANJANANANDA SARASWATI

Swami Niranjanananda was born at Rajnandgaon, Madhya Pradesh, in 1960. At the age of four he joined the Bihar School of Yoga and was initiated into Dashnami sannyasa at the age of ten. From 1971 he travelled overseas and toured many countries for the next 11 years. In 1983 he was recalled to India and appointed President of Bihar School of Yoga. During the following 11 years he guided the development of Ganga Darshan, Sivananda Math and the Yoga Research Foundation. In 1990 he was initiated as a paramahamsa and in 1993 anointed preceptor in succession to Swami Satyananda. Bihar Yoga Bharati was founded under his direction in 1994. He has authored over 20 books and guides national and international yoga programs.

SWAMI SATYASANGANANDA SARASWATI

Swami Satyasangananda (Satsangi) was born on 24th March 1953, in Chandorenagore, West Bengal. From the age of 22 she experienced a series of inner awakenings which led her to her guru, Swami Satyananda. From 1981 she travelled ceaselessly with her guru in India and overseas and developed into a scholar with deep insight into the yogic and tantric traditions as well as modern sciences and philosophies. She is an efficient channel for the transmission of her guru's teachings. The establishment of Sivananda Math in Rikhia is her creation and mission, and she guides all its activities there, working tirelessly to uplift the weaker and underprivileged areas. She embodies compassion with clear reason and is the foundation of her guru's vision.

Contents

Introduction

In order to understand the Upanishads, it is necessary to study the Vedas, and equally important to travel back into history and learn about the customs, races, civilizations, societies and cultures of those ancient times. Ancient India was once a vast country, covering Iraq, Iran, Afghanistan and Pakistan in the western region; Nepal, Sikkim, Bhutan, Tibet, some parts of western China and Asiatic Russia in the northern region; Bangladesh, Burma, Thailand, Laos and Cambodia in the eastern region; and Sri Lanka and the Lemurian continent in the southern region.

In prehistoric times many great civilizations flourished in the equatorial belt, and on the ancient Indian sub-continent various cultures developed side by side. Iraq and Iran were known as Aranya Vraja, and the Aranyak civilization developed there. Afghanistan was known as Gandhar Desh, which gave birth to the Gandhar civilization. Beside the Indus River, the Indus Valley civilization developed, and alongside the Saraswati River, the vedic culture evolved. The Dravidian race lived in the south-western region of the Indus River and the Magadhi culture flourished in the eastern region of this land.

These different civilizations belonged basically to the Aryan races in the north and the Dravidian races in the south. The Aryans developed the vedic culture while the

Dravidians may have developed the tantric culture, which is non-vedic in origin. In ancient times, the Aryans and Dravidians fought many bloody battles to settle in the land of their choice. In the course of time, these warring tribes compromised amongst themselves, demarcated their boundaries, developed their empires, acquired social skills, languages, scripts and spiritual ideologies, while maintaining their racial identity which was reflected in their customs, lifestyle and social conduct.

Vedic culture

The word *Arya* means 'noble', 'pure', 'one with spiritual values'. The Aryans had a polytheistic-monistic religion and philosophy. They worshipped and personified nature. It was their belief that they could influence and pacify nature through sacrifices performed to gods, who represented the different elements. In the Rig Veda the gods are classified as terrestrial, celestial and atmospheric. The hymns of the Rig Veda are expressions of primeval worship, pacifying and eulogizing personified aspects of nature, like Indra (thunder), Surya (sun), Vayu (wind), Usha (dawn) and so on.

Fire sacrifice was an important aspect of vedic culture. Fire is the most natural symbol of spirit hidden in matter, and fire offerings provide a natural way of communicating with the inner spiritual reality. In this respect, all of the ancient cultures were vedic in origin, as fire sacrifice was the most universal custom. It was an inherent part of the Greek, Roman, Celtic, German, Persian, Hebrew, Babylonian, Egyptian, Chinese and American Indian traditions, and their gods reflect its cosmic meaning. The fire ritual is part of the solar religion or the religion of light, which is found throughout the ancient world. Fire on earth represents the Sun in heaven as the immanent presence of the luminous, divine spirit.

According to vedic teachings, the Aryan race descended from Manu, the original man, who established the vedic culture along the banks of the Saraswati River in northern India. The Aryans were living in India well before 6000 BC, and vedic India was a pivot for the spread of spiritual culture throughout the world during these early times. The Aryan culture was not derived from Europe, the Middle East or Iran, but from the Himalayan region and the Saraswati and Gangetic planes. Civilization in these early times moved from the east to the west and not vice-versa. India, being larger and more fertile, was better able to support larger numbers of people. It was a more favourable region for the growth of civilization than the Middle East or the colder European countries to the west.

There is no archaeological evidence to support the theory that the Aryans invaded India. The vedic culture was a natural development of the early indigenous tribes of north-west India, and not of any invaders. The Vedas suggest that the Indus Valley civilization belongs to the late vedic period. Recent excavations at Mehrgarh, however, show that the vedic civilization goes back to 6000 BC, and that it did not develop from outside influences. Such sites reflect the earlier vedic age. There is no evidence of any Indo-Aryan invasion or conquest of the Indian sub-continent. All evidence refutes this. The vedic people were not nomadic invaders. Their place of origin, the Saraswati river region, is described in the Vedas during and before the Indus Valley civilization, but not after, when the Aryan invasions were supposed to have occurred.

Related ancient cultures

The ancient Persian culture was also Aryan and was very close to the vedic culture. Persians were originally *kshatriyas* or warrior tribes called *Druhyus*, who separated from the vedic culture. They moved out of India in the direction of

Afghanistan, and may have been the ancestors of the Indo-Aryan people. Vedic and Persian cultures often intermingled as they bordered each other. Afghanistan had both vedic and Persian influences. According to references in the *Zend Avesta*, the Persians first came from this area. The Zoroastrian religion arose in Afghanistan and spread to the west, displacing vedic-Aryans in Iran. As the Persians moved into Iran and the Middle East, they encountered and displaced earlier Aryan people, whose culture was closer to the vedic. The early Aryan people of the Middle East were Indo-Aryan, not Iranian. The Iranians were related invaders or reformers who took over a vedic culture which dominated the region from Iran to Syria by 1500 BC.

In ancient times the people from India to Egypt were part of the same culture, which became divided as time passed and values changed. The predominant worship was Sun worship, and vedic gods like Varuna, Mitra, Yama, Indra, Agni and Soma were worshipped. In this light, the Rig Veda may be considered the oldest authority of the Middle East. In it can be traced the origins of the spiritual cultures of this area, including Islam, Christianity, Judaism, and the ancient religions of Egypt, Assyria and Babylon, as well as of the Persians and Hittites. Its connection to the people of the world beyond these regions can also be traced.

The people of many pre-Christian tribes living in Europe three to four thousand years ago were also kindred spirits to the vedic-Aryans of India. The Celts, for example, were a spiritual people, speaking an Indo-European language which was very similar to Sanskrit. They were grouped into tribes which spanned the entire European continent, from Turkey to Britain and Ireland. Along with the Celts, other Baltic, Slavic, German and Nordic tribes, settling as far north as Iceland, had languages and spiritual traditions which were on a par with the early vedic culture. The fire sacrifice was also the central ritual of most of these cultures and many of

4

the gods, whom they worshipped, correspond directly to those of the vedic pantheon. A wide route from India through Afghanistan, across the Caucus Mountains and southern Russia, along the west coast of Europe, as far north as Iceland, marks the passage of the vedic culture, which was a major influence on the lifestyle and thought of the Indo-European races.

Transmission of knowledge

The vedic civilization developed by the Aryans was a broad culture of yogic and spiritual values, encompassing the whole of life. It was a multifaceted culture, containing monotheism, polytheism and non-theistic systems, which recognized the divine as one form, all forms and beyond all form. In this way, the vedic culture represents the spiritual values that have motivated all great religions and cultures from the beginning of time. All spiritual views, experiences and philosophies are acceptable within it and each is accorded recognition in its proper place.

This basic drive to attain spiritual enlightenment propelled some of the Aryans to dedicate themselves to the discovery of metaphysical truths beyond the realm of the senses, mind, matter and individuality. They became known as the *rishis* or seers who, in their enlightened state, heard certain mantras which were later compiled as the Vedas. The word *veda* means 'knowledge', 'wisdom'. Just as gravity existed before Newton, although the credit goes to him for discovering and explaining it logically, in the same way, the vedic mantras were heard and discovered in contemplative states by the seers, who later on described and explained them to their followers.

Therefore, the Vedas are known as *shruti*, meaning 'heard'. The process of committing to memory is known as *smriti*. I speak: you hear and memorize it. You speak and a third person memorizes it. Transfer of knowledge from mind to mind through speech is known as shruti and smriti. In this way, the Vedas were transmitted orally and retained in the memory in ancient times. They were written down only after the Aryans came in contact with the Sharda script.

Some scholars speculate that it was the Sharda script which eventually evolved into Sanskrit, while others hold the view that the Brahmi script was the original. From Sanskrit, various other Indo-European languages emerged. In the meantime the other Aryan tribes which had settled in different parts of Europe developed their own forms of language and script. This accounts for the similarities in speech that exist between Sanskrit and European languages such as Latin, German, French, Spanish and English, yet the script remains totally different: for example, Mother (English), Matri (Sanskrit), Mater (Latin), Madre (Spanish), Mutter (German).

Vedic timeline

The antiquity of the Vedas has been argued by historians and research scholars, such as Max Muller, B.G. Tilak and others. They all accept the fact that the vedic era in India started to decline sometime around 500 BC and the origin of vedic culture is lost in the remote past. Some historians have used astrological evidence found in the Rig Veda to set the date for the present version of the Vedas at around 4500 BC. Generally it takes a civilization about three to four thousand years to evolve and reach a peak of human experience and expression. If the Vedas were written down at the peak of the Aryan civilization, then the date of the early period of Aryan civilization would go back three to four thousand years from 4500 BC, thus taking the antiquity of the Aryan civilization to about 8000 BC.

It should not be construed here that, by assigning a date for the birth of the Aryan civilization, a date for the origin of the Vedas could be finalized. The beginning of the Vedas is lost in the remote past. The eternal message of the Vedas was passed from one mind to the next, from one generation to the next, from one civilization to the next. It was probably passed on to the Aryan civilization by the previous civilization as it breathed its last breath. Knowledge is eternal; man is not.

In the ancient scriptures, earthly time and years are divided into *yugas* or ages. According to various theories, we now live in the last yuga, which is the Kali yuga. According to scriptural as well as mathematical calculations, the duration of Kali yuga is approximately 432,000 years. Prior to the Kali age was the Dvapara yuga, which lasted for 864,000 years. According to Hindu mythology, Sri Krishna was born towards the end of Dvapara yuga. It was during this time that sage Krishna Dwaipayana, commonly referred to as Veda Vyasa, classified the Vedas. Therefore, it can also be construed here that the Vedas are more ancient than Sri Krishna.

Going back even further in time, prior to the Dvapara age, was the Treta yuga, which lasted for 1,728,000 years. According to Hindu myth, Sri Rama was born during this age. In the *Ramayana*, the great epic of the Hindus, it is mentioned that Sri Rama had studied the Vedas and the Vedangas. If the mythology is considered to be correct in account and coincides with the history of humanity, then we can safely say that the Vedas predate Sri Rama.

Tantric culture

Even before the Vedas came into the limelight, it can be hypothesized that another well-established philosophy existed in the Indian sub-continent, which was known as Tantra. The tantric system of ancient India was a highly developed universal philosophy and practical science which motivated and guided the individual to develop intuitive and esoteric experiences. The Vedas were vocal utterances

7

while the Tantras were esoteric experiences. The first cross-cultural exchange between the Vedas and the Tantras took place in the Indus Valley civilization at Harappa and Mohenjodaro.

We find that Harappa is an ancient tantric name. *Hara* is one of the names of Lord Shiva, the principle deity of the tantrics, and *Appa* in many of the Dravidian dialects, even today, means 'father'. Thus Harappa was the land of father Shiva. In ancient days Tantra had two divisions: one was philosophical and the other was practical. These in turn were divided into two branches, known as the *Shaiva* and the *Shakta* traditions of the Tantras.

As the Aryan thought mingled with the thought of the Dravidian civilizations in the sub-continent, the philosophy of the Vedas underwent a transformation. The Rig Veda, the first Veda of hymns to various personified deities, remained very much the same, while the second, Yajur Veda, the Veda of sacrifices and rituals, represents this period of transition in vedic thought. The third, Sama Veda, the Veda of priestly chants, was meant mainly for monks and priests of the ancient traditions, while the fourth, Atharva Veda, is a cross between the vedic and tantric traditions, combining the essence of both cultures.

VEDANGAS AND UPA-VEDAS

In order to study the Vedas and understand their meaning it is necessary to know how the Vedas are divided, interpreted and which text comprises part of which Veda. The Vedangas are the limbs or *angas* of the Vedas. The Vedas are divided into six Vedangas, which are classified as follows:
1. *Kalpa* – code of rituals
2. *Shiksha* – learning, training in pronunciation
3. *Vyakarana* – grammar used in the Vedas
4. *Chhanda* – metre used in chanting the Vedas

5. *Nirukta* – etymology
6. *Jyotish* – astrology.

1. Kalpa Sutras form a body of literature which deals with the vedic samskaras and rituals that govern the life of an individual from birth until death. These rituals number about forty. These books have been further classified as *Srauta Sutras* (dealing with major rituals and sacrifices), *Grihya Sutras* (dealing with domestic rites and rules), *Dharma Sutras* (dealing with the code of behaviour and conduct) and *Shulva Sutras* (dealing with the science of making geometrical and proportionate *vedis* or fireplaces to be used for different vedic rites and ceremonies). The major and most famous Kalpa Sutras in this age are the works of Ashwalayan, Sankhyayana, Parashar, Vaijavapa, Katyayan, Varah, Kathak, Baudhayan, Apastambha, Hiranyakeshi, Vaikhanas, Agnivesh, Manav, Bharadwaj, Jaimini, Gobhil, Khadir, Latyayan, Drahyayana, Arsheya, Vaitan and Kaushik.

2. Shiksha literature comprises the detailed description of mantras, sounds, phonetics, script (consonants and vowels) and pronunciation. At present the following Shiksha literature is available:
• Rig Veda – *Paniniya Shiksha*
• Krishna Yajur Veda – *Vyasa Shiksha*
• Shukla Yajur Veda – *Yajnavalkya, Vashishthi, and Mandavya Shiksha*
• Sama Veda – *Gautamia Lomashiya and Naradiya Shiksha*
• Atharva Veda – *Manduki, Galadrik, Mana Swara and Kramasandhan Shiksha.*

Other Shiksha literature includes: *Katyayani, Parashari, Keshawi, Amoghanandini, Madhyandini, Mallasharma, Swarankash, Shodash Shloki, Awasan Nirnaya, Swarabhakti Lakshan and Pratishashakhya Pradip.*

3. Vyakarana, or grammar, defines the rules of the language and its usage of words. The main treatises are *Shakatayana Vyakarana Shastras* and *Paniniya Vyakarana,* which have been commented on by many scholars such as Katyayana and Patanjali. Apart from these, Saraswata, Kamadhenu, Hemchandra, Prakrit, Jainendra, Shakal, Kashakritsna, Kalap, Mugdhabodha grammars and Prakrit Prakash are famous Vyakarana Shastras.

4. Chhanda, or vedic metre, is described in the following literatures: *Samavediya Gargyaprokta Upanidan Sutra, Pingala Naagaprokta Chhanda Sutra, Vedook Madhawakrit Chhandanukramani, and Chhandasutra of Jayadeva.*

5. Niruktas are the encyclopaedias of the Vedas. Most of the Niruktas are lost. Ancient Nirukta literatures were by Kashyap, Shakapuni and others; however, at present it seems that only Yaskara's Nirukta literature is available.

6. Jyotish or vedic astrology was used to define the position and influence of celestial bodies prior to vedic ceremonies and samskaras. Ancient works of persons such as Narada, Parashar, Vashishtha, Varahamihir, Aryabhatta, Brahmagupta, Bhaskaracharya and Lagadhacharya are famous for their exposition of the subject.

Subsidiary Vedas

Upa-vedas are the four subsidiary Vedas, which include:
1. *Ayurveda* – science of medicine
2. *Gandharvaveda* – science of music
3. *Arthaveda* – political science and economy
4. *Sthapatyaveda* – vedic architecture.

1. Ayurveda is a part of Atharva Veda. It describes the ancient science of medicine, diagnosis and treatment of disease, hygiene, anatomy, physiology and surgery. Some of the literatures of Ayurveda are: (i) *Ashwini Kumar Samhita,* (ii) *Brahma Samhita,* (iii) *Mala Samhita,* (iv) *Dhanwantari Sutra,* (v) *Soop Sutra,* (vi) *Jabali Sutra,* (vii) *Charaka Samhita,* and (viii) *Ashtanga Hridaya.*

2. Gandharvaveda belongs to Sama Veda. Various aspects of music, dance, drama and performing arts have been discussed, such as ragas, rhythms, scales, instruments, dance beats etc. The main literatures on these topics are (i) *Natya Shastra* by Bharat Muni, (ii) *Sangeet Ratnakar* by Sharangadeva, and (iii) *Sangeet Darpan* by Damodar.

3. Arthaveda is a part of Rig Veda. It deals with economy, political science and the principles of practical life. Some of the major texts of this Upa-veda are: (i) *Artha Shastra* by Kautilya, (ii) *Chanakya Sutras*, (iii) *Nitivakyamrita Sutra*, (iv) *Kamandak*, (v) *Shukaniti*.

4. Sthapatyaveda, also known as Vastu Vidya or Vastu Shastra, is a part of Atharva Veda. It deals with the ancient science of architecture and engineering as well as sculpture and painting. Some of the important texts include: (i) *Samarangana Sutradhara*, (ii) *Vishvakarma Prakasu*, (iii) *Aparajita Preccha*, (iv) *Manasara* and (v) *Silparatna*.

Vedic interpretation

Training in interpretation and understanding of the vedic texts was also given in various ways, apart from the Vedangas. There are six accepted methods for this purpose: (i) nirukta, (ii) historical, (iii) mythological, (iv) ritualistic, (v) scientific and (vi) intuitive.

1. *Nirukta* is etymology, explanation or interpretation of the purpose behind any word that is written or spoken. The reason for this is to expand the awareness and inspire the individual to inquire about the origin of vedic speech.
2. *Historical* means comparing a particular event which has been mentioned in the Vedas with known history.
3. *Mythological* means utilizing ancient and modern folklore of various tribes and cultures to explain the vedic truths.
4. *Ritualistic* means practising the moral, physical, social and psychic code and discipline of the Vedas.
5. *Scientific* means identifying vedic events with natural phenomena and explaining them in scientific terms. In

the Vedas relevant facts are found about mathematics, astronomy, geography, geology, hydrostatics, agriculture, weaving, germs causing epidemic diseases, etc. Scientific truths may be ascertained by identifying certain phenomena mentioned in the Vedas, such as celestial constellations or conjunctions, a particular climate which may have occurred in a certain period of history or pre-history, certain geological formations unearthed by excavations, descriptions of certain cloud formations, the principles of aerodynamics and aviation used in vedic times, the names of sages or kings who may have been historical figures. Many details and events are mentioned in descriptive form in the Vedas, which can be explained scientifically today.

6. *Intuitive method* is possible for those who have been able to attain mastery over their mental faculties through yoga, and have developed the capacity of intuitive interpretation while living a normal life as householders or scholars or by becoming a recluse or sannyasin.

VEDAS

The four Vedas are *Rik, Yajus, Sama* and *Atharva*. The four major texts contained within the Vedas are *Samhita, Brahmana, Aranyaka* and *Upanishad*. Some scholars claim that only the Samhita and Brahmana constitute the ancient Vedas, whereas Aranyaka and Upanishads were included into the vedic body at a later date. However, we are concerned with the books and texts that are considered to be a part of the Vedas, and we shall look at them from this viewpoint.

The **Rig Veda Samhita** is considered to be the oldest Veda, consisting of about 10,500 verses arranged poetically in one thousand hymns. *Samhita* or mantra are the hymns belonging to the earliest tradition of the Vedas. Another name for the Rig Veda Samhita is *Rik Vada*. The Rig Veda speaks of Aryan sentiment and thoughts, and the devas are the subject matter. The principal exponent of Rig Veda was Paila, disciple of the legendary classifier of the Vedas, Sage Krishna Dwaipayana, or Veda Vyasa. The major Upanishads belonging to this Veda are *Aitareya* and *Kaushitaki*.

Yajur Veda consists of sacrificial formulas for the priests and many of the chants were taken from the Rig Veda. The Yajur Veda is divided into two parts, *Krishna* and *Shukla*. This Veda consists of approximately 1984 verses and another name for its collection of mantras is *Brahma Vada*. The principal scholar to develop Yajur Veda was Vaishampayana, who was a disciple of Veda Vyasa. Samhitas of Krishna Yajur Veda are *Taittireya, Maitrayani* and *Kathak*, while the major Upanishads are *Taittireya, Maha Narayana, Katha, Shvetashvatara* and *Maitrayana*. Samhita of the Shukla Yajur Veda is *Vajasaneyi*, while the major Upanishads are *Brihadaranyaka* and *Ishavasya*.

Sama Veda contains chants and melodies chanted by priests, who were known as *Saamans*. With the exception of about seventy-five stanzas, the whole text seems to be borrowed from the Rig Veda. The Samhitas of Sama Veda contain chants primarily of devotion, worship and contemplation. The principal exponent of this Veda was Jamini, also a disciple of Veda Vyasa. This Veda is divided into two parts, known as *Uttara Saaman*, consisting of thirty Samhitas, and *Poorvi Saaman*, consisting of twenty-four Samhitas. The major Upanishads are *Chhandogya* and *Kena*.

Atharva Veda is the last and differs from the earlier three in that it combines the essence of both the vedic and tantric traditions. This Veda consists of about 6000 verses. It is quite popular as it contains many chants and prayers to eradicate calamities and diseases, but is equally important for its philosophical views. According to Max Muller, the real vedantic Upanishads are a part of Atharva Veda. The chants of this Veda are inspirational, cosmological, and

13

ritualistic in nature. The major Upanishads of Atharva Veda are *Mundak, Prashna, Mandukya, Atma, Garuda, Sarva, Pinda, Sara, Pranagnihotra* and others. The codifier of this Veda was Sumanta, also a disciple of Veda Vyasa.

Brahmana are an extension of Samhita, as they are very much attached to the various branches of the samhitas. They give a lengthy description and explanation of the rituals and mantras connected with the vedic sacrifices. Much of their explanatory matter is in the form of symbols or symbolic character. The sacrifice is symbolic as well as physical and gross, the purpose behind it being to sanctify man's life. Sacrifice takes place within man and through man, who believes, hopes, loves and has made his very existence an act of worship. In sacrifice and adoration, the sadhaka moulds his life in the framework of worship, prayer, activity, contemplation and action, of which he is the active and passive participant, helper and helped, actor and spectator.

Aranyaka is the third text contained within the Vedas. The word *aranya* literally means 'forest', and this text deals with the speculations and codes of conduct for spiritual life of the forest dwellers or *vanaprasthas*. The Aranyaka are known as the forest treatise. They represent a further step towards internalization, as forest dwellers could not perform the elaborate vedic rituals prescribed for householders. Instead a rigorous training and discipline is prescribed, whereby a substantial change occurs in the attitude towards life. This leads to detachment or vairagya and a more profound understanding about human relationships with the cosmic arrangements.

Upanishads are the final stage of vedic knowledge, which deal with the nature of the absolute reality. They were originally secret doctrines revealed in the post-vedic era and comprise the primary source books of the Vedanta philosophy. The word Vedanta consists of two words: *veda*

14

or *vidya,* meaning 'knowledge', and *anta,* meaning 'end'. In this context, vidya refers to experiential knowledge which is attained through the meditative process. Upanishads are also referred to as *Brahmavidya,* meaning experiential knowledge of the infinite, ever expanding consciousness.

Samhitas and Brahmanas can be *karma kanda,* the ritualistic aspect of the Vedas, or *jnana kanda,* the wisdom or intuitive aspect. Aranyaka is *upasana kanda,* the practical, contemplative aspect, and the Upanishads are *jnana kanda.*

UPANISHADS

The word *Upanishad* is comprised of three words: upa + ni + shad. *Upa* means 'near', *ni* 'attentively' and *shad* 'to sit'. So the term actually describes the situation in which these unique texts were transmitted. The student or disciple sat near the realized master and listened attentively as he expounded his experiences and understanding of the ultimate reality. This teaching was said to destroy the ignorance or illusion of the spiritual aspirant in regard to what is self and non-self, or real and unreal in relation to the absolute and relative reality. Adi Shankara, in his introduction to the *Taittiriyopanishad,* says: "Knowledge of Brahman is called Upanishad because it loosens the bonds of birth and death and destroys them altogether, and because it leads the seeker very near to Brahman wherein the highest God is seated."

During the period when the upanishadic texts were propounded, this knowledge of the ultimate reality was considered sacred and was not easily accessible to all. It was imparted on a very selective basis after the mental and spiritual calibre of the seeker had been tested and proven. Each Upanishad reflected the teachings and tradition of a realized master and was connected with a specific Veda and vedic school, or *shaka*. At one time the vedic schools and their respective Upanishads numbered 1,180, but today only 108 are generally known, although about two hundred are still extant. These texts contain the direct teachings of great scholars, sages and saints of their time and reflect the heights of their spiritual insight and understanding.

Four collections

The exact collection of Upanishads is difficult to ascertain from the Vedas. There are various views on this. Most researchers agree with four collections of the Upanishads, although it is quite difficult to ascertain whether they are a survey of all existing Upanishads or only of those which belong to Atharva Veda.

1. The first collection is found in *Muktikopanishad*, where Sri Rama appears as an incarnation of Narayana and instructs his devotee, Hanuman, that only *one* Upanishad is sufficient to liberate an individual, and that is *Mandukya Upanishad*. However, even after that, if there is still a thirst for knowledge, then a study of the ten major Upanishads is required. If there is yet a hankering for more knowledge then the thirty-two minor Upanishads should be studied. If there is still a yearning for deliverance then the hundred and eight Upanishads should be read.

The hundred and eight Upanishads are then enumerated in the following order:

1. *Isa*, 2. *Kena*, 3. *Prashna*, 4. *Katha*, 5. *Mundaka*, 6. *Mandukya*, 7. *Taittiriya*, 8. *Aitareya*, 9. *Chhandogya*, 10. *Brihadaranyaka*, 11. *Brahma*, 12. *Kaivalya*, 13. *Jabala*, 14. *Shvetashvatara*, 15. *Hamsa*, 16. *Arunika*, 17. *Garbha*, 18. *Narayana*, 19. *Paramahamsa*, 20. *Amritabindu*, 21. *Amritanada*, 22. *Atharvasiras*, 23. *Atharvasikha*, 24. *Maitrayani*, 25. *Kausitaki*, 26. *Brihajjabala*, 27. *Nrisimhatapaniya*, 28. *Kalagniruda*, 29. *Maitreya*, 30. *Subala*, 31. *Ksurika*, 32. *Mantrika*, 33. *Sarvasara*, 34. *Niralamba*, 35. *Shukarahasya*, 36. *Vajrasuchi*, 37. *Tejobindu*, 38. *Nadabindu*, 39. *Dhyanabindu*, 40. *Brahmavidya*,

16

41. *Yogatattwa,* 42. *Atmabodha,* 43. *Naradaparivrajaka,* 44. *Trisikhibrahmana,* 45. *Sita,* 46. *Yogachudamani,* 47. *Nirvana,* 48. *Mandala-brahmana,* 49. *Dakshinamurti,* 50. *Sarabha,* 51. *Skanda,* 52. *Tripad-vibhooti-mahanarayana,* 53. *Advayataraka,* 54. *Ramarahasya,* 55. *Ramatapaniya,* 56. *Vasudeva,* 57. *Mudgala,* 58. *Shandilya,* 59. *Paingala,* 60. *Bhikchhuka,* 61. *Maha,* 62. *Sariraka,* 63. *Yogashikha,* 64. *Turiyatitavadhuta,* 65. *Sannyasa,* 66. *Paramahamsa-parivrajaka,* 67. *Aksamalika,* 68. *Avyakta,* 69. *Ekaksara,* 70. *Annapurna,* 71. *Surya,* 72. *Aksi,* 73. *Adhyatma,* 74. *Kundika,* 75. *Savitri,* 76. *Atma,* 77. *Pasupatabrahma,* 78. *Parabrahma,* 79. *Avadhuta,* 80. *Tripuratapini,* 81. *Devi,* 82. *Tripura,* 83. *Katha,* 84. *Bhavana,* 85. *Rudrahridaya,* 86. *Yogakundali,* 87. *Bhasmajabala,* 88. *Rudraksha-jabala,* 89. *Ganapati,* 90. *Tarasara,* 91. *Darshan,* 92. *Mahavakya,* 93. *Panchabrahma,* 94. *Pranagnihotra,* 95. *Gopalatapini,* 96. *Krishna,* 97. *Yajnavalkya,* 98. *Varaha,* 99. *Satyayana,* 100. *Hayagriva,* 101. *Dattatreya,* 102. *Garuda,* 103. *Kalisam-tarana,* 104. *Jabali,* 105. *Saubhagyalakshmi,* 106. *Saraswati-rahasya,* 107. *Bahvrika,* and 108. *Muktika.*

2. The second collection is as mentioned in the Oupanekhat by Sultan Mohammed Dara Shikoh, who was the elder brother of Emperor Aurangzeb, and had translated the fortieth chapter of Yajur Veda, which was the *Ishavasya Upanishad,* from Sanskrit to Arabic. In the year 1656 AD, he collected many learned pundits and scholars from various corners of the country and commissioned them to translate the whole series of Upanishads into Persian.

His collection contains fifty Upanishads, which are in the original order according to the translators. They are as follows: 1. Tschehandouk *(Chhandogya),* 2. Brehdarang *(Brihadaranyaka),* 3. Mitri *(Maitrayani),* 4. Mandata *(Mundaka),* 5. Eischavasich *(Ishavasya),* 6. Sarb *(Sarva),* 7. Narain *(Narayana),* 8. Tadiw *(Tadew),* 9. Athrabsar *(Atharvasiras),* 10. Hensnad *(Hamsananda),* 11. Sarbsar *(Sarvasara),* 12. Kok'henk *(Kausitaki),* 13. Sataster *(Shvetashvatara),* 14. Porsch *(Prashna),* 15. Dehian band

(Dhyanabindu), 16. Maha oupanekhat *(Maha)*, 17. Atma pra boudeh *(Atmaprabodh)*, 18. Kioul *(Kaivalya)*, 19. Schat roundri *(Shatarudriyam)*, 20. Djog Sankha *(Yogashikha)*, 21. Djogtat *(Yogatattwa)*, 22. Shiw Sanklap *(Shiva Sankalpa)*, 23. Abrat Sak'ha *(Atharvashikha)*, 24. Atma *(Atma)*, 25. Brahm Badia *(Brahma-vidya)*, 26. Anbrat Bandeh *(Amritabindu)*, 27. Tidj Bandeh *(Tejobindu)*, 28. Karbheh *(Garbha)*, 29. Djabal *(Jabala)*, 30. Maha Narain *(Mahanarayana)*, 31. Mandouk *(Mandukya)*, 32. Pank *(Paingala)*, 33. Tschchourka *(Ksurika)*, 34. Pram hens *(Paramahamsa)*, 35. Arank *(Arunika)*, 36. Kin *(Kena)*, 37. Kiouni *(Katha)*, 38. Anandbli *(Anandavalli* from *Taittiriya)*, 39. Bharkbli *(Bhriguvalli* from *Taittiriya)*, 40. Bark'he Soukt *(Purusha Suktam)*, 41. Djounka *(Chulika)*, 42. Mrat Lankoul *(Mrityulangala)*, 43. Anbratnad *(Amritanada)*, 44. Baschakl *(Baskala)*, 45. Tschhakli *(Chagaleya)*, 46. Tark *(Taraka)*, 47. Ark'hi *(Arsheya)*, 48. Pranou *(Pranava)*, 49. Schavank *(Saunaka)*, and 50. Nersing'heb atma *(Nrisimha)*.

Out of this collection, twelve Upanishads belong to the earlier Vedas. Intermingled with these are twenty-six other Upanishads, which are recognized as part of Atharva Veda. Four passages are included from the *Vajasaneyi Samhita* of Yajur Veda and the remaining eight works appear to belong to Rig Veda.

3. The third collection is by Colebrooke, who, in 1876, selected fifty-two Upanishads which may have found recognition in scholarly circles. They are as follows: 1. *Mundaka*, 2. *Prashna*, 3. *Brahmavidya*, 4. *Ksurika*, 5. *Chulika*, 6. *Atharvasiras*, 7. *Atharvasikha*, 8. *Garbha*, 9. *Maha*, 10. *Brahma*, 11. *Pranagnihotra*, 12–15. *Mandukya with Gaudapada Karika*, 16. *Nilarudra*, 17. *Nadabindu*, 18. *Brahmabindu*, 19. *Amritabindu*, 20. *Dhyanabindu*, 21. *Tejobindu*, 22. *Yogashikha*, 23. *Yogatattwa*, 24. *Sannyasa*, 25. *Aruniya*, 26. *Kanthasruti*, 27. *Pinda*, 28. *Atma*, 29–34. *Nrisimhatapaniya*, 35–36. *Katha*, 37. *Kena*, 38. *Narayana*, 39–40. *Brihadnarayana*, 41. *Sarvopanisatsara*, 42. *Hamsa*, 43. *Paramahamsa*, 44. *Anandavalli*, 45. *Bhriguvalli*, 46. *Garuda*,

47. *Kalagnirudra,* 48–49. *Ramatapaniya,* 50. *Kaivalya,* 51. *Jabala,* and 52. *Ashram.*

4. The fourth collection is by Narayana, a Sanskrit grammarian and upanishadic commentator, who called himself a son of Ratnakar, and lived sometime around 800 AD. No other details are known about him. He selected the fifty-two Upanishads in the following order:
1. *Mundaka,* 2. *Prashna,* 3. *Brahmavidya,* 4. *Ksurika,* 5. *Chulika,* 6. *Atharvasiras,* 7. *Atharvasikha,* 8. *Garbha,* 9. *Maha,* 10. *Brahma,* 11. *Pranagnihotra,* 12–15. *Mandukya with Gaudapada Karika,* 16. *Nilarudra,* 17. *Nadabindu,* 18. *Brahmabindu,* 19. *Amritabindu,* 20. *Dhyanabindu,* 21. *Tejobindu,* 22. *Yogashikha,* 23. *Yogatattwa,* 24. *Sannyasa,* 25. *Aruniya,* 26. *Kanthasruti,* 27. *Pinda,* 28. *Atma,* 29–30. *Nrisimha,* 31. *Katha,* 32. *Kena* 33. *Narayana,* 34. *Mahanarayana,* 35–36. *Ramatapaniya,* 37. *Sarvopanisatsara,* 38. *Hamsa,* 39. *Paramahamsa,* 40. *Jabala,* 41. *Kaivalya,* 42. *Taittiriya,* 43. *Ashram,* 44. *Garuda,* 45. *Kalagnirudra,* 46–47. *Gopalatapaniya,* 48. *Krishna,* 49. *Vasudeva,* 50. *Gopichandan,* and 51–52. *Naradapurvatapini.*

Seven classifications

Classification of the Upanishads is a difficult task. It seems impossible to decide how many Upanishads there are in total. Therefore, any attempt to work with them has to be confined to a selection. This selection should not depend on a subjective appraisal of the Upanishad, but on an objective analysis of its subject and metaphysical connotations. In the *Encyclopaedia of Upanishads*, N. S. Subrahmaniam has classified the 108 Upanishads into the following categories:
1. *Major* – ten
2. *Vedanta* – twenty-five
3. *Saiva* – fourteen
4. *Shakta* – eight
5. *Vaishnava* – fourteen

19

6. *Yoga* – twenty
7. *Sannyasa* – seventeen.

YOGA UPANISHADS

The Yoga Upanishads represent an important cultural merging of the vedantic and tantric traditions, which were earlier conceived as opposed to one another, but are here shown to be complementary systems. Yoga has its ancient origins in Tantra, and the yogic practices and physiology are all based in this tradition. The Yoga Upanishads deal with the major yogic aspects of Tantra, such as: kundalini, laya, nada, mantra and hatha. These texts further detail and describe how the yogic practices culminate in the vedantic realization of the Self as Atma/Brahman, or one with the absolute reality.

The Yoga Upanishads were composed after the *Yoga Sutras* of Patanjali and form an important part of the classical yoga literature. Their number varies between twenty and twenty-two. The following texts are generally listed among this group: 1. *Advayataraka,* 2. *Amritanada,* 3. *Amritabindu,* 4. *Brahmavidya,* 5. *Darshana,* 6. *Dhyanabindu,* 7. *Hamsa,* 8. *Kshurika,* 9. *Maha Vakya,* 10. *Mandalabrahmana,* 11. *Nadabindu,* 12. *Pashupatabrahmana,* 13. *Shandilya,* 14. *Tejobindu,* 15. *Trishikhibrahmana,* 16. *Varaha,* 17. *Yoga Chudamani,* 18. *Yogakundali,* 19. *Yogaraja,* 20. *Yogashikha,* 21. *Yogatattwa.*

An exact time line for the upanishadic body of yogic literature is difficult to assign. The earliest Upanishads are certainly pre-Patanjali and were probably composed between the completion of the vedic hymns around 1000 BC and the Classical Yoga period which arose around 300 BC. There is no doubt that the Yoga Upanishads were composed later and belong to the post-Patanjali era because of the term *ashtanga yoga,* which is used in all of these texts. However, no

20

references to Patanjali or his *Yoga Sutras* are found in any of these Upanishads. In the early Upanishads, like *Brihadaranyaka* and *Chandogya*, different *vidyas* or meditative disciplines are described, but nowhere were they codified as in Patanjali's *Yoga Sutras*.

Therefore, when inter-rivalries arose between the different philosophical systems, including the Classical Yoga system, the vedantic thinkers must have felt the need to reveal these secret yogic doctrines in book form. This marks the emergence of the Yoga Upanishads. Although the time of compilation of these Upanishads is post-Patanjali, the vidyas or meditative disciplines contained within them are pre-Patanjali. The Yoga Upanishads were written by vedantic scholars in order to show that these vidyas and related practices were not borrowed from Patanjali but were known and practised from the ancient period.

YOGA CHUDAMANI UPANISHAD

Yoga Chudamani is the 'Crown Jewel of Yoga'. Chudamani is comprised of two words: chuda and mani. The word *chuda* means 'crown' and also refers to the tuft of hair which is worn at the top back of the head by the Brahmin priests. The word *mani* means 'jewel'. Yoga Chudamani is a unique and concise text comprised of one hundred and twenty-one mantras which deal with the practices of kundalini yoga as a means to attain the heights of Vedanta philosophy. The author and origins of this text are unknown, but it is connected with Sama Veda and probably dates back to the period between 700 and 1000 AD, when the ancient tantric tradition had regained popularity and was undergoing a period of revival.

Yoga Chudamani is an ancient text in which no clear demarcation between the early systems of hatha yoga and kundalini yoga is found. Some scholars have, therefore, related the practical contents of this text with hatha yoga,

21

whereas in context these practices are actually part of kundalini yoga, as they deal directly with the awakening of the pranas, nadis, chakras and kundalini. In early times, when the seers of the Upanishads were exposed to tantric theories and practice, kundalini yoga comprised all the practices of hatha yoga, except for the original six purifying practices, which were known as *shatkarma*.

Hatha yoga was regarded as a physical and pranic purification system, whereas kundalini yoga was an esoteric system which involved the awakening of latent psychic energies only known and practised by adepts. Gradually, over time, all the asana, pranayama, mudra and bandha components of kundalini yoga were absorbed into the system of hatha yoga, because of their physical nature. The relationship between hatha and kundalini yoga was often not recognized by later scholars and, therefore, the pranic and psychic emphasis of the practices was gradually lost. The *Yoga Chudamani* is, therefore, an important source of yogic literature which reminds us of the esoteric purpose of many kundalini yoga practices that have come to be regarded as hatha yoga.

Outline of the text

The text begins with the six limbs of yoga: asana, pranayama, pratyahara, dharana, dhyana and samadhi, and then goes on to describe the six chakras, sixteen *adharas* (bases), three *lakshyas* (aims) and five *vyomas* (spaces) of yoga. This part of the text has a strong affinity with the science of Tantra and deals in depth with the lower chakras – mooladhara, swadhisthana and manipura, which are often not mentioned in other upanishadic or classical yogic text because of their relation with the instinctive nature. Special emphasis is given to the origin, location and function of the ten major nadis, or energy channels, including ida, pingala and sushumna. The prana vayus are also discussed in detail and in relation to *jiva*, the soul, and *guna*, the constituents of Prakriti. Next the text provides a description of ajapa gayatri, which is an older vedic and upanishadic vidya showing the harmonious integration of these two ancient systems.

Following these detailed discussions on yogic physiology and ajapa gayatri, the kundalini shakti is described along with its pathway, method of awakening and the necessary dietary and disciplinary observances. The text further deals with the theory of the red and white bindus, *rajas* and *shukla*, which represent the vital and conscious as well as the female and male forces. This is an important tantric concept which actually completes the theory of kundalini, but has been omitted from many of the later yogic texts due to its association with the sexual aspects of Tantra. The processes of retention and reversal of the bindus are clearly described here along with the relevant practices utilized in the different stages of this process. In this context several important mudras and bandhas, such as khechari, vajroli, maha mudra, jalandhara, moola and uddiyana, are described in detail.

At this point the text takes a more vedantic turn and discusses the states of consciousness in relation to Pranava or Aum and how Brahman manifests in the form of Pranava. The meaning and symbology of Pranava are described in elaborate detail in accordance with the vedantic system of philosophy and practice. This discussion further points out the relation between the three major deities, the three shaktis or powers, and the three lokas or dimensions of existence, with the three letters, 'A', 'U' and 'M', comprising the Aum mantra. The importance of Pranava as an *upasana*, or meditative discipline, which leads the practitioner into the subtle sphere of nada yoga, is further explained along with its benefits.

After this, the text again takes a different turn. Pranava is followed by discussions on the importance of the control

23

and retention of prana, which result in longevity. In order to control and retain prana, the practice of pranayama is a necessity. Here the methods of pranava pranayama, chandra bheda, surya bheda, nadi shodhana and kumbhaka are described along with their particular esoteric significance and forms of concentration, which are not found in other yogic or upanishadic texts. Finally the text draws to a close with further discussion on the limbs of yoga, their benefits and progression, bringing it back again to the topic on which it had begun. By this time, however, the reader has become a participator in the yogic process, and not just an intellectual observer.

Yoga Chudamani is a manual of higher sadhana which is meant for advanced and initiated aspirants. It delineates the ancient path of kundalini awakening in its original and pure form, before the proliferation of more modern yogic literature. Mantra by mantra, the text points out the necessary means of transformation which lead to an experience of the deeper aspects of yoga sadhana and its culmination in the expansion of consciousness and self-realization. Thereby the text becomes a practical and experiential proof of the compatibility of Yoga and Vedanta, or the tantric and vedic systems of philosophy and practice.

REFERENCES

Tilak, B.G., *The Arctic Home in the Vedas,* Tilak Brothers, Pune, 1983

Panikkar, Raimundo, *The Vedic Experience 'Mantramanjari',* All Indian Books, Pondicherry, 1977

Deussen, Paul, translated by Bedekar, V.M. & Palsule, G.B., *Sixty Upanishads of the Veda,* Motilal Banarsidass, Delhi, 1980

Chand, Devi, (trans) *Atharvaveda,* 1st edn, Munshiram Manoharlal, New Delhi, 1982

Chand, Devi, (trans) *Samaveda,* 2nd edn, Munshiram Manoharlal, New Delhi, 1981

Chand, Devi, (trans) *Yajurveda,* 3rd edn, Munshiram Manoharlal, New Delhi, 1980

Subrahmaniam, N. S., *Encyclopaedia of the Upanishads,* Sterling Publishers Pvt. Ltd., New Delhi, 1985

Radhakrishnan, S., *Indian Philosophy,* George Allen and Unwin, London, 1966

Saraswati, Swami Satyananda, *Nine Principal Upanishads,* 2nd edn, Bihar School of Yoga, Munger, 1985

SHANTI MANTRA

ॐ आप्यायन्तु ममाङ्गानि वाक् प्राणश्चक्षुः श्रोत्रमथो बलमिन्द्रियाणि च
सर्वाणि। सर्वं ब्रह्मौपनिषदं माहं ब्रह्म निराकुर्यां मा मा ब्रह्म निराकरोत्।
अनिराकरणमस्त्वनिराकरणं मेऽस्तु। तदात्मनि निरते य उपनिषत्सु धर्मास्ते
मयि सन्तु, ते मयि सन्तु।

ॐ शान्ति: शान्ति: शान्ति: ॥

Om Aapyaayantu Mamaangaani Vaak Praanashchakshuh
Shrotramatho Balamindriyaani cha Sarvaani. Sarvam Brahma-
upanishadam Maaham Brahma Niraakuryaam Maa Maa Brahma
Niraakarot Aniraakaranam-Astu-Aniraakaranam me Astu.
Tadaatmani Nirate Ya Upanishatsu Dharmaaste Mayi Santu Te
Mayi Santu.

Om Shaantih, Shaantih, Shaantih.

Om. May all my organs and limbs become pure and strong.
May my speech, sense of smell, sight, hearing and all
instruments of experience become pure and strong. All the
Upanishads are the forms of Brahman, the highest reality.
May I never be separated from Brahman and may Brahman
not abandon me. May I always remain immersed in Brahman
so that I may imbibe the instructions of the Upanishads.
May peace be with all.

Om peace, peace, peace.

Invocation

The aspirant of higher spiritual knowledge invokes the
Shanti Mantra before commencement of the Upanishad.
This is the common method of entering the studies of
secret and higher doctrines. All the Upanishads begin with
an invocation in the form of a prayer to God and Guru. The
aspirant seeking spiritual revelation prays for physical and
mental health. It is an established concept in Indian tradition

26

that the body, senses and mind are the agents through which the transcendental reality is experienced. To dwell eternally in the realm of pure consciousness is the perpetual desire of the soul. Therefore, the aspirant prays for attunement with the supreme reality, the fountain of all knowledge, so that he may receive the instructions of the Upanishad and be able to realize them.

Mantra 1: Purpose of the Upanishad

योगचूडामणिं वक्ष्ये योगिनां हितकाम्यया ।
कैवल्यसिद्धिदं गूढं सेवितं योगवित्तमै: ॥ 1 ॥

Yogachoodaamanim Vakshye Yoginaam Hitakaamyayaa;
Kaivalya Siddhidam Goodham Sevitam Yogavittamaih. (1)

Anvay

Yoginaam: of the yogis; *Hitakaamyayaa*: with the desire for
well-being; *Yoga Choodamanim*: crown jewel of yoga; *Vakshye*:
I say (that), I give out; *Kaivalya*: emancipation; *Siddhi*: power
of; *Dam*: giver of; *Goodham*: secret (and); *Yogavittamaih*: by
the knowers of yoga; *Sevitam*: is practised.

Translation

For the benefit of yogis, I give out the crown jewel of yoga. It
is a secret (doctrine) which gives the power of emancipation
and is practised by those who are well-versed in yoga.

Commentary

The literal meaning of *Yoga Chudamani* is 'crown jewel of
yoga'. This text is one of the Yoga Upanishads that describes
the esoteric principles of yogic science. The purpose of this
Upanishad is to indicate a process of self-evolution through
the path of kundalini yoga. Mere intellectual concepts lead
nowhere in yoga. Practice is necessary and the techniques
referred to in this text must be mastered with the guidance
of a competent preceptor or Guru. Only those aspirants
who are initiated and have established themselves in the
preparatory and basic stages of yoga can practise the esoteric
aspects of yoga.

This mantra dictates that only those aspirants who are
already established in yoga will be following the instructions
of this Upanishad. Therefore, the doctrines presented here

have been termed as secret. The esoteric aspects of yoga cannot be understood or applied by the average mind. They are accessible only to those aspirants who progressively go through the higher stages of yoga and ultimately attain *kaivalya* or liberation. In the process of awakening, the aspirant evolves from one stage of practice, perception, knowledge and perfection, to the next.

Mantra 2: Six limbs of yoga

आसनं प्राणसंरोध: प्रत्याहारश्च धारणा ।
ध्यानं समाधिरेतानि योगाङ्गानि भवन्ति षट् ॥ 2 ॥

Aasanam Praanasamrodhah Pratyaahaaraashcha Dhaaranaa;
Dhyaanam Samaadhiretaani Yogaangaani Bhavanti Shat. (2)

Anvay

Aasanam: posture; *Praana*: vital energy; *Samrodhah*: effective control over; *Pratyaahaaraashcha*: sensory withdrawal and; *Dhaaranaa*: one-pointed concentration; *Dhyaanam*: meditation; *Samaadhih*: transcendental state; *Etaani*: these; *Yogaangaani*: limbs of yoga; *Shat*: six; *Bhavanti*: become.

Translation

Asana, pranayama, pratyahara, dharana, dhyana and samadhi are the six limbs of yoga.

Commentary

For the aspirant who is established in the path of yoga, *abhyasa* (continuous practice) is necessary. Abhyasa provides the means to constantly evolve in the spiritual path. The main difference between the two paths of raja yoga and kundalini yoga is that raja yoga starts with the disciplinary code of *yama* and *niyama*, whereas kundalini yoga starts straight away with the practice. Kundalini yoga is an integral part of the tantric system in which it is considered that through practice the level of consciousness will be raised and then the disciplines will become a natural part of life, rather than forced patterns of behaviour, causing suppression and guilt.

Therefore, the instructions on kundalini yoga, which are the main theme of this Upanishad, begin with asana and pranayama and not yama and niyama. The six limbs of kundalini yoga mentioned in this mantra are as follows:

1. Asana: pranic regulation through physical postures

Asanas are the basis for kundalini yoga because of their effect on the pranic system. They help to regulate and balance the energy throughout the body by removing energy blockages in the pranic channels and stimulating the chakras or energy centres located at different points along the spinal column. Accumulation of toxins, tensions or stiffness in any part of the body causes blockage of energy and imbalance of the entire system. Asanas are designed to systematically remove these obstructions and in this way they prepare the body for the awakening of the pranas, chakras and kundalini.

There are two main categories of asana: dynamic and static. In the context of this Upanishad, as well as other texts dealing with higher practices, asana refers to a posture which is meant for meditation. Sage Patanjali has described asana as a posture in which the body is able to remain steady and comfortable for a duration of time. To attain success in sadhana, the body must be steady, comfortable and tension-free. The sadhaka is required to maintain a state of physical harmony so that the mind can be focused without any external distractions.

2. Pranayama: pranic expansion through manipulation of the breath

There is a subtle connection between breath, prana and mind. For this reason, yogis initially instruct the aspirant to control the breath before attempting to direct the mental forces and awaken the pranic energy. Pranayama is mastered in four stages: (i) awareness of the breath, (ii) manipulation or control of the breath, and (iii) expansion of prana.

In the preliminary stage of pranayama, awareness of the breath is engendered and the breathing is made regular and rhythmic. As the breathing is synchronized, the energy flow is harmonized and the mind becomes peaceful. After attaining this initial awareness, control of the three aspects

31

of breath: (i) *puraka* (inhalation), (ii) *rechaka* (exhalation) and (iii) *kumbhaka* (retention), is developed through further techniques. In this way the energy channels are purified and balanced in preparation for pranic awakening. Control of breathing leads to expansion of prana, which is the culmination of pranayama.

Pranayama harmonizes the physical systems and keeps them in good health. It helps to keep the body light and free of toxins. Pranayama practice eventually leads the practitioner to mastery over the mind and senses by awakening and directing the force and flow of prana. For purification and awakening of prana throughout the system, there are twenty-one pranayama techniques, all of which are not described in any literature. These techniques should be learned from a proficient teacher or Guru, who can assess and observe the requirements and attainments of the aspirant.

3. Pratyahara: withdrawal of the senses

By withdrawing the senses from the external field of objective awareness to the field of inner reality, the mind is able to perceive the inner experiences and realize the subtle personality. In normal conditions the mind is diffused in its quest for material happiness. It is the nature of the mind to be extrovert, to run after the attractions and pleasures of the world. Vast amounts of energy are utilized in external pursuits that leave the mind fragmented and drained. In order to conserve and harmonize the mental force, the yogic aspirant channels the mental and sensory tendencies of his personality towards inner awareness and experience. Normally the mind follows the senses. In pratyahara, the senses are made to follow the mind. When mastery over the sensory organs is attained through pratyahara, the mental energies can be redirected for the awakening of chakras and kundalini.

4. Dharana: fixing the mind upon one single object or idea

In dharana, the faculties of mind, after being fully withdrawn, are focused at one point. In order to focus the mind, a base for concentration is necessary which can hold the mind absolutely steady. This base may be a symbol or idea. In kundalini yoga the different psychic passages, chakra symbols and their corresponding mantras are used for this purpose. By concentrating one-pointedly on a particular chakra or symbol, the energies inherent in that centre are awakened. This is the preparatory state for higher meditation.

5. Dhyana: spontaneous meditation or contemplation

When the psychic passages and centres awaken, the mental energy is heightened. The state of fusion is experienced between the practitioner and the object of contemplation. This state results in an uninterrupted flow of consciousness which becomes expansive and does not remain confined to one region or object of perception. In dharana, awareness is fixed at one point. In dhyana, the field of awareness becomes more extensive and luminous as the kundalini awakens and the energy field expands beyond its normal boundaries.

6. Samadhi: the transcendental state of equanimity

Here the consciousness is freed from the individual identity which it retains in dharana and dhyana, and attains the superconscious state. This state arises with the ascent of kundalini to sahasrara, the crown chakra, where it merges with the unqualified, universal state. Samadhi is the culmination of all religions, philosophies and yogas. Many names and terms have been given to this state, i.e. self-realization, liberation, nirvana, kaivalya, moksha. The names are different but the state is one and the same. It is an experiential state which must be realized by the aspirant internally and cannot be conceptualized or intellectualized. It is an experience of self-realization and inner attainment.

Mantras 3, 4a: Psychic physiology

एकं सिद्धासनं प्रोक्तं द्वितीयं कमलासनम् ।
षट्चक्रं षोडशाधारं त्रिलक्ष्यं व्योमपञ्चकम् ॥ 3 ॥
स्वदेहे यो न जानाति तस्य सिद्धि: कथं भवेत् ॥ 4a ॥

Ekam Siddhaasanam Proktam Dwiteeyam Kamalaasanam;
Shatchakram Shodashaadhaaram Trilakshyam Vyomapanchakam. (3)
Swadehe Yo Na Jaanaati Tasya Siddhih Katham Bhavet. (4a)

Anvay

Ekam: first; *Siddhaasanam*: adept's posture; *Proktam*: has been said; *Dwiteeyam*: next, secondly; *Kamalaasanam*: lotus posture (padmasana); *Shatchakram*: six psychic centres; *Shodasha*: sixteen; *Aadharam*: bases, supports; *Trilakshyam*: three aims; *Vyoma-panchakam*: five akashas (spaces, ethers); *Swadehe*: in one's own body; *Yah*: who; *Na*: no; *Jaanaati*: knows; *Tasya*: his; *Siddhih*: power, perfection; *Katham*: how; *Bhavet*: could be.

Translation

The first asana is siddhasana (the adept's pose). The next is kamalasana (padmasana or the lotus pose). How can one attain perfection if one does not know the six psychic centres, the sixteen supports, the three aims and the five akashas within one's own body?

Commentary

This mantra mentions two classical postures, *siddhasana* and *padmasana*, which are considered most important for meditation because they lock the body in a steady, balanced and upright position. With practice, these asanas can be maintained for long periods of time without strain and discomfort. Meditation requires the spinal column to be straight, and few asanas fulfil this condition. Further, in advanced stages of meditation the aspirant loses body

34

awareness and conscious control over the muscle structure of the body. Thus the meditative asana needs to automatically hold the body in a steady posture. Regarding these two meditation postures, Swami Satyananda Saraswati has said: "Without adopting a secure and steady asana, one cannot progress in meditation. The steadier you are in your asana, the more you will be able to concentrate with a one-pointed mind."

. In kundalini yoga these two meditative postures are used because of their effect on the psychic centres. In sustained practice of siddhasana, the lower centres of mooladhara and swadhisthana are stimulated and the vital airs in this region, which normally flow downward, are rechannelled to the higher centres in the brain for spiritual awakening. In padmasana there is no direct stimulation of the lower centres. However, sustained practice balances and aligns the nadis or energy channels and opens sushumna nadi, the pathway of kundalini, which connects all the psychic centres from mooladhara to sahasrara, thus deepening the meditative experience. Both of these postures activate the chakras and sushumna passage, and redirect the energy to the brain, which enables deeper concentration and develops awareness of the latent psychic faculties. Regular practice also facilitates the experience of the *akasha* or spacial dimension of the mind.

Along with adopting a steady posture as an aid to meditation, this mantra also emphasizes the need to develop subtle awareness of the *chakras* or psychic energy centres located in the body, which represent the pathway of evolution. Each chakra is a vortex of vital, conscious and elemental energy, around which our individual being takes its material form. The chakras act as energy transformers, stepping down the psychic energy for use by the organs and parts of the physical body, as well as switches for the latent faculties of the brain. Concentration on the psychic centres

35

while performing asanas and/or other yoga practices opens and activates these energy flows, facilitating the experience of higher planes of consciousness and energy which one is normally unaware of. The chakras are further described in the following mantras.

Next the mantra mentions the necessity of realizing the sixteen *adharas*, which are the physical supports or basic foundations that the body is dependent on for balance, motion, interaction and experience. In certain practices of pratyahara, knowledge of the adharas and concentration on them is used to internalize the awareness. Traditionally, the sixteen adharas have been identified as the main physical supports: 1. toes, 2. ankles, 3. knees, 4. thighs, 5. perineum, 6. genitals, 7. navel, 8. heart, 9. base of the neck, 10. throat, 11. tongue, 12. nose, 13. eyebrow centre, 14. forehead, 15. top back of the head and 16. crown.

The consciousness is to be rotated through these centres. This rotation is explained in pratyahara as the gradual withdrawal of consciousness from all the external centres of pain and distraction which keep it tied to the gross, material world. In the *Yajnavalkya Samhita*, Sage Yajnavalkya has instructed his disciple, Gargi, to develop awareness of these adharas and raise the prana through these centres from the toes to the crown. The consciousness has to ascend from toes to crown and then descend from crown to toes. Swami Satyananda Saraswati has also instructed yoga aspirants to perfect the experience of the adharas through the practice of yoga nidra, a technique of pratyahara, which he evolved and expounded.

Next the mantra refers to the *trilakshyas*, which are the three goals or objectives to be realized at the time of sadhana. These goals are known as: (i) *bahya lakshya*, (ii) *madhyama lakshya* and (iii) *antarika lakshya*. Generally aspirants have a physical, mental or spiritual objective in mind during sadhana. Bahya lakshya is the physical goal or the external

36

objective which is aspired for. Madhyama lakshya is the mental goal or the middle objective. Antarika lakshya is the spiritual goal or internal objective.

These lakshyas have been explained as the state of experience which one aspires for after attaining completion and perfection in sadhana. According to tradition, the external objective to be aspired for at the time of sadhana is the vision of a blue light located a few inches away from the tip of the nose. This is bahya lakshya sadhana where the consciousness attains the ability to visualize the subtle form of an object. Madhyama lakshya sadhana is awareness of the *panchakosha*, the five dimensions of human experience: (i) *annamaya* (material), (ii) *manomaya* (mental), (iii) *pranamaya* (vital), (iv) *vijnanamaya* (psychic) and (v) *anandamaya* (transcendental). Antarika lakshya is becoming aware of the energy flow in the psychic passage, visualization of and concentration on the psychic symbol and awareness of the psychic sound.

Finally, the mantra mentions the akashas, which are described by the yogic traditions as states of inner experience where the individual consciousness fuses its identity with the vast and expansive nature of Brahman. The word *akasha* is literally translated as 'space' or 'etheric dimension'. The vedic tradition describes five akashas, which are known as *vyoma panchaka*. These akashas are:

1. *Para Akasha*: the pure and formless space where consciousness merges with the universal consciousness.
2. *Apara Akasha*: the space which is in the form of darkness within and without. In the Christian tradition this space is described as the 'dark night of the soul'.
3. *Mahat Akasha*: the space in which consciousness manifests in the form of mental attributes and qualities.
4. *Tattwa Akasha*: the space, which pervades the dimension of the five elements, their attributes and nature.
5. *Surya Akasha*: the space in the dimension of the cognitive faculties.

37

The yogic tradition describes three akashas or etheric planes:

1. *Chidakasha*: the plane of infinite consciousness in the region of the head or ajna chakra. The aspirant fixes his consciousness in chidakasha by gradually raising it through each of the six chakras. In chidakasha, the effects of pratyahara, dharana and dhyana are experienced and realized. As the consciousness moves from the gross planes of experience to the subtler planes, traversing the chakras, it becomes more refined and able to absorb the transcendental reality.

2. *Hridayakasha*: the space in the region of the heart or anahata chakra where one experiences personality transformation after the awakening of energy within. In this state of perception the aspirant is aware of the subtle and gross nature of the personality at the same time.

3. *Daharakasha*: the deep etheric plane where energy is at rest in the manifest universe. This is the psychic dimension symbolically represented by the chakras and elements.

The yogic traditions indicate certain methods of realizing these etheric dimensions through different forms of practice. They also state that although various descriptions may be given in different texts, complete comprehension or realization of these dimensions will not take place except through systematic practice. However, the individual sadhana and its method must be learned from a Guru or preceptor, for in the final analysis these are matters of inner realization.

Mantras 4b, 5, 6a: Knowledge of the chakras

चतुर्दलं स्यादाधारं स्वाधिष्ठानं च षड्दलम् ॥ 4b ॥
नाभौ दशदलं पद्मम् हृदयं द्वादशारकम् ।
षोडशारं विशुद्धाख्यं भ्रूमध्ये द्विदलं तथा ॥ 5 ॥
सहस्रदलसंख्यातं ब्रह्मरन्ध्रे महापथि ॥ 6a ॥

Chaturdalam Syaadaadhaaram Swaadhishthaanam cha Shaddalam. (4b)
Naabhau Dashadalam Padmam Hridayam Dwaadashaarakam;
Shodashaaram Vishuddhaakhyam, Bhroomadhye Dwidalam tathaa. (5)
Sahasradala Samkhyaatam Brahmarandhre Mahaapathi. (6a)

Anvay

Aadhaaram: base, mooladhara; *Chaturdalam*: four petals; *Cha*: and; *Swaadhishthaanam*: one's own abode, swadhisthana; *Shaddalam*: six petals; *Syaat*: are; *Naabhau*: at the navel, manipura; *Dashadalam*: ten petals; *Padmam*: lotus; *Hridayam*: heart, anahata; *Dwadasha*: twelve; *Arakam*: petals; *Shodashaaram*: sixteen; *Vishuddha*: purification centre, vishuddhi; *Tathaa*: and; *Bhroomadhye*: eyebrow centre, ajna; *Dwidalam*: two petals; *Aakhyam*: has been said; *Mahaapathi*: on the sublime path; *Brahmarandhre*: at the fontanel; *Sahasradala samkhyaatam*: is the thousand-petalled lotus.

Translation

It has been said (of the six psychic centres), mooladhara, the base centre, has four petals. Swadhisthana, the centre of one's own self, has six petals. Manipura, the navel centre, has ten petals. Anahata, the heart centre, has twelve petals. Vishuddhi, the purification centre, has sixteen petals, and bhrumadhya, the eyebrow centre, has two petals. On the sublime path of Brahmarandhra (opening at the fontanel) is the thousand-petalled lotus (sahasrara chakra).

39

Commentary

The mantras have mentioned eight chakras altogether, including bindu and sahasrara. The first six chakras are located in the region of the spinal cord, from the base or perineum to the eyebrow centre. They are interconnected and energized through a network of energy channels called *nadis*. At the physical level the nadis correspond to the nervous system. The chakras are depicted symbolically as lotus flowers, each having a specific number of petals. Each lotus is of a particular colour, and contained within the pericarp are particular geometrical shapes and symbols relating to the level of energy contained within that centre.

The petals of each chakra represent the rays of energy or the number of pranic channels leading in and out of it. Each chakra is the centre of a particular *tattwa* (elemental energy), having a related geometrical form, *bija mantra* (seed sound), presiding *devi* and *devata* (female and male deities) with their respective *vahana* (vehicle) and certain associated qualities. The six chakras are briefly described as follows:

1. Mooladhara: the lowest chakra in the body. The word *moola* means 'root' and *adhara* means 'base', 'place', so mooladhara is the root centre. There are seven centres below mooladhara situated in the legs, which represent the lower instinctive levels of consciousness. The human

40

dimension begins from mooladhara. In yoga, mooladhara is depicted as a deep red lotus with four petals. In the centre of the lotus is a yellow square, representing the earth element, with the bija mantra *Lam* at the top. Inside the square is a red inverted triangle, representing *shakti*, or energy. Within the triangle is the smoky-coloured *swayambhu linga*, depicting the individual consciousness in a nebulous and dissipated state. The swayambhu linga is encircled by a red serpent coiled three and half times, which symbolizes the latent kundalini.

The triangle is riding on the back of an elephant with seven trunks. The elephant symbolizes the stability and solidarity of the earth and the seven trunks represent the *saptadhatu* or seven minerals, which are the essence of the earth. The seven trunks also relate to the *tanmatra* or sensory attribute of this centre, which is the sense of smell and the related *jnanendriya* or sensory organ, the nose. The associated *karmendriya* or organ of action is the organ of elimination. The *vayu* or vital air is *apana*, the energy flowing downward from the navel to the pelvic floor. The *loka* or dimension of experience is *Bhu*, the earth region. The presiding *devata* is Brahma, the creator of the universe, and the *devi* is Dakini, who controls the skin element of the body. The associated foods are proteins and meats. The yoga path is hatha and the operating force is gravity.

Mooladhara is called the root centre, which is situated at the perineum in the male body, midway between the sexual organ and the anal sphincter, about two centimetres inside. In the female body it is located at the inner surface of the cervix, which is the opening of the womb. It is also known as *moola prakriti*, the source of creation, because it is the seat of kundalini, the primal energy. Kundalini is the source of all energy in man and in the universe, whether sexual, emotional, mental, psychic or spiritual. Energy is one, although the psychic centres through which it manifests give it various

41

qualities and attributes. The awakening of this energy through practice, self-purification and concentration and its union with pure consciousness is the aim of yoga.

At the psychological level mooladhara is the centre of primitive and deep-rooted instincts in man's nature. It represents the expression of the kundalini energy through the instinct of survival or self-preservation. It is closely associated with the reproductive organs and the sexual drive, but here the primary motive is for progeny, which represents the recreation and continuity of oneself in the material world. When open, mooladhara provides the will to live in the physical dimension, physical vitality, grounding and stability. When blocked, the physical vitality is low, one is unable to establish a place in the world and avoids physical activity.

2. Swadhisthana: the second centre, situated at the sacrum. The literal meaning of *swadhisthana* is 'one's own abode'. This chakra is symbolized by a vermilion lotus with six petals. At the centre of the lotus is a silvery white crescent moon, representing the water element. Within the moon is the bija mantra *Vam* riding on a crocodile, representing the power of the subterranean element. The tanmatra or sensory attribute is taste, and the jnanendriya or related sensory organ is the tongue. The karmendriya or organ of action is

42

the genitals. The vayu is *apana* moving towards *samana*, which is indicated by the orange colour, yellow mixed with red. The loka is *Bhuwah*, the intermediate region between heaven and earth. The presiding devata is Lord Vishnu, the sustainer of the universe, and the devi is Rakini, controller of the blood element in the body. The yoga path is Tantra and the operating force is the attraction of opposites.

Swadhisthana chakra is located at the coccyx, at the base of the spinal column, a few centimetres above and behind mooladhara. Physiologically, this centre is associated with the urogenital system and the sexual drive, but here the primary motive is pleasure rather than progeny. From the desire for pleasure arises the need to hold on to the source of that pleasure, which results in attachment. Pleasure also leads to pain, so there is a continuous search for more pleasure and avoidance of pain. At this point in human evolution the creative energy is expressed through the desire for sexual union. The chakra point is associated with sexual power and when open, tremendous potency is experienced. The trigger-point or *chakra kshetram*, located in the front at the centre of the pubic bone, relates with attraction to the opposite sex and facilitates the giving and receiving of sexual pleasure.

At a deeper level swadhisthana is the seat of the unconscious mind, which is the storehouse of all *karmas* and *samskaras*, experiences and impressions. The unconscious is the substratum of individual existence and is far more powerful than the conscious. Mooladhara represents the manifest unconscious where the karmas and instincts are expressed as anger, greed, jealousy, passion, delusion, and so on. Swadhisthana is the unconscious in a potential state, where the karmas and samskaras remain in their seed form. Swadhisthana is considered to be a difficult centre to awaken due to the confusion and disturbance arising from activation of this unconscious material.

43

Every impression and experience is recorded and filed away in some deeper layer of the mind. All of these form the total unconscious and they influence the mind, although they are not consciously perceived. They also form our karmic inheritance and travel with the soul from life to life. Thus the seeds of birth and of rebirth are contained at swadhisthana. These formless impressions have great power and block the passage of kundalini. Even after awakening, the kundalini is said to return back to mooladhara again and again. Non-attachment to pleasure is the key which unlocks the gate of swadhisthana and enables the kundalini to pass through to manipura.

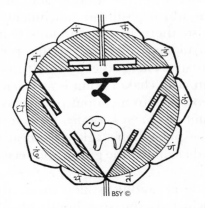

3. Manipura: the third centre, situated behind the navel. The word *mani* means 'jewel' and *pura* means 'city', so manipura is the city of jewels. This is the fire centre, the focal point of heat and vitality, depicted as a bright yellow lotus with ten petals. Within the lotus are a red triangle and the bija mantra *Ram*, riding on a ram, an aggressive beast that symbolizes the fire element. The tanmatra or sensory attribute is sight and the jnanendriya or related sensory organ is the eye. The karmendriya or organ of action is the feet. The vayu is *samana*, which is responsible for the

44

absorption of nutrients and distribution of vitality to the entire system. The loka is *Swaha*, the heavenly region. The presiding devata is Rudra, consumer of the universe, and the devi is Lakini, controller of the flesh element. The guna is rajas and the operating force is combustion. The associated food is starch. The yoga path is karma yoga.

Manipura is the centre of vitality in the physical body, where the heat necessary to maintain and support life is generated. Physiologically, it relates with the solar plexus, digestive organs and digestive fire. Psychologically, it is the centre of dynamism, power, control, status and ego identity. Here the creative energy is expressed through work, productivity, manipulation of others and attraction towards excitement. Manipura is also associated with the lower emotions, which may be negative, i.e. anger, hatred, fear, selfishness, or positive, i.e. courage, perseverance and the desire to win. Manipura chakra point is located behind the navel in the spine and is connected with physical health and resistance. When developed, it can become a powerful centre for pranic healing. The trigger point for manipura is located in the front at the navel and is associated with individual status, relationships and connections in life.

In some schools, manipura is regarded as the first centre and is believed to be the seat of kundalini. This is true in the sense that kundalini goes through a transformation when it passes through manipura. Mooladhara is the seat of kundalini and swadhisthana is the abode. However, it is from manipura that the awakening becomes stable and ongoing.

4. Anahata: the fourth chakra, situated behind the heart. The word *anahata* means 'unstruck'. All sounds in the created universe are produced by striking two objects together, which creates different vibrations or sound waves. That sound, which issues from beyond the material world, is the source of all sounds and is known as the *anahad nada*. This

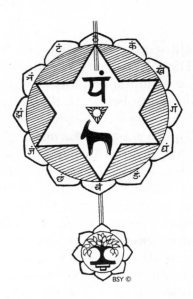

unstruck sound manifests at the heart centre, where it is perceived as the internal, unborn and undying vibration, the pulse of the universe. Anahata is also the centre of *hridayakasha*, the heart space, where the *jivatma* or individual soul resides.

Anahata is symbolized by a blue lotus with twelve petals. In the centre of the lotus is a hexagon formed by two interlacing triangles. Within the triangles is the bija mantra *Yam* riding on a black antelope, symbolizing the air element. The tanmatra or sensory attribute is touch or feeling. The jnanendriya or organ of perception is the skin, and the karmendriya or organ of action is the hands. The vayu is *sthoola prana* and the loka or dimension of experience is *Mahah*. The presiding devata is Isha, the Lord in an all-pervading form, and the devi is Kakini, ruler of the fat element in the body. The associated food is vegetable. The operating force is vibration and the yoga path is bhakti.

Physiologically, anahata is related with the cardiac plexus as well as the heart and lungs. Psychologically, it is the centre of higher emotions such as love, compassion, serenity and patience. By activating anahata, the lower emotions are transformed and one becomes free from the worldly and sensual desires associated with the lower centres. At this level of evolution, acts of sharing, uniting, motivating and inspiring others become a natural expression of the creative energy. Anahata chakra point, located behind the heart in the spine, is associated with harmony between the individual and divine will. The trigger point for anahata is located at the sternum and is associated with the capacity to extend feelings of love to others.

Anahata can become a very powerful healing centre when it is developed. It is also the centre for artistic ability and inspired speech. In relation to yoga, it is said that the physical energy is transformed to spiritual energy at anahata. So, one becomes a yogi with the awakening of anahata; before that one is a practitioner. Up to anahata one remains subject to the limitations of the fate or destiny with which one is born. However, when anahata opens one becomes the master of one's destiny, and whatever one thinks comes true. Therefore, the awakening of this centre requires mastery over the mind as well as positive thoughts, associations and ideals.

5. Vishuddhi: the fifth chakra, located in the throat region. This is the purification centre symbolized by a violet lotus with sixteen petals. In the centre is a large white circle with the bija mantra *Ham* seated upon a white elephant, symbolizing the element of ether or space. The tanmatra or sensory attribute is sound and the vayu is *udana*. The jnanendriya or organ of perception is the ear and the karmendriya or organ of action is the vocal chords. The loka, or dimension, is the experience of *Janah*. The presiding devata is *Ardhanarishwara*, the androgynous form of Lord Shiva and his consort Parvati, combined in one body. The devi is Sakini, who presides over the element of bone. The associated food is fruit and the yoga path is mantra and all forms of chanting.

Vishuddhi chakra is the bridge between the body and the head, the physical and the mental dimensions. Physiologically, it is associated with the thyroid, parathyroid, larynx and pharynx. Psychologically, it is centre of communication and creative expression. At this level arises the ability to discriminate between the lower mind and the higher mind, vidya and avidya, and thus to speak the truth. The trigger-point at the throat-pit relates with the assuming of personal responsibility for oneself and one's actions, and the ability to derive mental nourishment from one's experiences of life. The chakra point is associated with the assimilation of this nourishment and with one's sense of self within the social and professional arenas.

In relation to kundalini yoga, vishuddhi is the centre of purification where the *amrita* or divine nectar of immortality, which falls down from bindu at the top back of the head, is purified and becomes a powerful rejuvenating force. This nectar has a dual nature and acts as a poison also. In the higher centres the nectar remains undifferentiated. When vishuddhi awakens, it acts as a filter and removes the poison from the nectar. Otherwise the unpurified nectar falls unobstructed down to manipura where it is burnt up by the sun, resulting in disease, decay, old age and death. Vishuddhi is also linked with swadhisthana chakra and the sexual drive.

6. Ajna: the sixth chakra, located at the midbrain. This centre is known as *jnana chakshu* (the eye of wisdom), *bhrumadhya* (the eyebrow centre), *guru chakra,* the third eye, and the eye of Shiva. The word *ajna* means 'command'. This is the command centre from which instructions are received when the sadhaka enters deep states of consciousness beyond mental perception and cognition.

Ajna is depicted as a silver lotus with two petals, representing the sun and moon, ida and pingala, the vital and mental pranic flows which converge here. Ajna is the point of confluence where ida, pingala and sushumna merge into one stream of consciousness. The merging of these three forces represents the transcendence of duality, and hence of ego and individuality. This is symbolized by the black shivalingam, representing the causal state, with the bija mantra *Om* at the centre. The tanmatra, jnanendriya and karmendriya of this centre are all mind and the loka or region is *Tapah*. The presiding devata is Param Shiva, the formless consciousness, and the devi is Hakini, who controls *Mahat,* the subtle element of mind.

Ajna chakra is located at the top of the spinal column. Physiologically, it is associated with the brain and the pineal gland. Psychologically, it is synonymous with awareness and relates with the intellectual and psychic abilities. Activation and awakening of ajna increase the faculties of mind, such as intelligence, memory, will power, concentration and visualization. The trigger-point for ajna, located at the eyebrow centre, is also an important psychic centre known as *bhrumadhya* or *bhrukuti*. The trigger-point relates with the ability to understand mental concepts and the chakra-point is responsible for the implementation of ideas. On the subtle plane, ajna is the threshold between the mental and psychic dimensions. Like a doorway, it opens into higher realms of awareness beyond the manifest dimension. Ajna is also directly connected with mooladhara.

BSY ©

7. Sahasrara: the highest centre, at the crown of the head. It is not really a chakra in the sense that it has no attributes or corresponding associations. Sahasrara is the abode of superconsciousness, beyond all attributes. Its loka or dimension of experience is *Satya*, where the individual consciousness merges back into the absolute. The presiding devata is Parambrahma and the devi is Mahashakti or Adyashakti.

Yogis have visualized sahasrara as a resplendent lotus of a thousand petals. In the centre of the lotus is an effulgent shivalingam, symbol of pure consciousness. It is in sahasrara that the mystical union of Shiva and Shakti takes place, the fusion of cosmic consciousness with cosmic energy, the individual soul with the supreme soul. With the attainment of universal consciousness, the doorway to transcendental perception opens. The entrance to the dimension of higher reality is known as the *brahmarandhra*, the doorway to Brahma. This is the seat of bindu chakra, which is located at the fontanel, at the top back of the head.

Mantras 6b, 7, 8: Description of mooladhara

आधारं प्रथमं चक्रं स्वाधिष्ठानं द्वितीयकम् ॥ 6b ॥
योनिस्थानं द्वयोर्मध्ये कामरूपं निगद्यते ।
कामाख्यं तु गुदस्थाने पंकजं तु चतुर्दलम् ॥ 7 ॥
तन्मध्ये प्रोच्यते योनि: कामाख्या सिद्धवन्दिता ।
तस्य मध्ये महालिङ्गं पश्चिमाभिमुखम् स्थितम् ॥ 8 ॥

Aadhaaram Prathamam Chakram Swaadhishthaanam Dwiteeyakam. (6b)
Yonisthaanam Dwayormadhye Kaamaroopam Nigadyate;
Kaamaakhyam tu Gudasthaane Pankajam tu Chaturdalam. (7)
Tanmadhye Prochyate Yonih Kaamaakhyaa Siddhavandita;
Tasya Madhye Mahaalingam Pashchimaabhi Mukham Sthitam. (8)

Anvay

Aadhaaram: mooladhara; *Prathamam*: first; *Chakram*: psychic centre; *Swaadhishthaanam*: swadhisthana; *Dwiteeyakam*: is second; *Dwayoh madhye*: middle of both; *Yonisthaanam*: place of yoni; *Kaamaroopam*: place of desire, love; *Nigadyate*: is called; *Gudasthaane*: in anal region; *Kaama aakhyam tu*: by the name of Kama; *Chaturdalam*: four-petalled; *Pankajam*: lotus; *Tat madhye*: in the centre of that; *Kaamaakhyaa*: of the name of Kama; *Prochyate*: is said; *Yonih*: the source; *Siddhavanditaa*: worshipped by the siddhas; *Tasya*: its; *Mahaalingam*: great lingam; *Paschima abhimukham*: westward facing; *Sthitam*: is situated.

Translation

First (in sequence) is the adhara (mooladhara) chakra and the second is swadhisthana. Between the two (mooladhara and swadhisthana) is the seat of the yoni called kamaroopa. The four-petalled lotus in the anal region is known by the name of Kama. In the centre of the lotus is the kamayoni, which is worshipped by siddhas. In the centre of this yoni, the westward facing mahalinga is situated.

52

Commentary

In this description of mooladhara chakra, the references to yoni, mahalinga and kamaroopa are of symbolic significance. The word *kamaroopa* means the 'form of desire', which is said to be situated in-between mooladhara and swadhisthana. This refers to the close proximity and association of both centres with the reproductive organs and sexual drive. *Kandarpa vayu*, a manifestation of prana in the region of mooladhara, represents deep desire and is related with procreation. The presiding deity of mooladhara is Brahma, the creator. Therefore, the natural, inherent urge of mooladhara is to create. The will to create and its variety of expressions symbolize the creative will of Shakti in the form of kundalini.

The word *yoni* refers to the red inverted triangle where the kundalini energy resides inside the four-petalled lotus at mooladhara. The yoni or womb is the source of creation as well as of spiritual transformation. Siddhas or adepts revere this creative power, which manifests in nature as the inherent force of the divine. Worship, experience and realization of this creative power ultimately propel the sadhaka on the inner journey. The *mahalinga* situated in the yoni or triangle represents the level of consciousness within the sphere of creative energy at mooladhara. The word *maha* means 'great' and *linga* means 'subtle form of consciousness'.

At mooladhara, the consciousness which is obscured and dissipated by material associations and urges has also been symbolized as the *dhumra linga*. The word *dhumra* means 'smoky'. This gross form of consciousness, which is clouded over by desires and material associations, has to be purified and refined by the awakening of kundalini. With this awakening the veil of maya is lifted from the consciousness and it shines forth with its own inner light. Therefore, it is also called *swayambhu linga*, which means 'self-effulgent consciousness'. Westward facing (*paschima*) has been used to describe the position of the mahalinga in the yoni or triangle of mooladhara.

Three pranic channels or *nadis* known as *ida* (the lunar force), *pingala* (the solar force) and *sushumna* (the spiritual force) arise from the yoni, or triangle, directly above the mahalinga, and connect mooladhara with the other chakras and the brain. They have been described along with the other major nadis further on in the text. In the psychic body, pingala nadi emanates from the western side of the yoni or triangle and its function is to carry the vital force from the base chakra to the other chakras. The westward facing mahalinga, therefore, represents the influence of life force or physical energy on the consciousness at the level of mooladhara.

Mantras 9, 10: Description of manipura

नाभौ तु मणिवद्बिम्बं यो जानाति स योगवित् ।
तप्तचामीकराभासं तडिल्लेखेव विस्फुरत् ॥ 9 ॥
त्रिकोणं तत्पुरं वह्नेरधोमेद्ध्रात्प्रतिष्ठितम् ।
समाधौ परमं ज्योतिरनन्तं विश्वतोमुखम् ॥ 10 ॥

Nabhou Tu Manivadbimbam Yo Jaanaati Sa Yogavit;
Taptachaamikara Abhaasam Tadillekheva Visphurat. (9)
Trikonam Tatpuram Vahneradhomeddrat Pratishthitam;
Samaadhou Paramam Jyotiranantam Vishwatomukham. (10)

Anvay

Nabhau tu: in the navel; *Maniwat*: like jewel; *Bimbam*: shade, reflection; *Yah*: who; *Jaanaati*: knows; *Sah*: he; *Yogavit*: knower of yoga; *Tapta*: burning or heated; *Chaameekara*: gold; *Aabhaasam*: lustrous; *Tadit*: lightening; *Lekhaa eva*: like line; *Visphurat*: iridescent; *Tatpuram*: therein; *Medhraat*: at the point of origin of the nadis; *Adhah*: below; *Vahneh*: of fire; *Trikonam*: triangle; *Pratishthitam*: is situated; *Samaadhau*: in samadhi; *Paramam*: supreme; *Anantam*: eternal, infinite; *Vishwatomukham*: having mouth in all directions; *Jyotih*: light, flame.

Translation

In the navel is the reflecting jewel-like (manipura). One who knows this is the real knower of yoga. This (centre) is lustrous like heated gold and iridescent like a streak of lightning. Therein is the triangle, the seat of fire, below which is the medhra. By meditating in samadhi (on this region) (the yogi) sees the all-pervading light which is eternal.

Commentary

The word *manipura* means the 'jewelled city'. Jewels are very bright and are known to be powerful conductors of light and energy. Similarly, manipura is the centre or storehouse of prana and the seat of the fire element. One who knows this is said to be the real knower of yoga, because it is from manipura that actual spiritual awakening takes place. According to the yogic tradition, the kundalini force is generated at mooladhara, but the actual awakening takes place at manipura. The awakening of kundalini at mooladhara is like a trickle, whereas the awakening from manipura is like a blast. Kundalini is said to awaken from mooladhara, not once but many times, until the sadhaka is purified. Each time the kundalini rises a short distance and falls back. However, when the awakening takes place from manipura, it becomes ongoing and there is no longer any danger of falling back. Man is bound by the lower instincts until the awakening of manipura. From this point one's destiny is shaped by higher realization and there is no regression to the gross nature.

Manipura is described as situated two fingers width above the *medhra,* which is the nadi complex where the major nadis, or conductors of prana, originate. Manipura, like mooladhara, is an important centre of shakti, and this is represented by the red inverted triangle, symbolizing vital energy. At manipura, the kundalini energy is expressed in the form of fire and is known as *agni mandala.* The word *agni* means 'fire' and *mandala* means 'zone' or 'region'. So, manipura is the zone of fire and it is represented by the fiery red inverted triangle. When awakening takes place at manipura, this region is perceived as lustrous, like burnished gold, and iridescent, like lightning. Manipura is also symbolized by the sun, which is the source of illumination. Therefore it is said that by meditating in samadhi on manipura, the yogi experiences the dimension of pure spirit, which is the eternal, all pervading light.

Mantras 11, 12: Description of swadhisthana

तस्मिन्दृष्टे महायोगे यातायातो न विद्यते ।
स्वशब्देन भवेत्प्राण: स्वाधिष्ठानं तदाश्रयम् ॥ 11 ॥
स्वाधिष्ठानाश्रयादस्मान्मेद्रमेवाभिधीयते ।
तन्तुना मणिवत्प्रोतो योऽत्र कन्द: सुषुम्नया ॥ 12 ॥

Tasmindrishte Mahaayoge Yaataayaato Na Vidyate;
Swashabdena Bhavetpraanah Swaadhishthaanam Tadaashrayam. (11)
Swaadhishthaana Aashrayaadasmaan Meddramevaabhidheeyate;
Tantuna Manivatproto Yotra Kandah Sushumnayaa. (12)

Anvay

Mahaayoge: in highest state of yoga; *Tasmin drishte*: on seeing (experiencing) that; *Yaataayaato*: coming and going (birth and death); *Na vidyate*: does not remain; *Swashabdena*: by the word self; *Praanah*: vital force; *Bhavet*: becomes; *Tadaashrayam*: location thereof; *Swaadhishthaanam*: swadhisthana; *Asmaat*: its; *Swaadhishthaanaashrayaat*: because of location in swadhisthana; *Medhrameva*: indeed medhra; *Abhidheeyate*: is called, known; *Yah*: which; *Atra*: here; *Tantunaa*: with thread; *Manivat*: like gems; *Kandah sushumnayaa*: with the root of sushumna; *Protah*: tied, strung.

Translation

By realizing that in the highest state of yoga, (no trace of) coming and going (the cycle of birth and death) remains. By the word self the prana (life force) is understood, and swadhisthana becomes the place of prana. Because of its location swadhisthana is also known as medhra. That point, which is the root of sushumna, is like gems strung together.

Commentary

Swadhisthana chakra is the seat of the unconscious mind, which is also the domain of the *karmashaya*, the storehouse of karmas. These impressions which have accumulated in the consciousness since the beginning of time form a mental blockage and hinder the sadhaka from evolving further, keeping him enmeshed in the world of name and form, cause and effect, desire and repulsion. They also bind the individual soul to the continuous cycle of birth and death. Due to the karmas the soul is drawn back to the material dimension and suffers birth, disease, old age and death, life after life. This is known as bondage, from which yogins seek liberation.

The first mantra states that no trace of this cycle of 'coming and going' remains when the unconscious, or abode of the self, is realied in the highest state of yoga. Samadhi is the highest state of yoga, which occurs when the kundalini shakti awakens and ascends sushumna. Realization of swadhisthana in the highest state of yoga refers to the passage of kundalini through this centre. When the kundalini awakens swadhisthana, the unconscious is illumined and the karmas stored within it are purified and transcended. In this way, the karmic blockage is removed and no trace of 'coming and going', or transmigration, remains.

The mantra also refers to *swa-shabdha* in relation to swadhisthana. The word *swa* means 'self-manifest' and *shabdha* means 'word'. In the Bible it is said that 'in the beginning was the word, and the word was with God, and the word was God'. In Vedanta we also find the term *shabdha-brahman*, which means the 'word of reality', the first sound of the absolute, unmanifest. Similarly, here we find the term swa-shabdha, 'the self-arisen word', which manifests from the unconscious, without cause or beginning. One of the names of prana or life force is also *swa*. By meditating on swadhisthana in the highest state of yoga, one realizes the swa-shabdha, from which comes prana or life force responsible for all existence and creation. In this sense, swadhisthana may also be understood as the abode of prana.

In the next mantra, swadhisthana is given as the location of the *medhra*, which is the origin point for the major nadis or pranic channels. The medhra is described here as the root of sushumna nadi, the pathway through which kundalini ascends to sahasrara. The origin of sushumna is given as mooladhara in other references. This point is ambiguous due to the close proximity of the two centres. However, it is generally accepted that the sushumna arises from mooladhara, but is also rooted in the medhra along with the other major nadis. The gems strung together symbolize the confluence of nadis tied together at the medhra, as well as the psychic and spiritual experiences that arise at the time of kundalini passing through this centre. Witnessing the deep-rooted samskaras and archetypes and realizing them one at a time is the awakening of the unconscious mind.

Mantras 13, 14a: Agni mandala

तन्नाभिमण्डले चक्रं प्रोच्यते मणिपूरकम् ।
द्वादशारे महाचक्रे पुण्यपापविवर्जिते ॥ 13 ॥
तावज्जीवो भ्रमत्येवं यावत्तत्त्वं न विन्दति ॥ 14a ॥

Tannaabhi Mandale Chakram Prochyate Manipoorakam;
Dwaadashaare Mahaachakre Punyapaapa Vivarjite. (13)
Taavajjeevo Bhramatyevam Yaavat Tattwam Na Vindati. (14a)

Anvay

Tat naabhimandale: in that navel region; *Chakram*: centre;
Manipoorakam: manipura; *Prochyate*: called, known;
Dwaadashaare: twelve-petalled; *Mahaachakre*: great chakra;
Punyapaapavivarjite: unrelated to virtue or vice; *Taavat*: until;
Jeevah: embodied individual; *Evam*: thus; *Bhramati*: goes
through; *Yaavat*: so long as; *Tattwam*: element; *Na vindati*:
does not realize, attain.

Translation

In the navel region is the centre known as manipura, which
has twelve petals. As long as the individual does not realize
the element of this great chakra, which is beyond virtue and
vice (duality), he has to go through the cycles of birth and
death.

Commentary

Here manipura is symbolized as a lotus flower with twelve
petals, although in other texts it is said to have ten petals.
Manipura is the centre or storehouse of prana, the cause of
life and existence. The element of this chakra is fire, so it is
also known as *agni mandala*, the circle of fire. The circle is
symbolic of infinity, that which is without beginning or end.
So, the element of fire represents the eternal fire or spirit
which is beyond birth and death. At the physical level, this

fire is responsible for maintaining the digestive functions as well as regulating body heat. At the subtle level, it becomes the yogic fire which burns away all the impurities in the form of lower or instinctive tendencies and material associations and impressions.

Manipura is the centre where ego gratification depends on role, status and power in the outer world. This shift of awareness is based on duality, I versus other. There is great concern with social and professional constraints, whether one is inferior or superior, weak or strong, popular or unpopular. The mantra infers that this perception of duality, identification with vice and virtue, etc. will continue until the element of manipura is realized. Duality is dependent on the association of self or ego as a separate entity. As long as the individual identification prevails, there will be birth and death. With the awakening of agni mandala through the practices of kundalini yoga, the awareness is freed from ego associations and the pure consciousness shines forth like the light of the sun. Such a yogin no longer passes through the cycle of birth and death.

Mantras 14b, 15: Origin of the nadis

ऊर्ध्वं मेढ्रादधोनाभेः कन्दयोनिः खगाण्डवत् ॥ 14b ॥
तत्र नाडच: समुत्पन्ना: सहस्राणि: द्विसप्तति: ।
तेषु नाडीसहस्त्रेषु द्विसप्ततिरुदाहृता ॥ 15 ॥

Oordhwam Meddhraadadhonaabheh Kandayonih Khagaandavat. (14b)
Tatra Naadyah Samutpannaah Sahasraanih Dwisaptatih;
Teshu Naadee Sahasreshu Dwisaptatirudaahritaa. (15)

Anvay

Medhraat: from the medhra; *Oordhwam*: above; *Naabheh*: navel; *Adhah*: below; *Kandayonih*: root or base of the womb; *Khagaandavat*: like a bird's egg; *Tatra*: there; *Dwisaptatih*: seventy-two; *Sahasraani*: thousand; *Naadyah*: energy channels; *Samutpannaah*: emanate; *Teshu*: out of these; *Naadeesahasreshu*: from amongst thousands of nadis; *Dwisaptatih*: seventy-two; *Udaahritaa*: considered to be the principal ones.

Translation

From the medhra, (located) above the base of the womb and below the navel, which is the origin point of the nadis, and is shaped like an egg, seventy-two thousand energy channels emanate. From amongst these thousands of channels, seventy-two are considered to be principal.

Commentary

Prana is the etheric or vital force which pervades the entire cosmos and is responsible for all manifest existence. It comprises all beings, whether animate or inanimate, and nothing can live or exist without it. Though closely related to the air we breathe, it is not the same. Prana is subtler than air and can be defined as the energy force that is the substratum of every created object in the universe. In living beings this force is responsible for all life and movement,

62

whether physical, mental, psychic or spiritual. In human beings this life force is said to be generated by the kundalini shakti, which at man's present level of evolution is lying dormant at mooladhara chakra.

At the subtle level this pranic force is stored and transmitted to the related organs and parts of the body and brain by the chakras or psychic energy centres, which act as trigger points. This force is transmitted from the chakras through energy channels which are called nadis. The word *nadi* is derived from the Sanskrit root *nad,* which literally means 'to flow'. So nadis are energy currents or flows. In recent times the word nadi has been translated as nerve. Although nerves are said to be the closest physical correlate, nadis are not nerves for they are composed of subtle stuff. Nadis are not located in the physical body; they form the infrastructure of the vital or pranic body which gives life, movement and energy to the physical body.

The location of the origin point from which the nadis emanate is described as being below the navel and above the kandayoni. The navel is the physical location of manipura and the kandayoni is the location of mooladhara. So, the medhra is located between manipura and mooladhara chakras.

The word y*oni* means 'womb' and is symbolically depicted as a red inverted triangle. It is the seat of kundalini shakti, the latent spiritual force responsible for all manifestation and transformation. The word *kanda* means 'root' or 'base', and here it signifies the root plexus or mooladhara chakra, above which the nadis emanate in the psychic body. The medhra is situated just above the triangle or yoni at the opening of sushumna nadi, the path of energy flowing through the chakras or psychic centres, which represent the entire spectrum of human personality.

The nadis, or subtle channels of vital force, flow alongside the central canal of the spinal column and branch out at different psychic centres to vitalize different parts of the body. Some nadis also travel downward for maintenance of the lower extremities. It is stated in many of the ancient texts and also here in this mantra that there are seventy-two thousand nadis in the pranic body. A person who has developed psychic vision perceives these channels as currents of light. Out of the seventy-two thousand nadis, which flow throughout the pranic body, only seventy-two are considered to be important. The rest are subsidiary.

Mantras 16, 17: Ten major nadis

प्रधाना: प्राणवाहिन्यो भूयस्तासु दश स्मृता: ।
इडा च पिङ्गला चैव सुषुम्ना च तृतीयगा ॥ 16 ॥
गान्धारी हस्तिजिह्वा च पूषा चैव यशस्विनी ।
अलम्बुसा कुहूश्चैव शङ्खिनी दशमी स्मृता ॥ 17 ॥

*Pradhaanaah Praanavaahinyo Bhooyastaasu Dasha Smritaah;
Idaa cha Pingalaa Chaiva Sushumnaa cha Triteeyagaa.* (16)
*Gaandhaaree Hastijihvaa cha Pooshaa Chaiva Yashaswinee;
Alambusaa Kuhooshchaiva Shankhinee Dashamee Smritaa.* (17)

Anvay

Taasu: among them; *Bhooyah*: again; *Pradhaanaah*: principal; *Praanavaahinyah*: through which prana flows; *Dasha*: ten; *Smritaah*: are known; *Idaa*: ida; *Cha*: and; *Pingalaa*: pingala; *Cha eva*: and; *Triteeyagaa cha*: the third is; *Sushumnaa*: sushumna; *Gaandhaaree*: gandhari; *Hastijihvaa*: hastijihva; *Cha*: and; *Pooshaa*: pusha; *Cha eva*: and; *Yashaswinee*: yashaswini; *Alambusaa*: alambusa; *Kuhoo*: kuhu; *Cha eva*: and; *Dashamee*: the tenth; *Shankhinee*: shankhini; *Smritaa*: have been said.

Translation

Again, among these (seventy-two), the principal nadis for the flow of prana are ten. These are known as: ida, pingala and the third sushumna, gandhari, hastijihva, pusha, yashaswini, alambusa, kuhu and the tenth shankhini. So, they have been said.

Commentary

Some texts such as *Shandilya Upanishad, Gheranda Samhita, Hatha Yoga Pradipika* and *Yoga Sutras* describe fourteen major nadis and others ten. The number depends on individual observation and how the psychic body is perceived. This

65

text describes the ten main nadis mentioned above. Out of these, the first three, ida, pingala and sushumna are the most important and the others are of secondary importance. The location of the ten nadis is described in the following mantras.

Mantras 18, 19, 20: Location of the major nadis

एतन्नाडीमहाचक्रं ज्ञातव्यं योगिभि: सदा ।
इडा वामे स्थिता भागे दक्षिणे पिङ्गला स्थिता ॥ 18 ॥
सुषुम्ना मध्यदेशे तु गान्धारी वामचक्षुषि ।
दक्षिणे हस्तिजिह्वा च पूषा कर्णे तु दक्षिणे ॥ 19 ॥
यशस्विनी वामकर्णे चानने चाप्यलम्बुसा ।
कुहूश्च लिङ्गदेशे तु मूलस्थाने तु शङ्खिनी ॥ 20 ॥

Etannaadee Mahaachakram Gnaatavyam Yogibhih Sadaa;
Idaa Vaame Sthitaa Bhaage Dakshine Pingalaa Sthitaa. (18)
Sushumnaa Madhyadeshe tu Gaandhaari Vaamachakshushi;
Dakshine Hastijihvaa Cha Pooshaa Karne tu Dakshine. (19)
Yashaswini Vaamakarne Chaanane Chaapyalambusaa;
Kuhooshcha Lingadeshe tu Moolasthaane tu Shankhinee. (20)

Anvay

Etat: this; *Nadee mahaachakram*: great nadi complex; *Yogibhih*: by the yogis; *Sadaa*: always; *Gnaatavyam*: worth knowing; *Vaame bhaage*: on the left side; *Idaa*: ida; *Sthitaa*: is; *Dakshine*: on the right; *Pingalaa*: pingala; *Sthitaa*: is; *Sushumna*: sushumna; *Madhya deshe tu*: in the middle; *Gandhaaree*: gandhari; *Vaama*: left; *Chakshushi*: in the eye; *Dakshine*: in the right; *Hastijihvaa*: hastijihva; *Cha*: and; *Pooshaa*: pusha; *Karne tu*: of the ear; *Dakshine*: on the right; *Yashaswinee*: yashaswini; *Vaamakarne*: at the left ear; *Cha*: and; *Alambusaa*: alambusa; *Cha api*: also; *Aanane*: in the face; *Cha*: and; *Kuhoo*: kuhu; *Lingadeshe tu*: in the genitals; *Tu*: and; *Shankhinee*: shankhini; *Moolasthaane*: at the perineum.

Translation

The yogis should always be aware of this great nadi complex. Ida is on the left side and pingala on the right. Sushumna is in middle. Gandhari goes to the left eye and hastijihva to the right eye. Pusha goes to the right ear and Yashaswini to the left ear. Alambusa goes to the face region. Kuhu goes to genitals and Shankhini to the perineum.

Commentary

An important aim of yoga is to develop awareness and inner vision of the pranas and nadis. Ida and pingala are the two nadis which are responsible for vital and mental energy in the body and brain. They traverse the spinal cord alternately, originating from the left and right of mooladhara, just below the medhra, and link all the chakras together. Sushumna, which is the pathway for the ascent of kundalini, emerges from the centre of mooladhara and goes straight up through the psychic centres, piercing each one in turn. It is said that as long as sushumna remains in a dormant state, the human functions at the level of duality through the activity of chitta shakti and prana shakti, which flow transversely through the two major channels of ida and pingala. It is only when the kundalini or atma shakti awakens and flows through the sushumna nadi that the veil of duality is removed and one perceives the dimension of cosmic unity.

The remaining seven of the major nadis are the channels of prana which link the psychic centres with their related sensory organs. The cognition of the senses is dependent on the flow of prana to these organs. If the quantum of prana is less then the power of the senses is diminished, and if the quantum of prana is more then the senses are very sharp. A relatively large proportion of prana is required to empower the senses and connect their input to the brain. When prana flows to the eyes through gandhari and hastijihva nadis, the result is vision, perception of shape, form and colour. Pusha and yashashwini control the ears and perception of sound. Kuhu and shankhini channels direct the activities of procreation and excretion.

Mantras 21, 22a: Ida, pingala and sushumna

एवं द्वार समाश्रित्य तिष्ठन्ते नाडय: क्रमात् ।
इडापिङ्गलसौषुम्ना: प्राणमार्गे च संस्थिता: ॥ 21 ॥
सततं प्राणवाहिन्य: सोमसूर्याग्निदेवता: ॥ 22a ॥

Evam Dwaara Samaashritya Tishthante Naadayah Kramaat;
Idaa Pingala Soushumnaah Praanamaarge Cha Samsthitaah. (21)
Satatam Praana Vaahinyah Somasooryaagnidevataah. (22a)

Anvay

Evam: thus; *Dwaara*: passages; *Samaashritya*: dependent; *Naadyah*: nadis; *Kramaat*: systematically; *Tishthante*: are located; *Cha*: and; *Idaapingalaa*: ida, pingala; *Soushumnaah*: sushumna; *Pranamaarge*: in the path of prana; *Samsthitaah*: are located; *Soma*: moon; *Soorya*: sun; *Agnidevataa*: god of fire; *Satatam*: constantly; *Praanah vaahinyah*: continue to move the prana.

Translation

Thus these nadis are dependent and located systematically in the (various) passages of the body. Ida, pingala and sushumna are the paths of prana located in soma (moon), surya (sun) and agni (fire) devatas (illumined divinities) which continue to move the prana.

Commentary

Out of the seventy-two thousand nadis, the three most important are ida, pingala and sushumna; all the others are dependent upon them. Ida is the passive channel which is related with the moon, or mental energy, so it is known as *chandra* or *soma* nadi. The colour of ida is blue, and it is a negative or cooling current. Pingala is the active channel which is related with the sun, or vital energy, so it is known as *surya nadi*. The colour of pingala is red and it is a positive

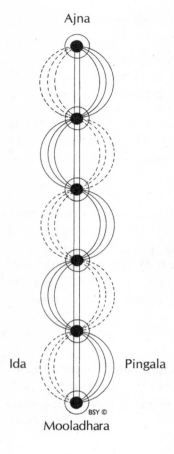

Ajna

Ida   Pingala

BSY ©

Mooladhara

or heating current. Ida emerges from the left of mooladhara and pingala from the right. They ascend the spinal pathway alternately, crossing over at each chakra point.

Ida and pingala nadis represent the dual or manifest forces of life. In yogic terms they are also known as the channels of *manas* or *chitta shakti*, the mental or conscious force, and *prana shakti*, the vital or physical force. When ida and pingala are purified, regulated and balanced, sushumna nadi, which represents the spiritual, unmanifest or unconscious forces, begins to flow. This mantra relates sushumna with *agni devata*, who represents the fiery, luminous quality of the spiritual force, which this nadi channels. Sushumna flows straight up through the centre of the spinal cord, from mooladhara to sahasrara, and is silvery in colour.

In yoga, sushumna is known as atma shakti, the spiritual force. It is this channel through which the ascending kundalini must pass at the time of spiritual awakening. Therefore, the preparatory practices of kundalini yoga involve purification and regulation of the nadis in general, and ida and pingala in particular, for the purpose of opening sushumna. This nadi must be flowing if there is to be success in meditation. If pingala flows predominantly, the body will be restless. If ida flows predominantly, the mind

70

will be restless. When sushumna flows, the mind enters a state of spontaneous absorption and kundalini, the spiritual force, rises through the chakras.

In physiological terms, ida and pingala correspond to the two aspects of the autonomic nervous system. Pingala corresponds to the sympathetic nervous system, which speeds up the heart, dilates the blood vessels, increases the respiration rate and intensifies the efficiency of the senses, thus extroverting the mind. Ida corresponds to the parasympathetic nervous system, which directly opposes the sympathetic nerves by reducing the heart beat, constricting the blood vessels, slowing the respiration and relaxing the system so that the mind and senses become relaxed and introverted.

The flow of prana through ida and pingala is completely involuntary and unconscious in most people. It only becomes conscious and subject to manipulation and control through systematic practice of hatha and kundalini yoga. Through these practices the quantum of vital and mental forces is regulated and increased, which brings about eventual mastery over the body and mind and opens the doors of the psychic and spiritual world.

Mantras 22b, 23a: Prana vayus

प्राणापानसमानाख्या व्यानोदानौ च वायव: ॥ 22b ॥
नाग: कूर्मोऽथ कृकरो देवदत्तो धनंजय: ॥ 23a ॥

Praana Apaana Samaanaakhyaa Vyaanodaanau cha Vaayavah. (22b)
Naagah Koormotha Krikaro Devadatto Dhananjayah. (23a)

Anvay

Praana: Prana; *Apaana*: apana; *Samaana*: samana; *Vyaana*: vyana; *Udaana*: udana; *Cha*: and; *Naagah*: naga; *Koormah-atah*: kurma; *Krikarah*: krikara; *Devadattah*: devadatta; *Dhananjayah*: dhananjaya; *Aakhyaa*: named; *Vaayavah*: vital airs.

Translation

The vital airs are named prana, apana, samana, vyana, udana, and naga, kurma, krikara, devadatta, and dhananjaya.

Commentary

The *prana vayus* refer to the vital airs, active in all beings, which are responsible for existence and life. Although the prana in the body is one force, it has traditionally been divided into five categories according to area and function. These are collectively known as the pancha (five) pranas: *prana, apana, samana, udana* and *vyana*. There are also five *upa-pranas* or secondary pranas: *naga, kurma, krikara, devadatta* and *dhananjaya*. The five pranas maintain the major body parts and functions, while the five upa-pranas are concerned with minor actions. Vayus or vital airs flow through these ten pranic fields. Each vayu is the movement associated with one pranic field and has the same name. For example, apana vayu is the movement within the apana energy field. The breathing process generates the vayus. By controlling the vayus, subtle manifestations of prana can be channelled.

72

Mantras 23b, 24: Location of the pancha vayus

हृदि प्राण: स्थितो नित्यमपानो गुदमण्डले ॥ 23b ॥
समानो नाभिदेशे तु उदान: कण्ठमध्यग: ।
व्यान: सर्वशरीरे तु प्रधाना: पञ्च वायव: ॥ 24 ॥

Hridi Praanah Sthito Nityamapaano Gudamandale. (23b)
Samaano Naabhideshe tu Udaanah Kanthamadhyagah;
Vyaanah Sarva Shareere tu Pradhaanaah Pancha Vaayavah. (24)

Anvay

Praanah: prana; *Hridi*: in the heart; *Sthitah*: located; *Apaanah*: apana; *Nityam*: always; *Gudamandale*: in the lower regions; *Samaanah*: samana; *Naabhideshe tu*: in the navel region; *Udaanah*: udana; *Kanthamadhyagah*: which moves in the throat region; *Vyaanah*: vyana; *Sarva shareere tu*: in the entire body; *Pradhaanaah*: principal; *Pancha*: five; *Vaayavah*: the vital airs.

Translation

Prana is located in the heart and apana is always in the lower regions. Samana is located in the navel region and udana in the throat region. Vyana moves in the entire body. These are the five principle vital airs.

Commentary

The mantra states that prana is situated in the heart region. The prana referred to here is *sthoola* prana or the physical manifestation of energy. This prana belongs to a specific part of the body located in the region between the larynx and diaphragm. It is associated with the respiratory tract, the heart and the oesophagus, together with the muscles and nerves that activate them. Prana is primarily an upward moving force which also moves downward. It is the force by which the breath is drawn in and then expelled, and food and liquid are swallowed.

73

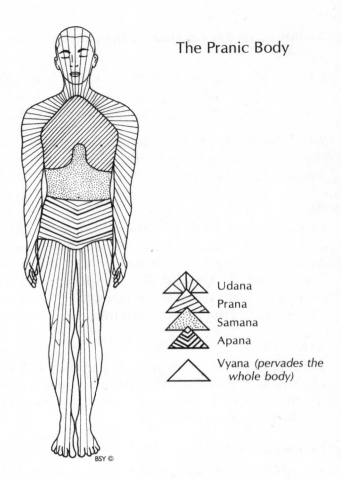

The Pranic Body

Udana
Prana
Samana
Apana
Vyana *(pervades the whole body)*

BSY ©

Apana flows in the lower regions between the navel and the perineum. It is a downward moving force which is responsible for the elimination of urine, faeces, gas, wind, sexual fluids, menstrual blood and the foetus at the time of birth. It provides energy for the functioning of the large intestine, kidneys, bladder, anus, genitals and womb.

Samana is located in the region between the diaphragm and navel. It controls the digestive system, including the stomach, small intestine, liver, pancreas and the secretions

74

of these organs. Samana is a lateral moving force which is responsible for the assimilation of nutrients as well as the heating and cooling of the body. It also activates the heart and the circulatory system.

Udana is a spiralling force which maintains the peripheral parts of the body, including the head above the larynx as well as the arms and legs. Thus the brain and all the sensory receptors: eyes, ears, nose, tongue and skin, as well as three organs of action: speech, hands and feet, are governed by this force. Without it we would be unable to think and act in the world.

Vyana is the all-pervasive force which moves in every direction throughout the body. It acts as a reserve force for the other pranas. If any prana becomes depleted, vyana steps in and maintains the balance. It regulates physical movement and coordinates the other vital energies. Vyana harmonizes and activates the limbs, associated muscles, ligaments, nerves and joints. It is also responsible for the erect posture of the body.

Mantras 25, 26: Function of the upa-pranas

उद्गारे नाग आख्यात: कूर्म उन्मीलने तथा ।
कृकर: क्षुत्करो ज्ञेयो देवदत्तो विजृम्भणे ॥ 25 ॥
न जहाति मृतं वापि सर्वव्यापी धनंजय: ।
एते नाडीषु सर्वासु भ्रमन्ते जीवजन्तव: ॥ 26 ॥

Udgaare Naaga Aakhyaatah Koorma Unmeelane Tathaa;
Krikarah Kshutkaro Gneyo Devadatto Vijrimbhane. (25)
Na Jahaati Mritam Vaapi Sarvavyaapee Dhananjayah;
Ete Naadeeshu Sarvaasu Bhramante Jeeva Jantavah. (26)

Anvay

Udgaare: bringing up as in vomiting, spitting and belching;
Naagah: naga; *Aakhyaatah*: named; *Tathaa*: and; *Unmeelane*:
in flickering the eyelids; *Koormah*: kurma; *Kshutkarah*: that
which causes sneezing; *Krikarah*: krikara; *Gneyah*: should
be known or understood; *Vijrimbhane*: in yawning; *Devadattah*: devadatta; *Sarva vyaapee*: all pervading; *Dhananjayah*:
dhananjaya; *Mritam vaapi*: even the dead body; *Na jahaati*:
does not leave; *Ete*: these; *Sarvaasu*: all; *Naadeeshu*: in the
nadis; *Jeeva jantavah*: all the living beings; *Bhramante*: move.

Translation

The energy which brings up as in belching, vomiting or
spitting is named naga. That which controls the flickering
of the eyelids is koorma. That which causes sneezing should
be known as krikara, and yawning as devadatta. The all-
pervading dhananjaya does not leave the body (immediately)
even after death. All these (upa-pranas) move through the
nadis in all the living beings.

Commentary

The five upa-pranas are vayus or winds concerned with the
minor actions of the body. Naga is responsible for bringing

up the contents of the stomach as in belching, eructation and vomiting. Kurma is the force which maintains the blinking of the eyes and keeps them moist. Krikara is responsible for sneezing, and devadatta for yawning. Dhananjaya maintains physical warmth and remains in the body even after death, causing rigor mortis. These five energies flow through the nadis of all living beings and help to maintain the internal harmony of the body.

Mantra 27: Jiva and prana

आक्षिप्तो भुजदण्डेन तथा यथोच्चलति कन्दुक: ।
प्राणापानसमाक्षिप्तस्तथा जीवो न तिष्ठति ॥ 27 ॥

Aakshipto Bhujadandena Tathaa Yathochchalati Kandukah;
Praanaapaana Samaakshiptastathaa Jeevo Na Tishthati. (27)

Anvay

Yathaa: as; *Bhujadandena*: with hands; *Aakshiptah*: thrown; *Kandukah*: ball; *Tathaa*: similarly; *Uchchalati*: goes up and down; *Praana apaana*: prana and apana; *Samaakshiptah*: thrown up in the same way; *Jeevah*: individual soul; *Na thisthati*: does not remain still.

Translation

Just as a ball goes up and down when thrown by hand, similarly, the individual soul is thrown up (and down) in the same way by the movement of prana and apana (and therefore) does not remain still.

Commentary

The word *jiva* means the individual soul or consciousness which experiences changes in the sensory world and is influenced by them. The changes are the experience of duality, such as heat and cold, sickness and health, happiness and misery, pleasure and pain, attraction and repulsion, life and death.

The cause of this duality at the physical level is said to be the breath. When the jiva is born into the human body it takes its first breath, which signifies its entry into life. From the first breath at birth until the last breath at death, the embodied soul is dependent on the breath as a source of life. Normally throughout a single lifetime, the human body breathes fifteen times in a minute, nine hundred

78

times in an hour and twenty-one thousand six hundred times in a day.

Breathing is a dualistic process involving two aspects or movements, inspiration and expiration. Prana represents the inspiration or active breath, and apana the expiration or passive breath. Prana and apana are the upward and downward moving forces which influence the manifest consciousness. Hence the jiva is tossed up and down with each continuous breath, like a ball which is thrown up and down by the hand. As long as the breath moves in and out, the metabolic processes of the body and the thought processes of the mind continue to function. The individual soul is constantly influenced by these processes and never remains still.

Under the influence of apana, the consciousness is drawn downward to mooladhara, which is associated with the grossest level of manifestation, the earth or material element. There it generates desires and interacts with the world. Under the influence of prana, the consciousness is drawn upward towards sahasrara, which is associated with ether, the subtlest element, and with the unmanifest dimension, where it experiences its higher nature. These two aspects of human life, the inner and the outer, the mundane and the spiritual, can be brought together and united through manipulation and cessation of the breath, which is an important aspect of kundalini yoga.

Mantra 28: Jiva and ida/pingala

प्राणापानवशो जीवो ह्यधश्चोर्ध्वं च धावति ।
वामदक्षिणमार्गाभ्यां चञ्चलत्वान्न दृश्यते ॥ 28 ॥

Praanaapaana Vasho Jeevo Hyadhashchordhvam Cha Dhaavati;
Vaamadakshina Maargaabhyaam Chanchalatvaanna Drishyate. (28)

Anvay

Praana apaana vashah: being under the influence of prana
and apana; *Jeevah*: individual soul; *Hi*: because of this;
Adhah cha oordhvam: down and up; *Cha*: and; *Vaama dakshina
maarga bhyaam*: through the left and the right passages;
Dhaavati: moves; *Chanchalatvaat*: because of its fast movement; *Na drishyate*: cannot be perceived.

Translation

Influenced by prana and apana, the individual soul ascends
and descends. It also moves through the left and the right
passages, but cannot be perceived because of its rapid
movement.

Commentary

The movement of prana and apana, inhalation and exhalation, as well as the flow of the left and right passages influence
the individual soul. In yoga, the left and right passages are
ida and pingala nadis respectively. These are the two major
energy channels within each individual which further
contribute to the duality in human nature. Ida is the lunar
channel, which represents the mental aspect of our nature,
and pingala is the solar channel, which represents the physical
or vital aspect. Together they rule all of the physical and
mental actions and interactions.

The mantra also states that the movement of jiva through
the left and right passages cannot be seen because of its

rapidity. The movement of jiva through ida and pingala is in the form of prana, which has no material existence as such. The word prana means energy or vibration in constant movement. The movement of this subtle vibration or force is very rapid and, therefore, it cannot be perceived by the naked eye. It is said that prana moves with the speed of light and is perceived as luminosity by yogis who have developed their inner vision. However, the breath influences the movement of prana through these two channels, and the breath can be manipulated and controlled.

The physical termination point of ida nadi is said to be at the left nostril and pingala nadi at the right. Normally, the breath is an autonomic process which flows without conscious regulation. The breath flows naturally in cycles of sixty to ninety minutes through one nostril and then the other, throughout the day and night. When the breath flows predominantly through ida, the left nostril, then the passive, mental force manifests, so the nature becomes quiet and subdued. When the flow changes to pingala, the right nostril, then the active, vital force manifests, so the nature becomes dynamic and restless. By manipulation of the breath through the alternate nostrils, the pranas are balanced and controlled. Then the jiva, or individual consciousness, can be perceived.

Mantra 29: Jiva and guna

रज्जुबद्धो यथा श्येनो गतोऽप्याकृष्यते पुनः।
गुणबद्धस्तथा जीवः प्राणापानेन कर्षति ॥ 29 ॥

Rajju Baddho Yathaa Shyeno Gatopyaa Krishyate Punah;
Gunabaddhastathaa Jeevah Praanaapaanena Karshati. (29)

Anvay

Yathaa: just as; *Rajjubaddhah*: tied by the string; *Shyenah*: falcon; *Gatah api aakrishyate*: could fly up but will be pulled down; *Punah*: again; *Tathaa*: similarly; *Guna baddhah*: bound by the gunas; *Praana apaanena*: by prana and apana; *Karshati*: is attracted by; *Jeevah*: individual soul.

Translation

Just as a falcon tied by the string flies up and is drawn back down, similarly, the jiva, bound by the gunas, is attracted by prana and apana.

Commentary

Jiva or the individual self is here compared to a falcon. Just as the falcon is bound by the string, so the jiva is bound by the *gunas* or attributes of *prakriti*, which govern every aspect of life.

Prakriti has three attributes or qualities: *sattwa* (balance), *rajas* (activity) and *tamas* (stability). In science, these three attributes represent vibration, motion and inertia. The three gunas interact with the pranas on the physical, subtle and causal dimensions. This interaction causes the consciousness to experience dissipation/concentration, peace/anxiety, heaviness/lightness and other physical, mental, emotional and psychic states. Due to the interaction of the gunas, the consciousness becomes dispersed and cannot remain steady and one-pointed.

This situation is described in the mantra by using the image of a falcon, representing the individual soul which is tied down by the strings of the gunas. Due to the attraction of prana, the falcon flies up as far as the strings will allow, and then again he is pulled downward by the force of apana. Similarly, the consciousness is limited and controlled by the gunas and fluctuates continuously between extroversion and introversion, dynamism and inertia. In this way, the self passes through innumerable rounds of birth and death until it is liberated from the bondage of prakriti and the gunas.

The *Yoga Sutras* state that the self or consciousness becomes free from the influence of prakriti, its attributes (the gunas) and the pranas, by passing through the different phases of evolution. The consciousness is said to be liberated when these influences cease to have any hold over it.

Mantras 30, 31a: Knower of yoga

प्राणापानवशो जीवो ह्यधश्चोर्ध्वं च गच्छति ।
अपान: कर्षति प्राणं प्राणोऽपानेन कर्षति ॥ 30 ॥
ऊर्ध्वाध: संस्थितावेतौ यो जानाति स योगवित् ॥ 31a॥

*Praanaapaana Vasho Jeevo Hyadhashchordhvam Cha Gachchhati;
Apaanah Karshati Praanam Praanopaanena Karshati.* (30)
Oordhvaadhah Samsthitaavetau Yo Jaanaati Sa Yogavit. (31a)

Anvay

Praana apaana vashah: influenced by prana and apana; *Jeevah
hi*: the individual soul; *Adhah cha oordhvam cha gachchhati*:
ascends and descends; *Apaanah*: apana; *Praanam*: prana;
Karshati: draws down; *Praanah*: prana; *Apaanena*: by apana;
Karshati: draws up; *Etau*: both of these; *Oordhva adhah*:
ascendance and descendence; *Samsthitau*: located; *Yah*: who;
Jaanaati: knows; *Sah yogavit*: he is the knower of yoga.

Translation

So the jiva, influenced by prana and apana, ascends and
descends, for prana draws apana up and apana draws prana
down. One who knows the significance of the ascending
and descending of jiva is the knower of yoga.

Commentary

According to the theory of pranayama, the involuntary
process of breathing, by which the jiva constantly moves up
and down, can be made voluntary by the introduction of
awareness. It is possible to attain mastery over the breathing
process and harmonize the flow of prana and apana through
breath awareness and control, coordination of the breath
with the mantra, and awareness of the pranic movement
within the body. Once this harmony and control is attained
through the practices of pranayama, it becomes possible to

84

observe and transcend the gunas, thus attaining liberation. So, in the mantra it is said that one who understands the significance of the ascending and descending of jiva is the knower of yoga.

Mantras 31b, 32, 33: Ajapa gayatri

हकारेण बहिर्याति सकारेण विशेत्पुनः ॥ 31b ॥
हंसहंसेत्यमुं मन्त्रम् जीवो जपति सर्वद ।
षट्शतानि दिवारात्रौ सहस्राण्येकविंशतिः ॥ 32 ॥
एतत्संख्यान्वितं मन्त्रम् जीवो जपति सर्वदा ।
अजपानाम गायत्री योगिनां मोक्षदा सदा ॥ 33 ॥

Hakaarena Bahiryaati Sakaarena Vishetpunah. (31b)
Hamsahamsetyamum Mantram Jeevo Japati Sarvadaa;
Shatshataani Divaa Raatrou Sahasraanyeka Vimshatih. (32)
Etat Samkhyaanvitam Mantram Jeevo Japati Sarvadaa;
Ajapaa Naama Gaayatree Yoginaam Mokshadaa Sadaa. (33)

Anvay

Hakaarena: with the sound 'Ha'; *Bahih*: out; *Yaati*: goes; *Sakaarena*: with the sound 'Sa'; *Vishet*: comes in; *Punah*: again; *Hamsahamsa iti amum*: making the sound of *Hamsa, Hamsa*; *Mantram*: sound vibration; *Jeevah*: individual soul; *Sarvadaa*: continuously; *Japati*: repeats; *Divaa raatrou*: during day and night; *Shatshataani*: six hundred and; *Sahasraani eka vimshatih*: twenty one thousand; *Etat samkhyaa anvitam*: with this number; *Mantram*: sound vibration; *Jeevah*: jiva; *Sarvadaa*: always; *Japati*: continues to repeat; *Ajapaa naama gaayatri*: is called the ajapa gayatri; *Sadaa*: always; *Yoginaam*: to the yogis; *Mokshadaa*: gives liberation.

Translation

With the sound *Ha* (the breath) goes out and with the sound *Sa* it comes in again, making the sound *Hamsa, Hamsa*. Thus the individual soul continuously repeats the mantra. Day and night this mantra is being repeated 21,600 times. When the jiva ceaselessly continues to repeat this number of mantras, it is called the ajapa gayatri, which always brings liberation to the yogis.

86

Commentary

Ajapa japa is a spontaneous form of mantra chanting coordinated with the breath for attaining concentration of mind and liberation of the Self. In the technique described above, the natural flow of breath is observed. As concentration deepens, it is possible to discern the soft hissing sound of the breath at the time of inhalation and exhalation. The sound heard during inhalation is similar to the syllable '*Sa*' and during exhalation to the syllable '*Ha*'. This sound which is produced by the breath has been accepted in yoga as a mantra or subtle sound vibration conducive for meditation. In the yogic texts it is explained that the mantra *Hamsa* or *Soham*, which represents the sound of the breath, also has a deeper esoteric meaning.

According to Samkhya and Tantra, the mantra *Hamsa* is symbolic of the Purusha/Prakriti or Shiva/Shakti tattwa. The '*Ha*' sound represents Purusha/Shiva, the positive or male principle and the '*Sa*' sound represents Prakriti/Shakti, the negative or female principle. The combination of the Shiva/Shakti or Purusha/Prakriti principles produces the mantra *Hamsa*. In this way, the entire manifest universe has evolved out of this sound vibration. The *Hamsa* mantra has been reversed in the vedantic tradition and is known as *Soham*. The difference is that in the *Hamsa* mantra the emphasis is on the outgoing breath or the Shiva principle, whereas in the *Soham* mantra the emphasis is on the ingoing breath or the Shakti principle.

When meditation on the breath and its mantra is performed for short durations, such as half an hour or one hour at a time, then it is called ajapa japa, or spontaneous mantra meditation. However, when the ajapa japa continues throughout the day and night without any break, then it is known as ajapa gayatri. It has been observed that over a twenty-four hour period, a person normally breathes about twenty-one thousand six hundred times. By maintaining unbroken awareness of each breath together with the *Hamsa* or *Soham* mantra for twenty-four hours continuously, without any fluctuation of the concentration, the highest level of spiritual experience is attained.

Ajapa japa is a complete meditation technique in itself which leads the practitioner from the preliminary stages of meditation to the final goal of emancipation. In this way, it is a method of great psychological and spiritual importance. In the initial stages it helps to balance and harmonize the pranas and the faculties of mind. Later on, this harmonized state acts as a springboard to attain higher spiritual experiences. In the final stages, when the ajapa gayatri becomes ongoing, it leads the consciousness to the ultimate reality.

Mantras 34, 35: Knowledge of ajapa gayatri

अस्या: संकल्पमात्रेण सर्वपापै: प्रमुच्यते ।
अनया सदृशी विद्या अनया सदृशो जप: ॥ 34 ॥
अनया सदृशं ज्ञानं न भूतं न भविष्यति ।
कुण्डलिन्यां समुद्भूता गायत्री प्राणधारिणी ॥ 35 ॥

Asyaah Sankalpa Maatrena Sarvapaapaih Pramuchyate;
Anayaa Sadrishee Vidyaa Anayaa Sadrisho Japah. (34)
Anayaa Sadrisham Gnaanam Na Bhootam na Bhavishyati;
Kundalinyaam Samudbhootaa Gaayatree Praanadhaarinee. (35)

Anvay

Asyaah: its; *Sankalpa maatrena*: only with awareness; *Sarva-paapaih*: from all sins; *Pramuchyate*: gets rid; *Anayaa sadrishee vidyaa*: knowledge like this; *Anayaa sadrishah japah*: japa like this; *Anayaa sadrisham gnaanam*: knowledge of this; *Na bhootam na bhavishyati*: neither was in the past nor will be in the future; *Kundalinyaam*: from kundalini shakti; *Samudbhootaa*: born of; *Gaayatree*: Gayatri; *Praanadhaarinee*: sustainer of prana.

Translation

Such knowledge as this, such japa as this, removes all sins only by its awareness. Knowledge of this existed neither in the past nor will it be in the future. This (ajapa) gayatri, born of kundalini, is the sustainer of prana.

Commentary

The importance of ajapa gayatri has been emphasized in these mantras. By this method the gross consciousness is transformed into pure consciousness; therefore, it is comparable to the highest knowledge. In the normal repetition of a mantra there is awareness of a particular sound produced verbally or mentally for a limited period of time. Whereas in ajapa gayatri the mantra is not produced verbally or mentally, but by the natural rhythm of the breath, which is a constant physical process. Use of the breath as the basis for mantra repetition allows the practice to go on effortlessly, so that the awareness of sound becomes continuous for all the twenty-four hours. This type of spontaneous japa brings about constant meditative awareness, which purifies all the mental impressions or samskaras and hence removes all sins.

Here we can understand sin as the negative impressions in the mind which accumulate at the subconscious and unconscious levels and influence the jiva to act in ways which are harmful for its own spiritual evolution and for the welfare of others. According to kundalini yoga these negative samskaras, which are stored in the *karmashaya,* subtle layers of impressions, at the level of swadhisthana chakra, form the primary obstruction to the upward passage of kundalini shakti. The mantra implies that this blockage is removed by the ajapa gayatri and hence kundalini shakti is able to ascend the sushumna passage unhindered.

The next mantra declares that knowledge of this ajapa gayatri existed neither in the past nor will it be in the future. This statement is a way of emphasizing the spontaneous quality of ajapa japa. That which has no existence in the past or future exists only in the present moment. Awareness of past and future implies mental or intellectual memory and rational conceptualization, whereas awareness of the present moment is purely spontaneous. Only that awareness which is experiential and free from intellectualization can be perceived by the pure mind, as it is without any illusive covering. The spontaneous experience of the present moment is only possible when the accumulation of negative impressions has been rooted out of the deeper levels of consciousness.

The mantra further states that this ajapa gayatri is born of kundalini. This spontaneous awareness of the mantra or

90

sound principle of the breath arises from the spiritual potential or kundalini. The unawakened mind dwells constantly in the state of duality, which is symbolized here by the terms past and future. The spontaneous experience of the present moment which is attributed to ajapa gayatri refers to the state of unified or transcended awareness, which is beyond duality. Hence ajapa gayatri is the natural quality or state of kundalini, and by bringing about this state consciously, one is able to activate the kundalini directly.

According to yoga, kundalini shakti is synonymous with mahaprana, the unmanifest aspect of prana which is responsible for all creation and life at the cosmic level. Ajapa gayatri, the spontaneous state of perception born of kundalini, is therefore described here as *pranadhaarani*, the base, the holder, the sustainer of prana, from which all manifestation or creation transpires.

Mantra 36: Kundalini shakti

प्राणविद्या महाविद्या यस्तां वेत्ति स वेदवित् ।
कन्दोर्ध्वे कुण्डलीशक्तिरष्टधा कुण्डलाकृतिः ॥ 36 ॥

Praanavidyaa Mahaavidyaa Yastaam Vetti Sa Vedavit;
Kandordhve Kundaleeshaktih Ashtadhaa Kundalaakritih. (36)

Anvay

Praanavidyaa: knowledge of prana; *Mahaavidyaa*: great knowledge; *Yah*: who; *Taam*: this; *Vetti*: knows; *Sah*: he; *Vedavit*: knower of Vedas, knower of reality; *Kandordhve*: above the root; *Kundaleeshaktih*: kundalini shakti; *Ashtadhaa kundalaakritih*: formed in eight circles.

Translation

Knowledge of prana is the great knowledge. One who knows this knows the reality. Above the root is the kundalini shakti, a serpent of eight coils.

Commentary

In this mantra *pranavidya*, the knowledge of prana, is said to be *mahavidya*, the great knowledge. Knowledge of prana is ultimately knowledge of kundalini, the cosmic prana which resides in a dormant state within each individual. Therefore, pranavidya arises through the process of kundalini yoga. The basis of this knowledge is awakening the cosmic energy potential and returning it to the source at sahasrara chakra, where it merges with Shiva, the pure consciousness, in the transcendental state. The mantra further states that one who knows this knows the Vedas or the reality. Such a yogi is able to perceive the ultimate truth directly.

The mantra next states that the kundalini shakti resides above the kanda. The word *kanda* means 'root', and all the nadis are said to spring from it. The term kanda is also synonymous with medhra, which was used previously in the mantras describing swadhisthana and manipura. In the *Hatha Yoga Pradipika* (3:113) the kanda is described as 'situated above the anus, one hand span high and four fingers breadth wide'. The kanda connects sushumna nadi to mooladhara in the space above the shivalingam. The dormant kundalini is generally symbolized as a small red serpent coiled around the shivalingam with its head resting on top, asleep. The reference to kundalini being above the kanda in this mantra indicates that the spiritual force has already begun to ascend sushumna.

Kundalini has been described as the serpent power, the primordial energy, which is electric, fiery and spiritual in nature. It is the cosmic power within the individual body, which links the individual with the divine. When this energy is awakened and manifesting, it is called Devi, Kali, Durga, Saraswati, Lakshmi etc., according to the state or degree of awakening. For example, Kali represents the state of uncontrolled cosmic forces in the early stages of awakening. Durga represents the controlled, channelled cosmic forces in the intermediate stages of awakening, and Saraswati represents the refined expression of cosmic energy at higher stages of awakening.

The word kundalini has been translated in different ways. The root of the word is *kundala,* which means 'coil'. From this definition the symbol of a coiled serpent was derived, which is described in the mantra. The word kundalini also comes from the root *kund,* which means pit, cavity or deeper place, i.e., *havan kund.* In this connotation, kundalini is that power which resides in a deeper place, i.e. mooladhara chakra. The unawakened kundalini remains in a dormant state at mooladhara, the lowest psychic centre, representing the element earth or matter. Here the cosmic force is fixed in matter, and thus unable to manifest its divine potentiality.

The mantra further describes kundalini as a serpent of eight coils. The eight coils symbolically represent the all pervading energy or force of the eight chakras of kundalini yoga: mooladhara, swadhisthana, manipura, anahata, vishuddhi, ajna, bindu and sahasrara. The eight coils also represent the *ashta siddhi* or eight psychic powers associated with the awakening of the chakras in their dormant potential. With the awakening of kundalini, i.e., the straightening of the coils, these eight siddhis become manifest.

The word siddhi also means paranormal accomplishment or perfection. These siddhis are mentioned in many yogic texts as the natural outcome of kundalini awakening at different stages or chakra levels. The eight siddhis are as follows:

1. *Animaa*: the ability to become infinitely small
2. *Mahimaa*: the ability to become infinitely large
3. *Garimaa*: the ability to become infinitely heavy
4. *Laghimaa*: the ability to become infinitely light
5. *Praaptih*: the ability to obtain whatever one wishes
6. *Praakaamyam*: the ability to obtain whatever one desires
7. *Vashitvam*: the ability to totally subjugate others
8. *Eeshitvam*: attainment of absolute supremacy.

Some yogic and tantric literatures have described kundalini as having three and half coils. There seem to be varying concepts regarding this aspect of the kundalini symbology. The texts which describe kundalini as having three and half coils refer to the three gunas: sattwa, rajas and tamas, as the binding force or form of manifest energy. Others state that three and half coils represent the manifestation of shakti as nada, bindu and beeja. *Nada* is the primal sound, the first vibration, rhythm, or movement produced by shakti in the process of creation. *Bindu* is the primal source, potential or point of manifest form, through which shakti creates, and *beeja* is the seed, agency, or medium through which creation takes place.

Some have described the three coils as representing the three aspects of shakti: *ichchha* (will), *kriya* (action) and *jnana* (knowledge). These three are necessary to create the world of name, form and idea. Others have identified the three coils with the three aspects of transcendental nature, which are omniscience, omnipresence and omnipotence.

Mantra 37: Pathway of kundalini

ब्रह्मद्वारमुखं नित्यं मुखेनाच्छाद्य तिष्ठति ।
येन द्वारेण गन्तव्यं ब्रह्मद्वारमनामयम् ॥ 37 ॥

Brahmadvaara Mukham Nityam Mukhenaachchhaadya Tishthati;
Yena Dvaarena Gantavyam Brahmadvaaram Anaamayam. (37)

Anvay

Nityam: eternal; *Brahmadvaara mukham*: passage to the door of Brahman (all pervading consciousness); *Mukhena*: with mouth; *Aachchaadya*: closing; *Tishthati*: lies; *Yena dvaarena*: through that passage; *Anaamayam*: free from suffering; *Brahmadwaaram*: to the door of Brahman; *Gantavyam*: could be reached or realized.

Translation

(The kundalini) lies eternally with its mouth closing the passage to the door of Brahman (all pervading consciousness). (By going) through that passage, one is freed from suffering when the door of Brahman is reached.

Commentary

The kundalini lies in a dormant state with its mouth over the passage of sushumna, which is referred to here as the passage to the doorway of Brahman. Brahman is the vedic parallel to Shiva; it means the ever-expanding consciousness, the transcendental or perfect state of being. According to Tantra, Shakti and Shiva are ever merged in the unmanifest dimension. This is symbolized by Ardhanarishwara, the divine androgynous aspect which embodies Shiva and Shakti in one form. At the individual level, the merger of Shiva and Shakti is symbolized at sahasrara chakra. From the state of ever expanding consciousness, kundalini shakti descends to mooladhara, the earth bound state of limited consciousness.

In the process of descent, the kundalini comes down through the sushumna passage, which links all the chakras together from sahasrara to mooladhara. The descent of Shakti through the chakras is responsible for manifestation. Sushumna is the pathway through which Shakti descends at the time of creation and ascends at the time of dissolution, when it returns to the source or state of perfect union with Shiva at sahasrara. The descent of Shakti is known as *srishti krama*, the creative process, and the ascent is known as *laya krama*, the dissolution process.

Therefore, it is the sushumna passage, through which kundalini descends at the time of creation and ascends at the time of dissolution, that links the gross and transcendental experiences in the course of human evolution. It is this pathway which is known as the passage to the door of Brahman. The terminal point of this passage is at mooladhara where the kundalini covers the opening of sushumna with her mouth, preventing any reversal or dissolution of the manifestation process. Thus the entire law of creation, preservation and destruction is under the control of shakti, prakriti or kundalini.

The mantra further states that one who ascends this passage is freed from suffering when the door of Brahman is reached. Suffering is the outcome of entrance into the manifest dimension. Man suffers because of the body, which is comprised of elements. As the kundalini ascends the sushumna, it awakens the major chakras relating with the *pancha bhootas* or five elements. In this process the chakras along with their corresponding elements are gradually transcended and the yogi is freed from suffering. The door of Brahman represents the unmanifest dimension or reality which is beyond the influence of the gunas and the formation of the elements.

Therefore, it is said that the kundalini both binds and liberates. This same force is the cause of both man's downfall and his liberation. According to *Hevajra Tantra*, "One must rise by that which one falls." So, to those who seek her unmanifest aspect, kundalini bestows liberation, and to those who seek her manifest aspect through material achievements and sensory enjoyments, she gives bondage. One receives his own due, according to his desires.

Mantra 38: Method of awakening

मुखेनाच्छाद्य तद्द्वारं प्रसुप्ता परमेश्वरी ।
प्रबुद्धा वह्नियोगेन मनसा मरुता सह ॥ 38 ॥

Mukhenaachchhaadya Taddvaaram Prasuptaa Parameshwaree;
Prabuddhaa Vahniyogena Manasaa Marutaa Saha. (38)

Anvay

Taddwaaram: that doorway; *Mukhena*: with mouth; *Aach-chhaadya*: closing; *Parameshwaree*: Parameshwari (kundalini); *Prasuptaa*: is resting, sleeping; *Manasaa*: mind; *Marutaa saha*: along with the wind, prana; *Vahniyogena*: yogic fire; *Prabuddhaa*: awakens.

Translation

Parameshwari (kundalini) is at rest, closing that doorway with her mouth. She can be awakened (through) the mind along with the prana by the fire of yoga.

Commentary

The kundalini is referred to by many names: *Kundalee* (the coiled one), *Kutilangee* (the crooked bodied), *Kundashakti* (the power of the depth, referring to mooladhara), *Bhujangee* (the female serpent), *Shakti* (primal force), *Devi* (goddess) etc. Reference to *Parameshwari* in the mantra indicates the supreme, non-decaying aspect of kundalini.

Even while manifesting in the gross body, the kundalini is experienced as a subtle, transcendental force, the essence of which is beyond change or destruction. This potential force has come to rest at mooladhara, closing the doorway of sushumna with its mouth. This state is indicative of man's great nascence, which can only be removed by the awakening and ascending of this transcendental force. As long as this force remains in the dormant state, man is aware of the external world of duality and asleep to the inner reality.

This force can be stimulated and awakened by the fire of yoga through the practices which harmonize and activate the mind and prana. The force of mind is known as *chitta shakti*, which flows through the ida passage, and the vital force is known as *prana shakti*, which flows through the pingala passage. The ascent of kundalini, or *atma shakti*, through the sushumna passage only takes place after the ida and pingala channels have been fully regulated and activated. There must be coordination between the mental (subtle) and vital (gross) forces. The whole system of yoga is based on principles and practices that help to attain this harmony, which is prerequisite to the awakening of kundalini.

The fire of yoga referred to here can be understood as the prana generated by yogic practices and lifestyle that are sustained over a period of time. This prana manifests throughout the body in the form of *tejas*, or physical lustre, and is stored at manipura, which is also known as *agni mandala*, the zone of fire. This yogic fire helps to prepare for the awakening of kundalini by burning up toxins in the system which block the free flow of prana and increasing the quantum of prana in the nadis. Some practices of kundalini yoga are designed to increase this yogic fire and others are used to explode it and send the force up sushumna to achieve a more ongoing awakening.

The kundalini awakens from manipura with a great surge because the yogic fire empowers it. Generally when the kundalini rises from mooladhara, it falls back after a short distance. However, when the yogic fire detonates this force, it never falls back. For this reason, some traditions consider manipura to be the starting point of kundalini awakening and not mooladhara.

Mantra 39: Rising of kundalini

सूचीवद्गात्रमादाय व्रजत्यूर्ध्वं सुषुम्नया ।
उद्घाटयेत्कवाटं तु यथाकुञ्चिकया गृहम् ।
कुण्डलिन्या तथा योगी मोक्षद्वारं प्रभेदयेत् ॥ ३९ ॥

Soocheevad Gaatramaadaaya Vrajatyoordhvam Sushumnayaa;
Udghaatayetkavaatam Tu Yathaa Kunchikayaa Griham;
Kundalinyaa Tathaa Yogee Mokshadvaaram Prabhedayet. (39)

Anvay

Soocheevad: like needle; *Gaatram*: body; *Aadaaya*: having; *Sushumnayaa*: through sushumna passage; *Oordhvam*: up; *Vrajati*: moves, goes; *Yathaa*: just as; *Kunchikayaa*: by a key; *Griham*: house; *Kavaatam*: door; *Udghaatayet tu*: opens; *Tathaa*: similarly; *Yogee*: yogi; *Kundalinyaa*: through kundalini; *Mokshadvaaram*: door of liberation; *Prabhedayet*: opens.

Translation

(When awakened) she goes straight up through sushumna passage, having a body like a needle. Just as a key opens the closed door of a house, similarly, the yogi opens the doors of liberation through (the awakening of) kundalini.

Commentary

When kundalini shakti awakens, she ascends the sushumna passage like a sharp needle, piercing all the psychic centres in turn. The needle is a long, thin instrument, which easily pierces through material. Similarly, the kundalini easily pierces through the different layers of material evolution. As kundalini ascends, the consciousness is gradually freed from the bondage of the elements, the gunas and prakriti, and attains purity. This purity or refinement enables one to experience the transcendental reality, which is also known as *moksha* or liberation.

101

The awakening of kundalini is furthermore said to be the yogic key to the door of higher consciousness. In mundane life this door remains locked and no one gains access to the inner chambers. However, with the key of kundalini the yogi is able to unlock the door and behold the infinite mansions of the mind. As such, the awakening of kundalini is a turning point in one's life, when one departs from the lower, manifest dimension to the unmanifest or absolute dimension of reality.

Regarding this event, Swami Satyananda Saraswati has said: "In evolution there have been definite demarcations when life developed from mineral to vegetable, from vegetable to animal, from animal to human. Now man lives in the lower mind through logic. Awakening of kundalini marks the departure from logic into the dimension of intuition and spiritual vision, where the ordinary mind becomes the supermind."

Mantra 40: Jalandhara bandha

कृत्वा संपुटितौ करौ दृढतरं बध्वाऽथ पद्मासनं
गाढं वक्षसि संनिधाय चुबुकम् ध्यानं च तच्चेष्टित् ।
वारंवारमपानमूर्ध्वमनिलं   प्रोच्चारयेत्पूरितं
मुञ्चन्प्राणमुपैति   बोधमतुलं   शक्तिप्रभावान्नर: ॥ 40 ॥

Kritvaa Samputitou Karou Dridhataram Badhvaatha Padmaasanam;
Gaadham Vakshasi Sannidhaaya Chubukam Dhyaanam Cha
Tachcheshtitam;
Vaaramvaaram Apaanam Oordhvam Anilam Prochchaarayet
Pooritam;
Munchanpraanamupaiti Bodhamatulam Shakti Prabhaavaan
Narah. (40)

Anvay

Kritvaa: by doing; *Atha padmaasanam*: sitting in padmasana;
Karou: hands; *Samputitou*: together; *Dridhataram*: more firmly;
Badhvaa: crossing (the legs); *Chubukam*: chin; *Gaadham*: firmly;
Vakshasi: against the chest; *Sannidhaaya*: pressing; *Tat*: That
(Brahman); *Dhyaanam*: meditation; *Cheshtitam*: should make
effort; *Vaaram vaaram*: again and again; *Apaanam*: apana;
Oordhvam anilam: ascending air; *Pooritam*: filling up fully;
Prochchaarayet: should move up and down, breathe in and
out; *Praanam*: prana; *Munchan*: leaving in this way; *Narah*:
man; *Shaktiprabhaavaat*: with the help of Shakti; *Bodhamatulam*: infinite knowledge; *Upaiti*: acquires.

Translation

Sit in padmasana, crossing (the legs) with the hands pressed
very firmly together (with the knees). Press the chin firmly
against the chest and meditate on That (Brahman). Again
and again breathe in and out, and raise the apana force to
the region of prana, filling it fully. In this way, with the
help of Shakti the practitioner acquires infinite knowledge.

103

Commentary

This verse describes jalandhara bandha as a practice of kundalini yoga. Steadiness of the body is essential for inner balance. Therefore, the instruction to sit in padmasana has been given here. When mastered, padmasana allows the body to remain steady for a long period of time, even when the consciousness becomes totally absorbed in higher states of meditation. As the body and mind are connected and control each other, steadiness of the body brings steadiness of mind. This steadiness is the first step towards productive meditation. Padmasana further helps to redirect the flow of apana upward.

Jalandhara bandha, the chin lock technique described in this mantra, is practised as follows:

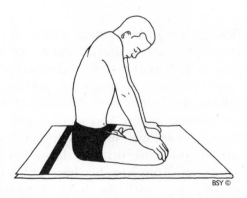

Sit in padmasana with the eyes closed. Exhale and take the awareness down to mooladhara. Inhale slowly and draw the breath together with the apana force upward through sushumna to the region of prana at the chest, filling it fully. At the end of inhalation, retain the breath inside at the chest and merge apana with prana.

Simultaneously, straighten the elbows and press both palms firmly against the knees. Hunch the shoulders forward slightly. Bend the head forward and press the chin tightly against the sternum, just below the throatpit. Remain in this pose, holding the breath inside for as long as is comfortably possible. Be aware of the build-up of energy at the chest.

Then release the chin lock. Lower the shoulders and bend the elbows. Raise the head. Exhale slowly, directing the breath and the awareness back down to mooladhara. This is one round. The practice may be repeated for five to ten rounds initially.

This version of jalandhara bandha has powerful effects on the pranas, nadis and chakras. It brings about the union of prana and apana, which is an important adjunct for the awakening of kundalini. Energy blockages are released along the sushumna channel by creating an upward flow of energy. Advanced practitioners may experience tightening of sushumna at this time. This is a psychic manifestation which indicates an increase of pranic energy. Jalandhara is an important technique for purifying and awakening vishuddhi chakra. It also activates *kurma nadi,* one of the major nadis terminating just below the throat pit. This nadi gives control over hunger and thirst, allowing the sadhaka to remain immersed in meditative states for long durations of time.

The mantra further states that by performing jalandhara bandha in this way, the practitioner will acquire infinite knowledge with the help of Shakti. By raising the prana and establishing it in the higher centres, the bondage of maya is gradually overcome and one is ultimately able to experience the ever-expanding consciousness.

Mantra 41: Instructions for the practitioner

अङ्गानां मर्दनं कृत्वा श्रमसंजातवारिणा ।
कट्वम्ललवणत्यागी क्षीरभोजनमाचरेत् ॥ 41 ॥

Angaanaam Mardanam Kritvaa Shramasanjaatavaarinaa;
Katvamla Lavanatyaagee Ksheerabhojanam Aacharet. (41)

Anvay

Shramasanjaata: produced by labour in the process of this practice; *Vaarinaa*: with water or perspiration; *Angaanaam*: of the body; *Mardanam kritvaa*: by rubbing; *Katu*: pungent; *Amla*: sour; *Lavana*: salty; *Tyaagee*: one who renounces; *Ksheera bhojanam*: milk based diet; *Aacharet*: should be taken in proper and reasonable quantity.

Translation

Perspiration produced by the exertion of this practice should be rubbed into the body. Renounce pungent, sour and salty (foods). Milk based diet should be taken in proper and reasonable quantity.

Commentary

The instructions given in this mantra apply to the practitioner of kundalini yoga in general and jalandhara bandha in particular. First, it is recommended to rub the perspiration produced by the exertion of the practice back into the body so that it is reabsorbed. This results in lightness and increases the energy of the body. Sweat contains a large proportion of salt. During intensive sadhana, consumption of salt is to be avoided. Hence, by rubbing the perspiration back into the body, salt is recycled back through the skin.

Diet plays an important role in kundalini sadhana. A sattwic diet is necessary in order to maintain the correct harmony and balance in the system which is favourable for spiritual awakening. Rajasic foods that are pungent, sour and salty should be avoided because they increase *pitta*, i.e., heat, bile and acid, which disturb the system and make the mind restless. If there is a preponderance of pitta in the system, then higher sadhanas will not give the desired result.

Furthermore, the techniques of kundalini yoga such as jalandhara bandha heat the system because they activate the pranas, nadis and chakras. Therefore, heating foods which are pungent, sour and salty must be avoided during these sadhanas, and a milk-based diet is recommended. Heating practices burn up the excess mucus in the system and the internal channels, especially the airway passages, and the bowels may become dry. Milk is a mucus forming food and its consumption is, therefore, recommended here to ensure internal lubrication of the body.

From early times fresh cow's milk was regarded as a pure and complete form of diet. A milk-based diet could provide sufficient protein, fat and other necessary nutrients which are used up in the course of intensive sadhana, during the awakening of the pranas and kundalini. A milk-based diet refers to a diet of milk products with very few additional items. When other foods are added to this diet, the sattwic quality is lost and it becomes rajasic or tamasic.

Another factor which must be considered regarding a milk-based diet is that in previous times ashrams and hermitages always kept their own cows, which were well tended by the womenfolk and free from disease. The milk produced by these cows was of a pure quality and was consumed in its natural state without any homogenization or pasteurization. Such milk was considered to be a complete and sattwic diet, and processed milk cannot be of the same quality. Unpasteurized milk is high in prana and contains many important properties which are lost in the pasteurization process. Therefore, pasteurized and processed milk products cannot be regarded as a complete and sattwic diet.

The mantra also points out the need for proper regulation of quantity in the diet of a sadhaka. Dietary regulation is advocated in many yogic texts, especially at the time of intensive sadhana. Excess fasting is undesirable as the body becomes weak and the practices cannot be performed properly. Excess food intake is also not recommended as the energy which fuels the metabolic process is rechannelled for spiritual awakening during intensive sadhana. Excess food ingested at this time, especially if it is rich and heavy, creates an unnecessary burden on the digestive organs. When food is not properly metabolized, toxins build up and produce a predominance of tamas in the system, which obstructs the awakening process.

Mantra 42: Three yogic disciplines

ब्रह्मचारी मिताहारी योगी योगपरायण: ।
अब्दादूर्ध्वं भवेत्सिद्धो नात्र कार्या विचारणा ॥ 42 ॥

Brahmachaaree Mitaahaaree Yogee Yogaparaayanah;
Abdaadoordhvam Bhavetsiddho Naatra Kaaryaa Vichaaranaa. (42)

Anvay

Yogee: yogi; *Brahmachaaree*: who practises sexual abstinence;
Mitaahaaree: who practises moderation in diet; *Yoga
paraayanah*: a regular practitioner of yoga; *Abdaat oordhvam*:
by the end of one year; *Siddhah*: adept, perfect; *Bhavet*:
should become; *Atra*: in this; *Vichaaranaa*: doubt; *Na kaaryaa*:
need not do.

Translation

The yogi who practises sexual abstinence, moderation in diet,
and is a regular practitioner of yoga, should become an adept
within one year. One need not have any doubt about it.

Commentary

The word *brahmacharya* means 'one who walks with God'. In
yogic parlance this term implies the practice of sexual
abstinence as a means to develop heightened awareness.
One who constantly expends the sexual fluids will not be
able to rechannel this vital energy upward for spiritual
awakening. Brahmacharya also refers to abstention from
sexual interaction as a means to maintain constant communion with Brahman or the absolute reality. However,
since yoga does not require the practitioner to renounce
family life, brahmacharya must also be interpreted as
moderation and regulation of marital relations.

Mitahara means moderation in diet. The yogi who is a
mitahari eats to live and does not live to eat. Moderation in

diet is necessary because all digestive functions are maintained by prana. The more food one eats, the more prana is required to digest it. Therefore, the yogi practises moderation in diet in order to avoid unnecessary expenditure of energy on digestion of food which is not required for the body processes. He is also careful to take light, pre-digested foods which require less time and energy to metabolize than heavy, spicy or acidic foods.

Yoga paraayana means regularity in yogic practice. Many people practise yoga, but very few are regular. Regularity is one of the most important disciplines to be cultivated in yoga. It is only through regular practice that success is attained and the goal of yoga is reached. One who practises much yoga without regularity will never become an adept. One who practises yoga with regularity purifies and awakens the nadis and chakras, so that kundalini can ascend the middle path without any difficulty.

The mantra states that the yogi who is able to practise the three disciplines: (i) moderation or abstinence in sexual interaction, (ii) moderation in diet and (iii) regularity in yogic practice, will surely become a *siddha* or adept by the end of one year. A siddha or adept is a yogi who has attained mastery or perfection of yoga and is able to manifest the siddhis or yogic powers at will. In order to be a siddha, the chakras and kundalini must be awakened at least to the level of anahata; otherwise siddhis may manifest, but not permanently or at will.

Mantra 43: Dietary regulations

सुस्निग्धमधुराहारश्चतुर्थांशावशेषितः ।
भुञ्जते शिवसंप्रीत्या मिताहारी स उच्यते ॥ 43 ॥

Susnigdhamadhuraahaarah Chaturthaanshaavasheshitah;
Bhunjate Shivasampreetyaa Mitaahaaree sa Uchyate. (43)

Anvay

Susnigdha: very soft; *Madhura*: sweet; *Aahaara*: food; *Chaturthaansha*: a quarter; *Avasheshitah*: leaving empty; *Shivasampreetyaa*: remembering the name of Shiva with devotion; *Bhunjate*: eats, takes; *Sah*: he; *Mitaahaaree*: mitahari; *Uchyate*: is said to be.

Translation

The diet (of a sadhaka) should be soft and sweet. One quarter of the stomach should remain empty. He who takes food (in this way) while remembering the name of Shiva is said to be mitahari.

Commentary

The mantra states that the diet should be soft and sweet because these are the qualities of sattwic food. Soft food is moist and does not require excess secretion of digestive enzymes and churning of the stomach to break it down. Sattwic foods, which are fresh, sweet and bland, provide maximum nutrition and require minimum digestive power to be absorbed. A sattwic diet helps to maintain balance in the system and is necessary for keeping the three disciplines mentioned in the previous mantra: brahmacharya, mitahara and yoga paraayana.

Leaving a quarter of the stomach empty is an important rule of yoga as well as of ayurveda. This science of life advocates that for proper digestion and absorption of

111

nutrients, half the stomach should be filled with solid food, one quarter with water and the remaining quarter should remain empty. The empty portion of the stomach is necessary to allow space for proper churning and digestion of the meal. This aids in fast and efficient metabolization of nutrients and insures the optimum health of the digestive system.

Another reason for these injunctions is that enjoyment of food should not be considered as a principal objective in life. Excess and tasty food should not be consumed due to greed or for the gratification of the senses. Generally, it is food ingested with greed or desire for taste that feeds the body. This greed is also a symptom of indiscipline. The yogi disciplines the mind, controls the urge for pleasure and maintains maximum health by correct dietary habits, which are necessary for advanced sadhanas.

The sadhaka also observes moderation in diet by accepting the meal as *prasad*,or a gift of the divine, to sustain and nourish the body. By remembering Shiva or God's name while taking food, one can change the mental attitude towards food from sensual pleasure to divine communion. Therefore, it is stated that one should remember God at meal times. Even in the *Bhagavad Gita*, a similar sentiment has been echoed in the statement: "Consider every action as sacrifice to God, for you are not the doer, nor the enjoyer." This attitude is known in yoga as *Ishwara Pranidhana*, surrender to God.

Constant remembrance of God during meals also implies that this becomes a time of inner silence and contemplation, rather than an extroverted social hour of chatting and dissipated thought. Social eating leads to unawareness, indiscipline and sensory indulgence, whereas contemplative mealtimes lead to discipline of the senses and awareness of intake. In this way the quantity of food in the stomach does not exceed the recommended one half for solids, one quarter for water and one quarter empty. In order to facilitate constant remembrance of God at mealtimes, mouna or silence should be practised while eating by sincere sadhakas, especially during periods of intensive sadhana.

Mantra 44: Bondage and liberation

कन्दोर्ध्वे कुण्डलीशक्तिरष्टधा कुण्डलाकृतिः ।
बन्धनाय च मूढानां योगिनां मोक्षदा सदा ॥ 44 ॥

Kandordhve Kundaleeshaktih Ashtadhaa Kundalaakritih;
Bandhanaaya Cha Moodhaanaam Yoginaam Mokshadaa Sadaa. (44)

Anvay

Kandordhve: above the kanda; *Kundalee shaktih*: kundalini shakti; *Ashtadhaa*: eight; *Kundalaakritih*: circular or coiled form; *Moodhaanam*: for the ignorant; *Bandhanaaya*: in the form of bondage; *Cha*: but; *Yoginaam*: for the yogis; *Sadaa*: always; *Mokshadaa*: one who grants liberation.

Translation

The kundalini shakti lies above the kanda in eight coils. For the ignorant it is the form of bondage, but for the yogis it always grants liberation.

Commentary

This mantra once again emphasizes that for those engrossed in the world kundalini is the cause of bondage, for it bars the opening of sushumna passage and prevents one from rising above the experience of matter. Here kundalini represents the dual aspects of evolution: creation and liberation. In the process of creation, kundalini descends from the unmanifest to the manifest dimension, from sahasrara to mooladhara. It is this aspect of creation which is responsible for man's bondage, limitation and ignorance. Kundalini shakti creates by descending and maintains the creation by remaining asleep at mooladhara.

The descent of kundalini is said to be the cause of *maya* or illusion. As kundalini descends, it becomes progressively more gross and limited, until no degree of freedom or self-

114

awareness remains. At mooladhara kundalini sleeps with its mouth closing sushumna and dreams the world of everyday wakeful life. In this state man is awake to the external world of name and form in which he retains a sense of individuality and self-centredness, and is asleep to the internal dimension of reality.

At a certain point in man's evolution, kundalini begins to awaken and arouses man from the dream. With the ascent of kundalini, man begins to experience the inner reality. The veil of maya is gradually removed as the boundaries of individuality are dissolved. With the rising of kundalini, one's self identification progressively expands to include the universe. Thus it is said to be the same kundalini which creates and binds the jiva in the body, and which also withdraws the bonds by revealing the process of liberation.

Mantra 45: Kundalini yoga practices

महामुद्रा नभोमुद्रा ओडच्चाणं च जलन्धरम् ।
मूलबन्धं च यो वेत्ति स योगी मुक्तिभाजनम् ॥ 45 ॥

Mahaamudraa Nabhomudraa Odyaanam Cha Jalandharam;
Moolabandham Cha Yo Vetti Sa Yogee Mukti Bhaajanam. (45)

Anvay

Yah yogee: the yogi who; *Mahaamudraa*: maha mudra; *Nabho-mudraa*: nabho mudra; *Odyaanam*: uddiyana; *Cha*: and; *Jalandharam*: jalandhara; *Cha*: and; *Moolabandham*: moola bandha; *Vetti*: knows; *Sah*: he; *Muktibhaajanah*: fit to attain liberation.

Translation

The yogi, who knows maha mudra, nabho mudra, and uddiyana, jalandhara and moola bandhas, is fit to attain liberation.

Commentary

This mantra mentions the major techniques of mudra and bandha, which form the practical aspect of kundalini yoga. These techniques are also found in hatha yoga. Such practices form an important part of kriya and kundalini yoga because they channel the flow of pranas in the system and awaken the kundalini shakti. This mantra names: maha mudra, nabho mudra, uddiyana bandha, jalandhara bandha and moola bandha as practices for attaining an inner awakening, and states that the yogi who knows them is fit to attain liberation. Each of these practices is described in the following mantras.

Mantra 46: Practice of moola bandha

पार्ष्णिघातेन संपीडच्च योनिमाकुञ्चयेद्दृढम् ।
अपानमूर्ध्वमाकृष्य मूलबन्धो यमुच्यते ॥ 46 ॥

Paarshnighaatena Sampeedya Yonimaakunchayeddridham;
Apaanam Oordhvamaakrishya Moolabandho Yamuchyate. (46)

Anvay

Paarshni: heel; *Ghaatena*: with pressure; *Yonim*: genital region; *Sampeedya*: pressing; *Dridham*: firmly; *Aakunchayet*: should contract; *Apaanam*: apana; *Oordhwam*: upwards; *Aakrishya*: drawing; *Yam*: which; *Moolabandhah*: moola bandha; *Uchyate*: is known as.

Translation

The heel should be pressing firmly against the genital region with pressure. One should contract (the perineum and) draw the apana vayu upward, which is known as moola bandha.

Commentary

This mantra describes the technique of moola bandha, which is so named because of the lock (*bandha*) it forms at the base (*moola*). In Sanskrit, the word moola means 'root'. Here this refers to the root of the spine or the perineum where mooladhara chakra, the seat of kundalini, is located. In this practice, mooladhara chakra is contracted and pulled upwards. This forces the apana vayu which normally flows downward below the navel to flow upwards in order to facilitate the awakening of kundalini. The technique is performed as follows.

Sit in the meditative pose of siddhasana. The lower heel should be pressing firmly against the genital region, midway between the genital organ and the anal sphincter, with pressure. The upper heel should press against the centre of the pubic bone just above the root of the genital organ. Place the palms of the hands on the knees.

Inhale deeply and retain the breath inside. Contract the muscles in the region of the perineum, at the centre of the pelvic floor, and draw them upwards. Simultaneously, draw the apana vayu upward to the region of prana, above the diaphragm in the chest.

Hold the contraction for as long as is comfortably possible and merge the apana and prana vayus. Then release the contraction of the perineum and slowly exhale. Allow the breath to normalize before beginning the next round.

Mantra 47: Benefits of moola bandha

अपानप्राणयोरैवं   क्षयान्मूत्रपुरीषयो: ।
युवा भवति वृद्धोऽपि सततं मूलबन्धनात् ॥ 47 ॥

Apaanapraanayoraivam Kshayaan Mootrapureeshayoh;
Yuvaa Bhavati Vriddhopi Satatam Moolabandhanaat. (47)

Anvay

Apaanapraanayoh: in apana and prana; *Evam*: thus; *Mootra pureeshayoh*: urine and excreta; *Kshayaat*: because of being less; *Satatam*: always, regular; *Moolabandhanaat*: with the practice of moolabandha; *Vriddhopi*: even an old man; *Yuva*: young; *Bhavati*: becomes.

Translation

Apana (fuses) with prana, thus the urine and excreta become less. With regular practice of moola bandha, even an old man becomes young.

Commentary

The practice of moola bandha reverses the apana vayu which normally flows downward from the navel to the perineum and unites it with prana vayu in the chest region. This redistributes the energy from the lower to the higher centres and aids in the sublimation of sexual energy and establishment of brahmacharya. Moola bandha symbolizes the ultimate aim of yoga, which is to find and experience the source of creation (moola prakriti) and redirect it upward by contracting mooladhara chakra and restraining the modifications of the mind.

Physiologically, moola bandha stimulates intestinal peristalsis whereby constipation and piles are effectively removed. Rechannelling stagnant energies in the reproductive region deals effectively with male and female disorders

119

of the urogenital tract. This practice also relieves depression, neurosis and psychosis resulting from accumulation of unreleased energy in the reproductive region.

The mantra further states that even an old man becomes young wth regular practice of this technique. This occurs because the apana energy which is normally lost in the elimination process is reversed by moola bandha and directed upward. The fusion of apana and prana also fans the fire element in the system, which activates samana, allowing all the ingested food to be fully digested, absorbed and metabolized by the system.

Food which is completely metabolized is converted into energy and produces fewer wastes and toxic residues. That energy is then distributed throughout the system by vyana vayu. The quantity of waste matter is gradually reduced as more nutrients and fluids are absorbed, rather than being excreted. In this way, the system is regenerated and does not suffer from disease or old age. Thus the verse says that even an old man becomes young by regular practice of moola bandha.

Mantras 48, 49: Uddiyana bandha

ओडचाणं कुरुते यस्मादविश्रान्तम् महाखग: ।
ओड्डियाणं   तदेव   स्यान्मृत्युमातङ्गकेसरी ॥ 48 ॥
उदरात्पश्चिमं   ताणमधोनाभेर्निगद्यते ।
ओडचाणमुदरे बन्धस्तत्र बन्धो विधीयते ॥ 49 ॥

Odyaanam Kurute Yasmaadavishraantam Mahaakhagah;
Oddiyaanam Tadeva Syaanmrityu Maatangakesaree. (48)
Udaraatpashchimam Taanam Adhonaabheh Nigadyate;
Odyaanamudare Bandhastatra Bandho Vidheeyate. (49)

Anvay

Vishraantam: after much rest; *Mahaakhagah*: great bird; *Yasmaat*: just as; *Odyaanam*: uddiyana bandha; *Kurute*: is practised; *Oddiyaanam*: uddiyana bandha; *Mrityumaatanga*: for the elephant of death; *Tat eva*: like; *Kesaree*: a lion; *Syaat*: is; *Adhonaabheh*: (region) below the navel; *Udaraat*: from abdomen; *Pashchimam*: towards the back; *Taanam*: drawing; *Odyaanam*: uddiyana bandha; *Nigadyate*: is practised; *Tatra*: there; *Udare*: in the abdomen; *Bandhah*: because of binding, contracting; *Bandhah vidheeyate*: (that) bandha is practised.

Translation

Just as a great bird takes to flight after a long rest, similarly uddiyana is to be practised. Uddiyana is like a lion challenging the elephant of death. Drawing the abdomen below the navel towards the back is called paschimottana. Uddiyana is also practised by binding this region of the abdomen. Therefore, because of the binding or contracting it is called uddiyana bandha.

Commentary

The meaning of the word *uddiyana* is to 'raise up' or 'fly upward', therefore, the image of a bird is used here to describe the practice. The bird which flies in the air is a symbol of prana, so the movement of prana shakti in the physical body is described as a bird. The bird depicted in the first mantra is *mahakaga*, the great bird, which further implies that uddiyana is a powerful practice able to raise a substantial force to the highest point. After resting, the great bird takes to flight; similarly, the practitioner rests before drawing in the abdomen, enabling the prana vayu to fly up the sushumna. Rest is required before each round because uddiyana bandha is a strenuous practice.

In uddiyana the lower portion of the abdomen is pulled back and up underneath the ribcage. This contraction stimulates the solar plexus and creates a suction which reverses the flow of prana and apana and unites them with samana. Repeated practice awakens manipura chakra and forces the combined vayus to enter sushumna, so that they fly upward to sahasrara. At the same time, the alternate upward and downward movements of prana and apana are arrested. Manipura is said to be the storehouse of prana or vitality. When this vital force is awakened and directed upward to the higher centres, the entire system is rejuvenated and physical diseases are removed. Hence the first mantra describes the practice of uddiyana as a lion which is able to challenge the elephant of death.

The second verse describes the practice of uddiyana as drawing the abdomen as far back as possible. The full practice is performed as follows:

Sit in siddhasana or padmasana with the palms of the hands on the knees. Close the eyes and relax for a few moments. Breathe in deeply through the nose, filling the lungs. Exhale fully, emptying the lungs. Hold the breath outside.

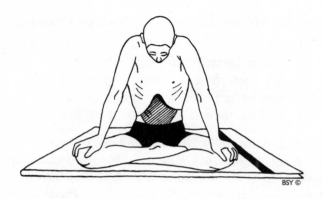

Raise the shoulders, straightening the elbows. Press down on the knees with the palms of the hands. Bend the head forward so that the chin touches the sternum, just above the throat pit. Pull the abdominal muscles backward toward the spine and then upward.

Hold the abdominal contraction with the breath outside for as long as you can comfortably. Then release the contraction, bend the elbows and lower the shoulders. Slowly raise the head and exhale. Rest for a few moments, allowing the breath to normalize, and feel the effects of the practice.

Uddiyana bandha is one of the most powerful practices for awakening the kundalini. It should be performed under the guidance of a competent teacher.

Mantras 50, 51: Significance of jalandhara bandha

बध्नाति हि शिरोजातमधोगामि नभोजलम् ।
ततो जालन्धरो बन्ध: कण्ठदु:खौघनाशन: ॥ 50 ॥
जालन्धरे कृते बन्धे कण्ठ दु:खौघनाशने ।
न पीयूषं पतत्यग्नौ न च वायु: प्रधावति ॥ 51 ॥

Badhnaati hi Shirojaatam Adhogaami Nabhojalam;
Tato Jaalandharo Bandhah Kanthaduhkhaughanaashanah. (50)
Jaalandhare Krite Bandhe Kanthaduhkhaughanaashane;
Na Peeyoosham Patatyagnau Na Cha Vaayuh Pradhaavati. (51)

Anvay

Shirojaatam: produced in the head; *Adhogaami*: (that is) going down; *Nabhojalam*: water of the sky; *Badhnaati hi*: (which) binds or prevents from falling; *Tatah*: that; *Jaalandharo bandhah*: (is said to be) jalandhara bandha; *Kantha duhkhau*: (which) throat trouble; *Aghanaashanah*: destroys all; *Jaalandhare bandhe*: (of) jalandhara bandha; *Krite*: by doing (and); *Kantha duhkhau*: throat trouble; *Aghanaashane*: with the destruction of; *Peeyoosham*: nectar; *Agnau*: in the fire; *Na patati*: does not fall; *Cha*: and; *Vayuh*: breathing; *Na pradhaavati*: does not run hither and thither.

Translation

That (is said to be) jalandhara bandha, which binds or prevents the water of the sky produced in the head from falling down (and which) destroys all troubles of the throat. By doing the practice of jalandhara bandha, along with the destruction of throat problems, the nectar does not fall into the fire, nor does the breath move in and out.

Commentary

Jalandhara bandha is performed by pressing the chin firmly against the sternum, as described in Mantra 40. By this practice, the glands situated in the throat as well as the organs of speech are compressed and toned, thereby removing all throat problems. Physiologically, this technique closes the windpipe and compresses various organs, including the sinus receptors which are located in the throat region. These receptors are sensitive to the blood pressure in the jugular vein. If the pressure is high or low, these receptors send messages to the brain and heart to slow down or speed up. In jalandhara bandha these receptors are compressed for a regular duration of time, which slows down the heart rate and induces tranquillity of brain and mind. Similarly, anxiety, stress and anger are also relieved.

By this compression the thyroid and parathyroid glands are toned and massaged, thus improving their functioning, which has a wide influence over body growth, metabolism and sexual development. The throat connects the brain with the digestive and assimilative process. The thyroid gland secretes the hormone thyroxin (T4), which is responsible for the rate of nutrient consumption, cell turnover and tissue ageing. By squeezing this gland the nerve stimuli and blood flow are promoted and secretor responses modulated. Jalandhara bandha is, therefore, a means to consciously regulate the rate of metabolism. The influence of thyroxin pervades the body's tissues right down to the cellular level, where it activates the enzyme and oxidation processes.

In kundalini yoga, jalandhara bandha plays an important role in raising the prana and arresting the process of decay in the body. The ancient yogic texts speak of a cavity in the head region called bindu visarga, which is situated at the top back of the head below sahasrara chakra. The term *bindu visarga* is translated as 'the falling drop'. In chakra symbolism bindu is represented by the moon, which is constantly dripping minute secretions of *amrita* or nectar. This life giving fluid drops down from the cavity of bindu to *lalana*, a minor chakra at the back of the throat which stores the nectar. From lalana, the nectar falls down to vishuddhi chakra and then further to manipura where it is burnt up in the metabolic processes, providing heat and energy for the entire body.

With regular practice of jalandhara bandha, this fluid or nectar, which flows down from the cavity of bindu visarga at the top back of the head, is held within the region of vishuddhi chakra where it is purified instead of being burnt up by the fire at manipura. The purification of the nectar takes place only when the nectar is held for some period at vishuddhi chakra. By this process the nectar of life is converted into a higher form of energy which does not dissipate, but is used to rejuvenate the body and brain at the cellular level.

The mantra also states that during the practice of jalandhara the breathing process ceases to fluctuate. With the stilling of the breath, the mind and body are also stilled and the practitioner is able to experience that transcendental state which is beyond duality and mental cognition.

Mantra 52: Practice of khechari mudra

कपालकुहरे जिह्वा प्रविष्टा विपरीतगा ।
भ्रूवोरन्तर्गता दृष्टिमुद्रा भवति खेचरी ॥ 52 ॥

Kapaala Kuhare Jihvaa Pravishtaa Vipareetagaa;
Bhroovoh Antargataa Drishtih Mudraa Bhavati Khecharee. (52)

Anvay

Kapala kuhare: cavity of the head; *Vipareetagaa*: inverted; *Jihvaa*: tongue; *Pravishtaa*: put in, entered; *Bhroovoh*: (and) of both the eyebrows; *Antah*: in the middle; *Drishtih*: sight; *Gataa*: fixed; *Khecharee mudra*: khechari mudra; *Bhavati*: is.

Translation

When the tongue is folded back and entered into the cavity of the head, and the sight is fixed in-between the eyebrows, that is khechari mudra.

Commentary

The practice of khechari mudra, as described in the above mantra, is also known as *nabho mudra*. Swami Sivananda has called this practice lambhika yoga, the word *lambhika* referring to the suspended part of the soft palate. There are two forms of khechari mudra – raja yoga and hatha yoga. The raja yoga form is the easiest and can be performed by anyone. It is done by folding the tongue back so that the under surface touches the upper back portion of the soft palate. Then the tip of the tongue is inserted into the nasal orifice at the back of the throat, if possible. The position of the tongue should be maintained for as long as is comfortable. At first it will be necessary to release the tongue every now and then to relax it, and then resume the mudra. With practice, however, the tongue will automatically ascend into the sinuses to stimulate vital nerve centres in the brain.

The form of khechari described in the traditional hatha yoga texts involves the gradual cutting of the frenulum and elongation of the tongue. This form of khechari is only to be attempted by advanced practitioners under the guidance of a Guru. It requires perseverance and patience. First, the tongue has to be elongated, which is done by holding it with a piece of cloth and gently massaging, stretching and rolling it from side to side. Then the frenulum is cut very gradually week by week with surgical methods or by rubbing it with abrasive materials. During this process the tongue is massaged daily by milking it for long periods of time with butter or oil.

This process is continued for many months until the tongue becomes very long. Then it is possible to fold it back and slide it up through the nasal cavity at the back of the throat. In this way the ida and pingala nadis are effectively blocked and lalana chakra, at the back of the throat, is stimulated. There is a close relationship between lalana and bindu visarga at the top back of the head, where the moon energy resides. Stimulation of lalana causes the nectar or ambrosial fluid to drip down from bindu to permeate the entire body. When the tongue is fully elongated, which may take many years, the tip reaches the eyebrow centre, internally activating ajna chakra. In this regard, the mantra states that the sight or concentration becomes fixed between the two eyebrows.

Ajna chakra is referred to in many traditions as the mythological third eye located midway between the two eyebrows. The two physical eyes gaze outward at the manifest world and are associated with the vision of duality, whereas the third eye gazes inward at the unmanifest dimension and is responsible for the vision of unity, the cosmic or universal vision, which transcends duality. The third eye is associated with meditation and direct experience, relating to the underlying nature of consciousness, energy and existence.

In the final stage of khechari mudra, the tip of the tongue reaches ajna chakra and the sight becomes fixed on the internal dimension revealed by the third eye, also known as *divya chakshu,* the divine eye, or *jnana chakshu,* the eye of knowledge.

Mantras 53, 54, 55: Benefits of khechari mudra

न रोगो मरणं तस्य न निद्रा न क्षुधा तृषा ।
न च मूर्छा भवेत्तस्य यो मुद्रां वेत्ति खेचरीम् ॥ 53 ॥
पीडचते न च रोगेण लिप्यते न स कर्मभि: ।
बध्यते न च केनापि यो मुद्रां वेत्ति खेचरीम् ॥ 54 ॥
चित्तं चरति खे यस्माज्जिह्वा चरति खे यत: ।
तेनेयं खेचरी मुद्रा सर्वसिद्धनमस्कृता ॥ 55 ॥

Na Rogo Maranam Tasya Na Nidraa Na Kshudhaa Trishaa;
Na Cha Moorchaa Bhavettasya Yo Mudraam Vetti Khechareem. (53)
Peedyate Na Cha Rogena Lipyate Na Sa Karmabhih;
Badhyate Na Cha Kenaapi Yo Mudraam Vetti Khechareem. (54)
Chittam Charati Khe Yasmaajjihvaa Charati Khe Yatah;
Teneyam Khecharee Mudraa Sarva Siddhanamaskritaa. (55)

Anvay

Yah: who; *Khechareem mudraam*: khechari mudra; *Vetti*:
knows; *Tasya*: him; *Rogah*: disease; *Maranam*: death; *Nidraa*:
sleep; *Na*: do not trouble; *Na*: nor; *Kshudhaa trishaa*: hunger,
thirst; *Na cha*: and nor (him); *Moorchaa*: swoon; *Bhavet*:
becomes; *Yah*: one who; *Khechareem mudraam*: khechari
mudra; *Vetti*: knows; *Sah*: he; *Rogena*: by disease; *Na peedyate*:
does not suffer; *Na cha*: and nor; *Karmabhih*: by karmas;
Lipyate: is attached; *Na cha*: and nor; *Kena api*: by anybody
or anything; *Badhyate*: is bound; *Yasmaat*: by which; *Chittam*:
consciousness; *Khe*: in the sky, cosmic space; *Charati*: rotates,
moves; *Yatah*: by which; *Jihvaa*: tongue; *Khe*: in the head
cavity; *Charati*: moves; *Tena*: by that; *Iyam*: this; *Khecharee
mudraa*: khechari mudra; *Sarva siddha*: by all the siddhas;
Namaskritaa: is homaged, respected.

Translation

Disease, death, and sleep do not trouble him who knows
khechari mudra, nor hunger and thirst, nor swoon. One

130

who knows khechari mudra does not suffer from disease, nor is he attached to karmas, nor bound by anybody or anything. All the siddhas pay homage to khechari mudra by which one is able to rotate the consciousness in the cosmic space by moving the tongue into the cavity of the head.

Commentary

Through the practice of khechari mudra, one drinks the nectar which drips down from bindu visarga and becomes free from disease, death and the desire for sleep. Disease and death are the result of a gradual dissipation and waning of the vital force until the body and brain are no longer able to sustain health or life. By drinking the nectar which falls down to lalana, the yogi is able to access a more subtle and refined level of energy. This acts within the system like the mythological fountain of youth, rejuvenating the body and brain at the cellular level and removing disease and ageing, which are the causes of death.

This potent fluid which drips down from bindu visarga is able to maintain all the life functions in itself, without the need for more gross forms of energy such as food and drink. In India, there have been many instances of persons who were able to maintain life without any intake of food or drink over a period of years. This is possible when the subtle life forces are accessed in their pure state, as in the practice of khechari mudra. The necessity for food and drink is one of the biggest obstacles in intensive sadhana. The yogi is forced to interrupt his sadhana in order to obtain food and drink. When intensive sadhana is interrupted, it takes a long time to again resume the same depth of concentration.

Digestion is also a problem during intensive sadhana. The physical system that is geared for sustained meditation functions at a lower metabolic rate, so a longer period is required for digestion after meals are taken. If any sadhana is undertaken during the time when food is digesting, gastric

131

problems will result. Poor digestion causes toxins and gases to build up in the system, which affect the sadhana adversely. Drinking the nectar in khechari mudra allows the body and mind to be nourished by a subtle form of prana. Thus the yogi is freed from all hunger and thirst and able to pursue higher sadhana uninterrupted.

Sleep is another obstacle during intensive sadhana. When the mind is introverted for long periods of time, there is a tendency to become dull. Then the yogi is troubled by the constant desire for sleep. During the time of sadhana, excess sleep makes the system tamasic and prevents the yogi from awakening the higher dimensions of consciousness. A regular amount of sleep is required by people living in the world to counteract stress and fatigue. During this period of rest and introversion, the body and mind repair themselves and prepare for the next day's onslaught. However, sleep becomes unnecessary for a yogi, whose system is free from disease, degeneration and decay. Only those who are unable to control the degeneration process require sleep.

Finally, the mantra states that the yogi who knows khechari mudra will be untroubled by *moorcha*, which means 'faint' or 'swoon', as in an unconscious trance state. Faint or swoon is somewhat akin to sleep in that both involve the unconscious state. Both imply total cutting off of the sensory perceptions from the outside world, but without the requisite awareness that is necessary for conscious meditation. The purpose of kundalini yoga is to experience the unconscious consciously and this is what is achieved through mastery of khechari mudra.

The second mantra states that one who knows khechari no longer comes under the influence of Shakti or Maya. He does not suffer from disease nor is he attached to karma nor bound by external situations. Here it is implied, first of all, that one who drinks the nectar by the practice of khechari mudra is unaffected by the suffering of the body. He views the body as one would a rented vehicle, without any feeling of identification or ownership. Therefore, if the body is diseased he does not suffer. He is not concerned because he identifies himself with the higher dimension, the state of universal awareness, which is beyond duality and the finite experience of body and mind. The body and mind function within the confines of time and space, ida and pingala, but it is possible to transcend these poles of duality. Normal psycho-physiological functioning undergoes a change and restructuring, so that supernormal functioning takes place.

Secondly, by drinking the nectar in the practice of khechari mudra, one is freed from attachment to karma. The word *karma* means 'action'. All actions, whether performed physically, mentally, psychically or spiritually, consciously or unconsciously, are karmas. Furthermore, these karmas are stored as residual impressions in the deeper layers of consciousness, where they colour and influence every aspect of life from birth to death. Many scriptural texts state that karma is the cause of bondage to maya and to the cycle of birth and death. Therefore, the main objective of yoga is to free oneself from the bondage of karma and hence from the illusory veil of Maya, Shakti or Prakriti.

In the previous mantra reference was made to fixing the concentration at the point between the eyebrows. In the final stage of khechari mudra, when the tip of the tongue stimulates ajna chakra at the top of the nasal orifice, the inner vision associated with this psychic centre is awakened. Freedom from the influence of karma and destiny is only possible at the level of ajna chakra, where the identification with the external world of duality or the manifest dimension of existence is transcended. The practice of khechari mudra ultimately awakens ajna chakra, and consequently one is freed from the attachment of karma.

One who is freed from the attachment of karma functions by different laws. He is free in the real sense; to soar in the unmanifest, infinite space unbound by the manifest world, by external situations, by anyone or anything. Hence the next mantra states that the accomplished yogis and siddhas pay homage to the practice of khechari mudra by which they are able to rotate the consciousness through the boundless space of eternity. Time and object are concepts of the finite mind and the laws of nature. The finite mind is the product of nature. If the consciousness is expanded beyond the limits of the finite mind and natural phenomena, the consciousness will enter the realm of the infinite.

Mantra 56: Bindu

बिन्दुमूलशरीराणि सिरा यत्र प्रतिष्ठिता: ।
भावयन्ति शरीराणि आपादतलमस्तकम् ॥ 56 ॥

Bindumoola Shareeraani Siraa Yatra Pratishthitaah;
Bhaavayanti Shareeraani Aapaadatala Mastakam. (56)

Anvay

Bindu: bindu; *Shareeraani*: of the whole body; *Moola*: original cause; *Yatra*: where; *Siraa*: nerves and blood vessels; *Pratishthitaa*: is situated; *Aapaada tala*: from the toes; *Mastakam*: to the head; *Shareeraani*: of the body; *Bhaavayanti*: is viewed.

Translation

The bindu is viewed as the original cause of the whole body. It is situated in the nerves and blood vessels and sustains the entire physical structure from the toes to the head.

Commentary

The word *bindu* means a 'point' or 'drop'. Bindu is considered to be the nucleus or the abode of matter. It is the point from which all creation manifests the potency ready to create. In Tantra shastra the *parabindu* or supreme aspect of bindu is equated with Shiva and Shakti, abiding in sahasrara chakra as the undivided, undifferentiated principle. Thus parabindu represents the first, subtlest manifestation of creation. Creation implies vibration, movement and action. The parabindu, therefore, divides itself into three principles: (i) *nada* – the primal vibration, (ii) *bindu* – the primal point or emanation of creation, and (iii) *bija* – the creative power. So, it is said that at the time of creation the entire universe emanates from bindu, which is the first point of individual ideation and objective form, and at the time of dissolution it returns to bindu.

135

In yogic terminology the concept of bindu has several different meanings:

1. *Bindu chakra,* which is situated in the top back of the head and is an important centre of awakening in kundalini yoga
2. *Drop of nectar or ambrosia,* which falls down from bindu chakra and rejuvenates the entire system
3. *Semen or seed* potential in human beings
4. *Vital energy* which creates and sustains the physical system.

This mantra states that bindu is the cause of physical existence and describes the location of the bindu at the physiological level. In the physical context, bindu would normally be considered as the semen or seed which contains the entire human potential in concentrated form. Here, however, bindu is visualized throughout the nerves and blood vessels of the physiological system from the toes to the head.

Every cell of the body depends upon the nerves and blood vessels for sustenance and integration with the rest of the body. This implies that the bindu is not only the seed but also the vital source of life at the cellular level which sustains and links every cell to the whole. The establishment of the bindu at the cellular level brings this abstract and transcendental concept of creation down to the physical plane where it can be experienced and understood by the mind and senses. It also implies that as bindu is the necessary agent for rejuvenation, it is possible to rejuvenate the body at the cellular level by controlling and preserving the bindu.

Mantras 57, 58: Retention of bindu

खेचर्या मुद्रितं येन विवरं लम्बिकोर्ध्वतः ।
न तस्य क्षीयते बिन्दुः कामिन्यालिङ्गितस्य च ॥ 57 ॥
यावद्बिन्दुः स्थितो देहे तावन्मृत्युभयम् कुतः ।
यावद्बद्धा नभोमुद्रा तावद्बिन्दुर्न गच्छति ॥ 58 ॥

Khecharyaa Mudritam Yena Vivaram Lambikordhvatah;
Na Tasya Ksheeyate Binduh Kaaminyaalingitasya cha. (57)
Yaavadbinduh Sthito Dehe Taavan Mrityubhayam Kutah;
Yaavadbaddhaa Nabhomudraa Taavadbindurna Gachchhati. (58)

Anvay

Khecharyaa: with khechari; *Yena*: by which; *Lambikaa*: suspended part of the soft palate; *Oordhvatah*: from above; *Vivaram*: like cavity; *Mudritam*: is closed; *Kaaminya aalingitasya cha*: even in the embrace of a woman; *Tasya*: his; *Binduh*: bindu; *Na ksheeyate*: is not lost; *Yaavat*: as long as; *Binduh*: bindu; *Dehe*: in the body; *Sthitah*: is retained; *Taavat*: until then; *Mrityu bhayam*: fear of death; *Kutah*: from where; *Yaavat*: as long as; *Nabho mudraa*:with nabho mudra (khechari mudra); *Baddhaa*: is bound; *Taavat*: until then; *Binduh*: bindu; *Na gachchhati*: is not wasted.

Translation

One who closes the cavity of the palate from above with khechari will not lose the bindu even in the embrace of a woman. As long as bindu is retained in the body, from where arises the fear of death? Bindu is not wasted as long as it is bound by nabho mudra.

Commentary

The actual source of bindu is in the higher centres of the brain, in the region of bindu chakra. However, due to the influence of desire and passion the bindu falls down to the

137

lower regions. There it is burnt up by the fire at manipura or falls lower to the reproductive centres where is it transformed into sperm and ova. At the higher level, bindu exists as a drop of amrita or nectar of immortality. At the intermediate level, it exists as prana which maintains the digestive and metabolic processes. At the lower level, it exists as a drop of sexual fluid or seed which is secreted from the male and female reproductive organs at the time of orgasm.

Normally, the sexual act takes place when the bindu falls from the higher centres due to the influence of desire and passion. During emission the bindu is ejected through the sexual organs by the active force of apana, the downward moving prana. In this way the bindu is expended for the pursuit of pleasure or the regeneration of life. However, there is a third form of sexual interaction practised for the purpose of spiritual awakening in which the partners unite without losing the bindu. In order to utilize the sexual act for spiritual upliftment, both partners must control their emotions and passions and perfect certain practices of kundalini yoga which reverse the downward flow of apana and retain the bindu.

According to this mantra, khechari mudra is one such practice. By folding the tongue back and closing the cavity of the palate, the bindu does not fall, even in the embrace of a woman. The science of Tantra, from which kundalini yoga was derived, teaches that sexual suppression or abstention does not result in retention of the bindu. In order to retain the bindu it is necessary to establish control at the point of origin and prevent it from falling down to the lower centres where it would normally be dissipated. The yogi who is indifferent to desire and passion can thus use khechari mudra to retain the bindu, even during sexual interaction. In this way, the yogi avoids the loss of bindu, even while maintaining a sexual relationship.

This second mantra states that there will be no fear of death as long as the bindu is retained in the body. *Abhinivesha*

138

or fear of death is one of the five *kleshas* or basic causes of suffering described by Sage Patanjali in the *Yoga Sutras*. It is one of the most fundamental motivating forces governing the human personality and behaviour. Fear of death stems from the falling of bindu, which results in the identification of the self with the physical body. The loss of bindu, especially during the sexual act, strongly reinforces this identification. When a yogi can control the bindu, preventing its fall and release even during sexual interaction, identification with the body ceases, and the consciousness is freed from the fear of death.

Retention of the bindu is prescribed for three reasons. Firstly, the bindu is the source of creation and of individual manifestation, so its retention is necessary for the maintenance of life. Tantra states that retention of the bindu leads to immortal life and loss of the bindu leads to degeneration and death. Secondly, when the bindu is retained and exploded at the higher centres, spiritual experiences manifest and human nature becomes divine. Thirdly, the process of regeneration can only be carried out by retention of the bindu. As long as the bindu is preserved, there is no possibility of death due to disease or degeneration.

Preservation of the bindu gives the benefits of physical strength, power, heat, vitality, resistance, brilliance, endurance and the ability to decide one's own destiny. Loss of the bindu results in weakness of the body and gradually leads to degeneration, disease, old age and death. This is a very important consideration for the yogi who performs intensive sadhanas in order to merge himself with the *atma* while still living in the body. The body is the instrument for achieving perfection in sadhana, therefore, the yogi wishes to preserve it for as long as possible in order to reach his goal. If death intervenes before the goal is reached, the yogi must come back and start again. For this reason preservation of the bindu is emphasized in kundalini yoga, which is a higher form of sadhana.

The mantra further states that as long as nabho mudra (khechari mudra) is practised, there is no loss or dissipation of bindu. The bindu will be prevented from falling down to the lower centres. Therefore, it will not be wasted or lost, which is what would happen otherwise in the normal course of life.

Mantra 59: Raising bindu by yoni mudra

ज्वलितोऽपि यथा बिन्दु: संप्राप्तश्च हुताशनम् ।
व्रजत्यूर्ध्वं गत: शक्त्या निरुद्धो योनिमुद्रया ॥ 59 ॥

Jwalitopi Yathaa Binduh Sampraaptashcha Hutaashanam;
Vrajatyoordhvam Gatah Shaktyaa Niruddho Yonimudrayaa. (59)

Anvay

Yathaa: if; *Gatah*: falling down; *Binduh*: bindu; *Sampraaptah cha hutaashanam*: merges in the fire; *Jwalitopi*: while burning; *Yonimudrayaa*: with the practice of yoni mudra; *Niruddhah*: after being prevented; *Shaktyaa*: because of its power; *Oordhwam*: upward; *Vrajati*: raised.

Translation

If bindu falls down and merges in the fire (of manipura), even while burning, after being prevented (from dissipating further), it can be raised upward by the practice of yoni mudra because of its power.

Commentary

Regular loss of the bindu takes place at the level of manipura, where it is burnt up by the gastric and metabolic fire. This is why moderation in diet and discipline in lifestyle are recommended as an important adjunct to higher sadhanas. This mantra states that even if bindu falls down to the region of agni, at manipura chakra, it should be again raised to the higher centres by the practice of yoni mudra.

The agni or fire element at manipura chakra represents rajas, the dynamic quality of life. When the bindu falls from vishuddhi to manipura, what actually happens is that its sattwic, nectarine qualities which illumine the body and mind and bestow immortality are transmuted into rajas. Due to the influence of desire and passion, the bindu falls

141

down further to the centres below manipura which are concerned with instinctive and tamasic qualities. When the bindu falls down to swadhisthana and mooladhara it becomes a poison, causing suffering, disease and death.

In previous mantras the practice of khechari mudra was prescribed for preventing the fall of bindu from the higher regions. Here the method indicated for reversing the fall of bindu to the region of agni or manipura is yoni mudra. The word *yoni* refers to the female reproductive organ, which is the source of creation at the individual as well as the universal level. So, yoni mudra is that attitude which invokes the power of creation. Therefore, the mantra states that, even if the bindu is already in the process of being burnt by the fire, the yogi can still prevent further dissipation and raise it upwards to the higher centres by the power of yoni mudra.

Yoni mudra is also known as shanmukhi mudra. The word *shanmukhi* means 'seven gates', which refers to the seven sensory apertures in the head, i.e. two eyes, two ears, two nostrils and mouth. So, shanmukhi mudra is the attitude in which the seven gates are closed. Yoni mudra or shanmukhi mudra is performed as follows:

Sit in a meditative posture such as siddhasana or padmasana. Raise the hands in front of the face with the elbows pointing sideways. Close the ears with the thumbs, the eyes with the index fingers, the nostrils with the middle fingers, and the mouth with the ring fingers above the upper lip and the little fingers below the lower lip. The fingers should close the seven gates gently but firmly.

Release the middle fingers, which are blocking the nostrils and inhale slowly and deeply. At the end of inhalation, again close the nostrils with the middle fingers and practise *antar kumbhaka*, internal breath retention. While holding the breath inside, concentrate on *bindu visarga* at the top back of the head.

142

By closing the sensory apertures, the state of *pratyahara* or sensory withdrawal is produced. The awareness is thus shifted from the external to the internal dimension and focused at bindu. Furthermore, antar kumbhaka, or internal breath retention, performed during the practice activates the prana vayu in the region of the chest and reverses the flow of apana vayu, causing it to rise upward and unite with prana. The upward movement of apana and prana vayus raises the bindu which has fallen into the lower regions. Withdrawal of the senses and focusing the awareness at bindu then restores the fallen bindu to its source.

There is a vital connection between the breath and the falling of bindu. As long as the breath moves, the bindu moves. When the breath is arrested, the bindu remains stationary in its original location. That is also why breath retention is performed in yoni mudra.

Mantra 60: White and red bindu

स पुनर्द्विविधो बिन्दुः पाण्डरो लोहितस्तथा ।
पाण्डरं शुक्लमित्याहुर्लोहिताख्यं महाराजः ॥ 60 ॥

Sa Punardvividho Binduh Paandaro Lohitastathaa;
Paandaram Shuklamityaahuh Lohitaakhyam Mahaarajah. (60)

Anvay

Sah: that; *Binduh*: bindu; *Punah*: again; *Dvividhah*: is of two types; *Paandarah*: white; *Tathaa*: and; *Lohitah*: red; *Paandaram*: white; *Shuklam*: shukla; *Iti*: this; *Aahuh*: is known as; *Lohitah*: red; *Mahaarajah*: maharaja; *Aakhyam*: is called.

Translation

That bindu is again divided into two types, paandara (white) and lohita (red). The white is called shukla and the red is called maharaja.

Commentary

According to Tantra, the bindu exists in two forms, the white and the red. The white bindu is related to the principle of consciousness or to Purusha or Shiva, and the red bindu to the principle of energy or to Prakriti or Shakti. Within each individual, the white bindu originates at the seat of the moon or bindu visarga, and the red at the seat of the sun or manipura chakra. In this mantra the white and red bindus are referred to as *shukla* and *maharaja*. Although the white and red bindus are present in each individual, the white bindu is said to predominate in the male body and the red bindu in the female body.

When the white bindu falls, it is transformed into semen or male reproductive fluid. When the red bindu falls, it becomes menstrual fluid. By specific practices of kundalini yoga, the semen produced by the male body can be trans-

144

muted back into shukla or consciousness. Similarly, the menstrual fluid produced by the female body is transmuted back into maharaja or energy. This transformation process is possible because, at a subtle level, these two energies exist in seed form as the two bindus, white and red. It is necessary to retain these bindus by a process of sublimation, so that the progressive awakening of the higher spiritual forces is not obstructed.

Mantra 61: Merger of the two bindus

सिन्दूरव्रातसंकाशं   रविस्थानस्थितं   रज: ।
शशिस्थानस्थितम् शुक्लं तयोरैक्यं सुदुर्लभम् ॥ 61 ॥

Sindooravraata Sankaasham Ravisthaana Sthitam Rajah;
Shashisthaana Sthitam Shuklam Tayoraikyam Sudurlabham. (61)

Anvay

Sindoora: of vermilion; *Vraata samkaasham*: like a heap of; *Rajah*: red bindu; *Ravisthaana*: in the place of the sun; *Sthitam*: is situated; *Shuklam*: white bindu; *Shashishthaana*: in the place of the moon; *Sthitam*: is situated; *Tayoh*: of both of them; *Aikyam*: merges; *Sudurlabham*: very difficult.

Translation

The red bindu, which is like a heap of vermilion, is situated in the place of the sun and the white bindu is situated in the place of the moon. The merger of both (bindus) is difficult.

Commentary

These mantras refer to the merging of the red and white bindus which are inherent within each individual. At the physical level the bindu is related with the reproductive system. Rajas is described as bright red in colour, which refers to the menstrual fluid. However, the ovum is the actual physical manifestation of bindu in the female body. The ovarian follicle, which nurtures and surrounds the ovum, is responsible for the menstrual cycle. The menses and vaginal secretions are dependent manifestations of the ovum because the ovarian follicle secretes the hormones, oestrogen and progesterone, which induce the proliferation of the uterine lining and its expulsion during menstruation.

Therefore, the red bindu or rajas is related with the female reproductive cycle at the physical level. At the pranic level, however, rajas corresponds with *prana shakti*, the vital force, which is represented by the sun and also by the colour red. In kundalini yoga, manipura chakra behind the navel is the solar centre. It is also the storehouse of prana and the centre of fire, or agni mandala, symbolized by a red inverted triangle. The mantra states that rajas is situated at the place of the sun, which can thus be equated with manipura.

Shukla, the white bindu, is represented at the physical level in the male body as spermatozoa, which are supported in the medium of the seminal fluid. The spermatozoa become the bindu when the semen is sublimated. In the sublimation process, neither fluid nor energy is lost from the body. However, it is not the retention or release of seminal fluid which is important here, but the conservation of energy that is utilized in its production.

According to the mantra, the seat of shukla is the moon, which is related with mind or *chitta shakti,* the mental or conscious force. In kundalini yoga, the moon is represented at two levels of evolution: at the instinctive level in swadhisthana chakra and at the higher mental level in bindu visarga. In the chakra symbology also, the moon is depicted at both centres. Therefore, the white bindu relates to the production of semen at the swadhisthana level, and to the secretion of *amrita* or nectar, which drips down from the moon at the level of bindu visarga. So, the seat of the white bindu is at the moon, which corresponds to both swadhisthana and bindu, depending upon the context.

The mantra states that the merger of both the white and red bindus is difficult. At this point we need to draw another analogy. According to hatha yoga, which forms the foundation for kundalini yoga, the lunar or mental force corresponds to ida nadi and the solar or vital force corresponds to pingala nadi. These two energies function independently like positive and negative polarities. It is only possible to unite them when a third neutral force is brought into the picture. That neutral force is sushumna nadi, the spiritual channel, which flows straight up through the centre of the spinal passage, while ida and pingala flow up spirally on either side.

The difficulty in uniting rajas and shukla, sun and moon, or ida and pingala, arises because sushumna is normally in a dormant or tamasic state. Sushumna is the pathway for the ascending kundalini and hence its activation is a prelude to all spiritual experience. First, sushumna must be opened and purified and then kundalini can be awakened. According to hatha yoga, the union of sun and moon takes place at ajna chakra where the three nadis, ida, pingala and sushumna, unite before making the final ascent to sahasrara chakra, the abode of Shiva or supreme consciousness, at the crown of the head.

In order to open sushumna, the ida and pingala passages, which carry the solar and lunar or the vital and mental forces, must first be purified and regulated. Secondly, they must be activated and awakened. The union of these forces at ajna chakra enables the yogi to access all the higher mental faculties and qualities. In kundalini yoga, the union of shukla and rajas, or ida and pingala, at ajna is achieved through the practices of mudra, bandha and kriya. By these practices the pranas are activated and raised through the two nadis from mooladhara to ajna chakra. This pranic awakening also activates the kundalini energy, which then rises towards its higher abode.

Mantra 62: Brahma and shakti

बिन्दुर्ब्रह्मा रज: शक्तिर्बिन्दुरिन्दू रजो रवि: ।
उभयो: सङ्गमादेव प्राप्यते परमं पदम् ॥ 62 ॥

Bindurbrahmaa Rajah Shaktih Bindurindoo Rajo Ravih;
Ubhayoh Sangamaadeva Praapyate Paramam Padam. (62)

Anvay

Binduh: bindu; *Brahmaa*: (is) Brahma; *Rajah*: rajas; *Shaktih*:
is Shakti; *Binduh*: bindu; *Indoo*: is the moon; *Rajah*: rajas;
Ravih: is the sun; *Ubhayoh*: of both; *Sangamaat*: with the
merger; *Eva*: only; *Paramam padam*: the highest state;
Praapyate: is attained.

Translation

The (shukla) bindu is Brahma and rajas is Shakti. Bindu is
the moon and rajas is the sun. By uniting the two, the
highest state is attained.

Commentary

This mantra refers to shukla, or the white bindu, as Brahma,
and to rajas, the red bindu, as Shakti. Brahma is the divine
conscious force responsible for creation at all levels, from
subtle to gross and from cosmic to individual. At the physical
level, Brahma corresponds to semen at the region of swadhisthana chakra. Semen is required in order to procreate
new life forms. At the subtle level, Brahma corresponds to
the moon or consciousness and to amrita, the nectar of
immortality which drips down from the moon for the purpose
of creation and sustenance at the psychic level, where the
individual first emerges from the unmanifest state.

Rajas is said to be Shakti because it is equated with the
manifest nature and qualities of creation. Brahma is the
creator and Shakti is the creation. At the physical level, rajas

149

or Shakti is represented by the menses, which nourishes the embryo of new life forms in the womb. At the subtle level, rajas is the sun, which represents the prana shakti or vital force responsible for maintenance of life at the physical and mental levels.

When the two forces of sun and moon merge at ajna, the spiritual experience dawns. Shakti merges with Shiva (Brahma). The dimension of Shiva, the pure consciousness, is from ajna up to sahasrara chakra. At bindu visarga, the centre of the moon, shukla (Brahma) resides in the form of *nada*, the primordial vibration. At ajna, shukla is experienced as the mind. The dimension of rajas (Shakti) is from mooladhara to manipura (the sun). The awakening of prana within the body is stabilized at this level.

The awakening of prana involves the withdrawal of both bindus from mooladhara and swadhisthana chakras. Brahma and Shakti, which formerly manifested through these centres as reproductive power, sensual desire and passion, manifest through manipura chakra as willpower (*ichchha shakti*) and the power of action (*kriya shakti*). The merger of Brahma and Shakti at manipura brings about the awakening of prana shakti, which in turn activates the kundalini. From manipura, the energy of Brahma, Shakti and kundalini, or ida, pingala and sushumna are raised through anahata and vishuddhi to ajna, where their merger takes place again, awakening the power of knowledge (*jnana shakti*). From ajna, Brahma and Shakti ascend to bindu visarga as one potential force, which is known as *Parabindu*.

Will is transcended sensuality and passion, and enlightenment is transcended mind. Will and higher awareness evolve from the instincts, desires and lower mind through the merger of Brahma and Shakti or shukla and rajas, first at manipura and then at ajna.

150

Mantra 63: Divine body

वायुना शक्तिचालेन प्रेरितं च यथा रज: ।
याति बिन्दु: सदैकत्वं भवेद्दिव्यवपुस्तदा ॥ 63 ॥

Vayunaa Shaktichaalena Preritam Cha Yathaa Rajah;
Yaati Binduh Sadaikatvam Bhaveddivya Vapustadaa. (63)

Anvay

Yathaa: when; *Vayunaa*: of pranic energy; *Shaktichaalena preritam cha*: moved with the force of; *Rajah*: rajas; *Sadaa*: for all time to come; *Binduh*: of bindu; *Ekatvam*: union; *Yaati*: attains; *Tadaa*: then; *Vapuh*: body; *Divya*: divine; *Bhavet*: becomes.

Translation

When rajas is moved by the force of vayu, it attains union with bindu, then the body becomes divine for all time to come.

Commentary

In kundalini yoga the process of transformation and self-realization is achieved through manipulation and awakening of the prana and chakra systems, and not through control and concentration of the mind. The above mantras give an indication of this procedure. Rajas, or prana shakti, is associated with the sun and has its seat at manipura chakra. However, it manifests as a procreative force in the region of the womb or swadhisthana chakra, where it is sustained by apana vayu, the pranic force which normally flows downward from the navel to the perineum. The different mudras and bandhas of kundalini yoga can reverse the downward flow of rajas, so that it unites with the sun at manipura chakra.

In this way, the storehouse of prana at manipura is gradually activated and awakened by the force of rajas.

151

Then, by further techniques of kundalini yoga, the awakened prana or rajas is directed into sushumna where it rises upward with great force and merges with the bindu. This process can be equated to the awakening of kundalini shakti at manipura. Therefore, it is said that with the awakening of kundalini at mooladhara, the prana shakti rises upward like drizzle, but when kundalini awakens from manipura, it arises in a gush.

By the merging of rajas with the sun or prana at manipura, the awakening of kundalini becomes established and ongoing. The kundalini awakening which takes place from mooladhara is never permanent. The prana shakti rises upward for a short distance and then falls back down again time after time due to the gravitational pull of material identifications and associations. There is not sufficient force to push through the major instinctive and karmic barriers formed by the lower psychic centres. However, once the kundalini force is awakened from manipura chakra by the merging of rajas with the sun, there is no further falling back and rajas rises unimpeded up the sushumna to unite with bindu.

By the union of rajas with bindu, the body is said to become divine for all time to come. The body that is divine for all time must be totally rejuvenated as well as immortal. Divination of the body refers to the process of cellular illumination which has been an aspect of kundalini/kriya yoga from ancient times. Bindu in the form of semen and ova has the power to create as well as sustain. If it is retained and redirected back to its source, then it has the power to rejuvenate the entire system. If rajas is united with bindu at the reproductive level, then new life is produced. However, if this union takes place in the higher region at the source of bindu, then these combined fluids or forces give birth to the manifest divine or spirit body, which is non-decaying and immortal.

The *Shiva Samhita* states: "Know that the seminal fluid is the moon and the menstrual fluid is the sun. It is necessary to unite the two within one's own body. In fact, I (Shiva) am the seminal fluid and the menstrual fluid is Shakti. When the two are united in the body of a yogi, he attains a divine body." (4:86,87)

Mantra 64: Attainment of yoga

शुक्लं चन्द्रेण संयुक्तं रज: सूर्यसमन्वितम् ।
तयो: समरसैकत्वं यो जानाति स योगवित् ॥ 64 ॥

Shuklam Chandrena Samyuktam Rajah Soorya Samanvitam;
Tayoh Samarasaikatvam Yo Jaanaati Sa Yogavit. (64)

Anvay

Chandrena: with the moon; *Samyuktam*: united; *Shuklam*: white;
Soorya samanvitam: united with the sun; *Rajah*: rajas; *Tayoh*: of
both of them; *Samarasa katvam*: full merger; *Yah jaanaati*: (one)
who knows; *Sah yogavit*: he is the knower of yoga.

Translation

Rajas is united with the sun and shukla with the moon. The
one who knows the full merger of both, he is the knower of
yoga.

Commentary

This mantra presents a very practical view of the aim of yoga
and the actual process involved in achieving it. A yogi is not
simply a person who practises yoga or even teaches yoga. A
yogi is he who has attained the fullness of yoga. The word
yoga itself is the key to the meaning of this mantra. Yoga
means 'union'. Many texts have defined yoga as the union
of the lower self with the higher, the *jivatma* with the
paramatma, but how this union is to be achieved is never
clear. Some texts say it is to be achieved through the yogic
practice of meditation and leave it at that. Others give no
method or process at all. This mantra gives the method of
attainment in kundalini yoga by uniting rajas, or prana
shakti, with the sun at manipura, and shukla, or chitta
shakti, with the moon at bindu. Then the awakened rajas is
raised to bindu where a full merger of the two is achieved.

Here it may also be noted that the practices of kundalini yoga were derived from the ancient science of Tantra. In the tantric texts sexual practices known as *maithuna* (practised by couples) or *chakra pooja* (practised by a group sitting in a circle) were also included to bring about the reversal of rajas and the awakening of kundalini. When Tantra fell into disrepute, the practices for kundalini awakening were removed and made into a separate branch of yoga. At this time, sexually related practices were rejected outright as they were regarded as demoralizing and anti-spiritual, especially when performed illicitly and by unmarried couples. So these practices remained as a part of tantric science and were never combined into the system of kundalini yoga that was accepted by the vedic tradition and included in the Yoga Upanishads.

This mantra may be understood to contain some reference to the ancient tantric system of kundalini awakening. The exoteric aspect of sexual union in kundalini yoga was rejected completely, but the esoteric or subtle aspect was accepted, in the sense that each individual contains both male and female propensities within himself/herself. In other words, each aspirant embodies the principles of Shiva (consciousness) and Shakti (energy), or moon (mind) and sun (prana), and the merging of these two aspects of being results in the highest state of yoga. This mantra states that he is a yogi who experiences the full merger of sun and moon, by merging rajas with the sun and shukla with the moon. He realizes the full attainment of yoga by awakening the kundalini force and establishing it in the higher centres.

Goraksha Satarka echoes similar thoughts: "Bindu is Shiva (consciousness) and rajas is Shakti (energy). Bindu is the moon (ida and mind) and rajas is the sun (pingala and prana). From the mingling of the two, one obtains the highest state. Shukla bindu (semen) is joined with the moon (bindu visarga) and rajas (prana) is joined with the sun (manipura). One who knows how to unite the two is an adept." (74 & 76)

Mantra 65: Maha mudra

शोधनं नाडिजालस्य चालनं चन्द्रसूर्ययो: ।
रसानां शोषणं चैव महामुद्राऽभिधीयते ॥ 65 ॥

Shodhanam Naadijaalasya Chaalanam Chandrasooryayoh;
Rasaanaam Shoshanam Chaiva Mahaamudraa Abhidheeyate. (65)

Anvay

Naadijaalasya: network of nadis, entire nadi structure;
Shodhanam: for purification; *Chandrasooryayoh*: of the moon
and sun; *Chaalanam*: for the movement; *Cha eva*: and also;
Rasaanaam: vital body fluids; *Shoshanam*: for absorption;
Mahamudraa: the great mudra; *Abhidheeyate*: method is
taught.

Translation

The method taught for purification of the entire nadi
structure governing the movement of the moon and the sun
and absorption of the vital fluid is maha mudra.

Commentary

This mantra refers to maha mudra, which is a technique of
hatha yoga as well as kundalini/kriya yoga. The kriya yoga
practice involves the entire range of asana, pranayama, mudra
and bandha. Maha mudra is generally performed with an
interrelated practice known as maha bheda mudra (the
great piercing mudra), which is not mentioned in this mantra.
Together these two practices supercharge the whole system
and induce a state of spontaneous meditation.

By the combined practice of asana, pranayama, mudra
and bandha in these techniques, the entire nadi structure is
balanced, purified and awakened, thereby balancing the
whole mind and body system. The flow of pranic energy in
the sushumna channel is cleared and stimulated, increasing

awareness, inducing clarity of thought and removing nervous depression.

These practices further govern the movement of prana and bindu in the moon and sun centres. Regular practice of maha mudra and maha bheda mudra prevents the bindu from falling and reverses the bindu even after it has fallen. By preserving the bindu from being burnt by the sun or passed out through the semen and ovum, the *rasas* or vital body fluids are reabsorbed. This leads to greater mental and vital power, which can be utilized for regenerating the system or awakening the higher mental faculties.

Mantras 66, 67: Maha mudra method

वक्षोन्यस्तहनुः प्रपीडच्च सुचिरं योनिं च वामाङ्घ्रिणा
हस्ताभ्यामनुधारयन्प्रसरितं पादम् तथा दक्षिणम् ।
आपूर्य श्वसनेन कुक्षियुगलम् बद्ध्वा शनै रेचये-
देतद्व्याधिविनाशिनी सुमहती मुद्रा नृणां प्रोच्यते ॥ 66 ॥
चन्द्रांशेन समभ्यस्य सूर्यांशेनाभ्यसेत्पुनः ।
या तुल्या तु भवेत्संख्या ततो मुद्रां विसर्जयेत् ॥ 67 ॥

Vakshonyastahanuh Prapeedya Suchiram Yonim Cha Vaamaang-
hrinaa Hastaabhyaam Anudhaarayan Prasaritam Paadam Tathaa
Dakshinam:

Aapoorya Shvasanena Kukshiyugalam Baddhvaa Shanai Rechayet
Etad Vyaadhi Vinaashinee Sumahatee Mudraa Nrinaam Prochyate.
(66)
Chandraamshena Samabhyasya Sooryaamshenaabhyasetpunah;
Yaa Tulyaa Tu Bhavetsankhyaa Tato Mudraam Visarjayet. (67)

Anvay

Vakshah nyasta hanuh: pressing the chin in the throat cavity;
Yonim: genital (perineum); *Vaama anghrinaa*: with left leg;
Prapeedya suchiram: pressing firmly for a long time; *Tathaa*:
and; *Hastaabhyaam*: by the two hands; *Prasaritam*: stretched;
Dakshinam paadam: right leg; *Anudhaarayan*: held; *Kukshi-*
yugalam: both parts of the abdomen; *Shvasanena*: with breath;
Aapoorya: filling up; *Baddhvaa*: holding; *Shanaih*: slowly;
Rechayet: should be exhaled; *Nrinaam*: for men; *Etat*: this;
Vyaadhi vinaashinee: destroyer of all disease; *Sumahatee*: very
important; *Mudraa*: mudra; *Prochyate*: has been called;
Chandra amshena: through the moon; *Samabhyasya*: practising
well; *Punah*: again; *Soorya amshena*: through the sun; *Abhyaset*:
should practise; *Tu*: and; *Yaa*: when; *Tulyaa*: equally;
Sankhyaa: number; *Bhavet*: becomes; *Tadaa*: then; *Mudraam*:
mudra; *Visarjayet*: should be released.

Translation

Press the chin into the throat cavity. Press the perineum firmly with the left foot for a long duration. Stretch the right leg in front on the ground and hold the (right) toes with both hands. Draw in the breath, filling up both parts of the abdomen completely. After holding the breath, it should be slowly exhaled. This mudra is very important for men and it is the destroyer of all diseases. Practise well through the moon and again through the sun. When the number of rounds becomes equal, then the mudra should be released.

Commentary

These mantras deal with the technique of maha mudra in which maha bheda mudra also forms an integral part. Although only maha mudra is named here, we can infer that originally both techniques were included in this practice. Later on, the method was divided into two parts and separate names given for each part. Maha bheda mudra, which means 'the great piercing attitude', supplements maha mudra, and the two practices are performed consecutively.

It is a peculiarity of the kriyas that upon commencement the head is bent forward so that the chin presses the throat cavity. In both maha mudra and maha bheda mudra the sitting posture of utthanpadasana is described. In other kriyas, different sitting postures are utilized. According to the mantra, utthanpadasana is performed by pressing the perineum firmly with the left foot and stretching the right leg in front. Then bend forward and hold the right toes with both hands.

Next the instructions say to draw in the breath, filling up both parts of the abdomen completely. In the process of yogic breathing, the upper and lower abdomen is expanded by filling up the lower and middle lobes of the lungs completely. This form of deep breathing is necessary to

159

oxygenate the system so that kumbhaka or breath retention can be performed easily without becoming breathless.

The instruction continues that after holding the breath, it should be exhaled slowly. The kriya yoga version of maha mudra also utilizes ujjayi pranayama, which has not been mentioned in the mantra. However, in ujjayi the exhalation is more pronounced and performed slowly. In the practice of maha mudra, the capacity to breathe slowly and deeply and to hold the breath for a duration of time, both inside and outside as in antar and bahir kumbhaka, is very important.

The next mantra says to practise well through the moon and again through the sun. 'Practise well through the moon' relates to the practice of maha mudra, in which shambhavi and khechari mudras are incorporated. Maha mudra deals with the preservation and reversal of the bindu in the higher centres before it falls down to manipura. 'Practise well through the sun' relates to maha bheda mudra, in which nasikagra mudra and uddiyana and moola bandhas are incorporated to reverse the bindu which has fallen down to manipura and the lower centres.

Hence, 'practise well through the moon and then through the sun' means during internal kumbhaka, apply shambhavi and khechari mudras and moola bandha, which is the technique of maha mudra. Then again during external kumbhaka, apply nasikagra mudra and uddiyana and moola bandhas, which is the technique of maha bheda mudra. The mantra further says to perform each variation for an equal number of rounds and then release the mudra. Although the method of maha mudra was later on divided into two separate practices, it is still stated in kriya yoga that the two practices, maha mudra and maha bheda mudra, are to be performed consecutively for the same number of rounds.

The mantra also adds that maha mudra is an important practice for men, and that it eradicates all diseases. The practice is important for men because the male reproductive system is easily influenced by erotic stimuli from both external and internal sources, causing the bindu to fall and semen to be produced. The female system, on the other hand, functions according to a monthly cycle in which menses and ovum are produced only once and on regular days, whether there is erotic stimuli or not.

Therefore, these practices can be used by males to preserve the bindu in the higher centres and to reverse the flow of the bindu even after it has fallen down to the lower centres. In this way, the male energy or *veerya* is not lost through excess production and emission of semen. The falling of the bindu to the lower centres and its escape from the body through the semen is the original cause of disease, ageing and death. So, by reversing this process, the practitioner is thereby able to eradicate all diseases as well as ageing and death.

Today we find the practices of maha mudra and maha bheda mudra described in greater detail, although the key points remain the same. There are several reasons why the original practice differs somewhat from the modern version. First of all, we must take into account that from early times up to the present day, the practices of kundalini yoga were transmitted only in secret to the most worthy disciples and aspirants.

Therefore, such teachings were rarely put into writing, and when they were, certain omissions were made so that the practices would still remain secret to some extent and could only be revealed fully by the Guru or realized master to initiated aspirants. Furthermore, these practices have been refined over the ages, since the time when they were described in this Upanishad.

The following passages contain the instructions for these practices according to the teachings of Swami Satyananda Saraswati.

Maha Mudra in Utthanpadasana

Sit with the right leg stretched in front, bend the left knee and press the left heel into the perineum, midway between the anal sphincter and the sexual organ. For women the heel should press against the inside of the vagina. Adjust the position so that you feel comfortable. Place both hands on the right outstretched knee. This posture is called utthanpadasana.

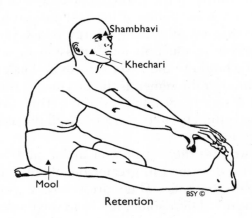

Retention

Hold the spine upright. Fold the tongue into khechari mudra and maintain it throughout the practice. Open the eyes and exhale deeply. Hold the breath and bend the head forward. Become aware of the pressure at mooladhara chakra applied by the left heel. Repeat mentally: mooladhara, mooladhara, mooladhara.

Inhale with ujjayi pranayama and ascend the frontal passage with the breath and awareness. Be aware of each chakra kshetram in turn: swadhisthana, manipura, anahata, vishuddhi and bindu.

As the awareness moves from vishuddhi to bindu, bend forward and grasp the toes of the outstretched right foot with both hands. Raise the head so that it is slightly back.

162

Fix the awareness at bindu. Hold the breath inside and mentally repeat: bindu, bindu, bindu.

While continuing to hold the breath inside, perform moola bandha and shambhavi mudra. Rotate the awareness from the eyebrow centre to the throat to the perineum, repeating: 'shambhavi, khechari, mool', three or more times.

Release shambhavi and moola bandha. Return to the upright position with the two hands on the outstretched right knee. Bring the awareness back to bindu.

Exhale slowly with ujjayi pranayama and unmani mudra. Allow the awareness to descend the spinal passage with mental awareness of each chakra point in turn: ajna, vishuddhi, anahata, manipura, swadhisthana and mooladhara. When the awareness reaches mooladhara chakra, the exhalation should be terminated. This is one round.

Practise four times with the right leg outstretched, four times with the left leg outstretched and then four times with both legs outstretched.

Maha Bheda Mudra in Utthanpadasana

The basic posture is the same. Sit with the right leg stretched in front, bend the left knee and press the left heel into the perineum, midway between the anal sphincter and the sexual organ. For women, the heel should press against the inside of the vagina. Adjust the position so that you feel comfortable. Place both hands on the right outstretched knee. This posture is called uttanpadasana.

Hold the spine upright. Fold the tongue into khechari mudra and maintain it throughout the practice. Open the eyes and exhale deeply. Hold the breath and bend the head forward. Become aware of the pressure at mooladhara chakra applied by the left heel. Repeat mentally: mooladhara, mooladhara, mooladhara.

Inhale with ujjayi pranayama and ascend the frontal passage with the awareness. Be aware of each chakra kshetram in turn: swadhisthana, manipura, anahata, vishuddhi and bindu.

As the awareness moves from vishuddhi to bindu, raise the head so that it is slightly back. Fix the awareness at bindu. Hold the breath inside and mentally repeat: bindu, bindu, bindu.

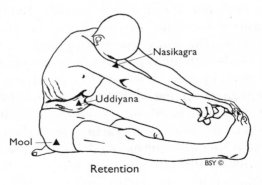

Retention

Exhale with ujjayi pranayama and unmani mudra, allowing the awareness to descend the spinal passage through ajna, vishuddhi, anahata, manipura, swadhisthana and mooladhara chakra points.

When the awareness reaches mooladhara, the exhalation should be terminated. Retain the breath outside and bend forward. Clasp the toes of the right foot with both hands. Perform jalandhara, moola and uddiyana bandhas and nasikagra mudra. Rotate the awareness from the nose tip to the abdomen to the perineum, repeating 'nasikagra, uddiyana, mool' three or more times.

Release nasikagra, moola, uddiyana and jalandhara, but keep the head slightly forward. Return to the upright position and bring the hands back to the outstretched right knee. Bring the awareness back to mooladhara. This is one round.

Practise four times with the right leg outstretched, four times with the left leg outstretched and then four times with both legs outstretched.

164

Combining the two practices

When the practices of maha mudra and maha bheda mudra have been mastered, it will again be possible to combine them into one practice, as they were originally taught. This means that during the same round both moon and sun rotations are performed. The 'shambhavi, khechari, mool' rotation follows inhalation during internal kumbhaka; and after exhalation, the 'nasikagra, uddiyana, mool' rotation is performed during external retention. However, this combination requires great proficiency of all the elements of the practice and should not be undertaken without guidance.

Note: For detailed explanation of all the subsidiary practices included in these techniques refer to *Asana Pranayama Mudra Bandha* by Swami Satyananda Saraswati, published by Yoga Publications Trust.

Mantra 68: Maha mudra and digestive fire

नहि पथ्यमपथ्यं वा रसा: सर्वेऽपि नीरसा: ।
अतिभुक्तं विषं घोरं पीयूषमिव जीर्यते ॥ 68 ॥

Nahi Pathyamapathyam Vaa Rasaah Sarvepi Neerasaah;
Atibhuktam Visham Ghoram Peeyooshamiva Jeeryate. (68)

Anvay

Pathyam apathyam vaa: wholesome or unwholesome; *Sarve*: all; *Neerasaah*: tasteless; *Api*: also; *Rasaah*: tasteful; *Atibhuktam*: overeating; *Nahi*: does no harm; *Visham ghoram*: gross poison; *Peeyooshamiva*: like nectar; *Jeeryate*: is digested.

Translation

By the power of this mudra, wholesome or unwholesome foods are digested and all tasteless things also become tasteful. Overeating does no harm and even poison is digested like nectar.

Commentary

This mantra states that the digestive power is greatly increased by the practice of maha mudra. In order to qualify this point, it should be remembered that maha mudra in this context also includes the practice of maha bheda mudra. The purpose of maha bheda is to activate the lower chakras, especially mooladhara and manipura in order to reverse the bindu. Within this practice there is a combination of several subsidiary techniques. Nasikagra mudra and moola bandha stimulate mooladhara chakra and redirect the downward flow of apana upward to manipura. Uddiyana bandha activates the solar energy at manipura and also directs it upward.

Therefore, maha bheda is a powerful practice for activating and awakening agni mandala. It raises the digestive fire

166

to such an extent that all ingested food can be easily digested, whether wholesome or unwholesome. Even tasteless items become tasteful when the digestive prana is high. It is said that Sage Agastya was able to drink the sea dry by the power of his awakened manipura. Later, he also digested the poisonous demon Vatapi, who had entered his stomach in the form of a goat which had been cooked by Vatapi's brother Atapi, into a tasty dish of mutton and offered to the sage with the intent of killing him. When the sage had finished the meal, Atapi called to his brother, "Come out Vatapi, come out." But Agastya patted his stomach and replied, "No, Vatapi will not come out; I will digest him whole where he is."

So, by the practice of maha bheda mudra, the power of digestion and assimilation can be increased to such an extent that the sadhaka can even consume deadly poison as if it were nectar and remain unaffected. Of course, it would take many years to achieve this level of digestive power and that is not the actual intention of the practice. Rather, it is meant to redirect the prana and bindu for higher spiritual awakening. The implication is that by accidental consumption of unwholesome or excess food no harm is done. It does not mean that the sadhaka should exercise no restraint at all in diet.

Mantra 69: Maha mudra removes disease

क्षयकुष्ठगुदावर्तगुल्माजीर्णपुरोगमा: ।
तस्य रोगा: क्षयं यान्ति महामुद्रां तु योऽभ्यसेत् ॥ 69 ॥

Kshayakushtha Gudaavarta Gulmaajeerna Purogamaah;
Tasya Rogaah Kshayam Yaanti Mahaamudraam Tu Yobhyaset. (69)

Anvay

Mahamudraam: of mahamudra; *Tu*: then; *Yah*: who; *Abhyaset*: practises; *Tasya*: his; *Kshaya*: tuberculosis; *Kushta*: leprosy; *Gudaavarta*: fistula; *Gulma*: tumour; *Ajeerna*: indigestion; *Purogamaah rogaah*: all possible future ailments; *Kshayam yaanti*: cured and prevented.

Translation

Tuberculosis, leprosy, fistula, indigestion and tumour are cured, and all possible future ailments prevented for those who practise maha mudra.

Commentary

This mantra states that freedom from disease can be gained by the practice of maha mudra. Diseases such as tuberculosis, leprosy, fistula, indigestion and tumour, which were prevalent and considered to be incurable around the time when this Upanishad was written, are said to be cured by this practice, and all possible future ailments prevented. The reason why the combined practice of maha mudra and maha bheda mudra cures and prevents disease is threefold.

Firstly, it stimulates the prana shakti in the frontal and spinal energy circuits from mooladhara to bindu chakras and removes energy blocks from the pranic and psychic systems. Secondly, it brings about the fusion of prana and apana with samana at manipura, releasing vast amounts of energy into the system, which could not be accessed previously. Existing diseases are permanently eradicated due to the dramatic increase of energy and even diseases which could possibly manifest at some future time are prevented. Thirdly, the combined practices of maha mudra and maha bheda mudra prevent the bindu from falling and redirect the bindu upwards even if it has fallen. The fall of the bindu is said to be responsible for the onset of ageing and of all diseases. By the reversal of this process, all diseases are prevented and removed.

Mantra 70: Maha mudra bestows great powers

कथितेयं महामुद्रा महासिद्धिकरी नृणाम् ।
गोपनीया प्रयत्लेन न देया यस्य कस्यचित् ॥ 70 ॥

Kathiteyam Mahaamudraa Mahaasiddhikaree Nrinaam;
Gopaneeyaa Prayatnena Na Deyaa Yasya Kasyachit. (70)

Anvay

Iyam: this; *Kathita*: mentioned earlier; *Mahaamudra*: maha-mudra; *Nrinaam*: for men; *Mahaasiddhikaree*: bestower of great powers; *Prayatnena*: with care; *Gopaneeyaa*: should be kept secret; *Yasya kasyachit na deyaa*: not taught to anyone.

Translation

This maha mudra, which was mentioned earlier, is the bestower of great powers for men. It should be kept secret, with care, and not taught to anyone.

Commentary

The activating effects of maha mudra can be experienced throughout the entire system at many levels. Physiologically, the digestive capacity is raised. Pranically, the vital energy is generated and circulated in the nadis and psychic passages. Psychologically, the mind and senses are brought under control, resulting in greater power of concentration and development of inner awareness. Psychically, the chakras and kundalini are activated, purified and awakened. With the awakening of the chakras and kundalini, siddhi is attained. The word *siddhi* means 'perfection in yoga'. It is also used for psychic powers or attainments which come as a result of this perfection. With the attainment of siddhi, the yogi becomes a *siddha*, an adept or master of yoga.

The eight siddhis attained through mastery of kundalini yoga are also mentioned in Mantra 36, and include the

170

following abilities: to become as small as an atom; to become weightless; to become as large as the universe; to become heavy; to reach any place at will; to remain under water for long periods; to maintain the body and youth indefinitely; to control all objects, organic and inorganic; to create and destroy at will. Some other siddhis obtained through awakening of the chakras and kundalini include: acquisition of hidden treasure; freedom from fear of the elements; freedom from disease; ability to enter another's body at will; knowledge of past, present and future; full knowledge of the scriptures.

The text further states that these powers are bestowed on men and there is no mention of women here. This qualification was given in view of the social structure during upanishadic times, as well as the location of the bindu in the male and female systems. In the male body the shukla (white) bindu emanates from the moon in the form of amrita, the nectar of life, and drips down from bindu visarga to vishuddhi. Due to natural propensities, it falls down to manipura where it is burnt up by the sun and then further down to the lower centres where it is transformed into semen and escapes from the body. Although the bindu falls in the natural process of life, it can still be reversed by the practices of kundalini yoga and reunited with its source at bindu visarga.

The nature of the female system differs in this respect. It relates with rajas, the red bindu, which is established in the lower centres and associated with the reproductive system and menstrual cycle. Rajas is united with the sun at manipura, which means that the natural tendency of women is to create and support life. Women do not need to transcend the material world in order to undergo spiritual experience. Their inner receptivity is enhanced through the natural processes of life, especially the production of children, resulting in direct experience of the higher reality. Therefore,

171

in the past women generally did not seek to perform practices to derive spiritual awakening and powers. However, should a woman chose to rechannel her force to the higher centres, she can undergo a more powerful awakening than a man can because rajas is stronger than shukla, especially in the lower centres. This is why a female counterpart was often sought in the tradition of Tantra.

The mantra also states that the practice of maha mudra should be kept secret with care and not taught to anyone. When any practice of great power is discussed or shared publicly, it loses its potency. In the *Hatha Yoga Pradipika* it states that: "Yogis who wish to attain perfection keep the practice highly secret. In order to be powerful it must be kept secret. If it happens to be revealed, it becomes powerless." (1:11) The practices performed for spiritual awakening are not a matter for idle talk. They are important for one's higher evolution and, therefore, of great value to oneself. So, the practice of maha mudra should be guarded carefully and not revealed to anyone.

Furthermore, when a powerful technique is given to the wrong person or group of persons, it can produce more harm than good, either by incorrect application or misuse of powers gained by it. So the mantra states that the practice should not be taught to anyone. All the practices of hatha and kundalini yoga were originally transmitted by masters or adepts and performed in secret. Maha mudra, being one of the most powerful of these techniques, is especially recommended to be practised in secret and not to be taught to anyone. Even today the practices of kundalini yoga are regarded as highly esoteric and are taught only by realized masters or by transmission and should not be performed by the unprepared or uninitiated.

Mantra 71: Padmasana

पद्मासनं समारुह्य समकायशिरोधरः ।
नासाग्रदृष्टिरेकान्ते जपेदोंकारमव्ययम् ॥ 71 ॥

Padmaasanam Samaaruhya Samakaaya Shirodharah;
Naasaagra Drishtirekaante Japedonkaaram Avyayam. (71)

Anvay

Padmasanam: in padmasana; *Samaaruhya*: sitting properly; *Samakaaya shirodharah*: keeping the head and body straight; *Ekaante*: in a solitary place; *Naasaagradrishtih*: keeping the attention firmly fixed on the nose; *Avyayam*: eternal; *Omkaaram*: of Aum; *Japet*: should repeat.

Translation

Sitting properly in padmasana, with the head and body straight, fix the attention firmly at the tip of the nose and continuously repeat the Aum mantra in a solitary place.

Commentary

Padmasana, also known as *kamalasana*, is a classical meditation posture. The words *padma* and *kamala* both mean 'lotus'. In this posture, the body is locked firmly in a balanced position and physical movement is reduced to a minimum. When mastered, padmasana enables the practitioner to hold the body steadily for long periods. As the body and mind are interrelated, steadiness of the body induces steadiness of the mind. Steadiness of body and mind is the first requisite for higher meditation. This posture also balances the flow of prana and directs it upward through sushumna from mooladhara to sahasrara, thus helping to awaken the kundalini. In the *Hatha Yoga Pradipika* (1:47) padmasana is referred to as 'the destroyer of disease'. The verse also says that 'ordinary people cannot achieve this posture; only the wise can do so'.

173

To practise padmasana, sit with the legs extended in front of the body. Bend one knee and place the foot on top of the opposite thigh. The sole of the foot should be facing upwards and the heel should touch the pelvic bone. Bend the other knee and place that foot on top of the opposite thigh. Both knees should touch the ground in the final position. Keep the head and spine straight, and shoulders relaxed. Place the hands on the knees in chin or jnana mudra.

The mantra says this practice should be performed in a solitary place in order to remain undisturbed. In such a place one should sit properly in padmasana, then fix the attention at the tip of the nose. Nasagra or nasikagra drishti is a form of concentration which has special implications in kundalini yoga because it stimulates mooladhara chakra due to its relation to the sense of smell.

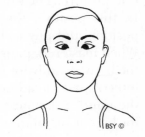

To perform nasikagra drishti, open the eyes slightly and focus them on the nose tip without straining. Try to see a double outline converging at the tip of the nose, forming an inverted V. Concentrate on the apex of the V to the exclusion of all other thoughts.

The mantra concludes the instruction for padmasana by saying to take up continuous japa of the mantra Aum. This implies that padmasana is not just a physical posture, but a meditation practice in itself which leads to the highest stage of spiritual awakening. The mantra Aum is synonymous with maha prana or kundalini shakti. There are many forms of Aum chanting which have different effects on the brain and nervous system. The correct technique for each individual must be learned under the direction of a competent master.

Sitting in padmasana with the concentration focused at the nose tip while repeating the Aum mantra is an important practice of meditation. By the methods of kundalini yoga described in this text the aspirant is gradually led into the state of concentration and meditation. In yogic sadhana, meditation is of prime importance for it enables the practitioner to go beyond the mind and ego, senses and sensory objects, pranas and elements, to experience the union of the self with the absolute reality in samadhi. The basic idea of meditation is that one should not struggle for illumination, but learn to still the body, pranas, senses, emotions, vrittis, mind and intellect. Only then will the light shine.

Meditation is an art, a science and a psychoanalytical technique of realizing the structure of personality and discovering the self, layer by layer. Therefore, the system of raja yoga describes the progression of meditation in four stages:

1. *Pratyahara*: withdrawal of the mind from the world of name, form, idea and objects
2. *Dharana*: controlling mental dissipation and distraction, and fixing the mind upon the object of concentration and contemplation
3. *Dhyana*: one-pointed awareness devoid of mental perception and fluctuation, which eventually culminates in the next stage

4. *Samadhi*: total fusion of the individual self with the transcendental self.

The practice described in this mantra begins at the stage of dharana, one-pointed concentration, culminating in dhyana, spontaneous meditation. The gradual transformation of dissipated awareness into concentration and concentration into meditation aims to make one aware of the dual tendencies of mind and their influence on behaviour and action. After such realization takes place, the mind attains equipoise and harmony. In this state, the duality of mind and prakriti are transcended and the aspirant is able to experience the Aum mantra, which is a symbolic representation of the transcendental state. All the traditional scriptures of ancient India have described meditation on Aum as the highest technique of self-discovery. In this technique the reflection of the macrocosmic and microcosmic experiences is seen.

Mantra 72: Dimensions of consciousness

विश्वो हि स्थूलभुङ्नित्यं तैजस: प्रविविक्तभुक् ।
आनन्दभुक्तथा   प्राज्ञ: सर्वसाक्षी पर: ॥ 72 ॥

Vishwo hi Sthoolabhuk Nityam Taijasah Praviviktabhuk;
Aanandabhuk Tathaa Praajnah Sarva Saakshee Parah. (72)

Anvay

Vishvah: ruler of the conscious state; *Hi*: also; *Sthoolabhuk*: enjoyer of the gross; *Nityam*: always; *Taijasah*: ruler of the subconscious state; *Praviviktabhuk*: enjoyer of the subtle; *Aanandabhuk*: enjoyer of bliss; *Tathaa*: and; *Praajnah*: ruler of the unconscious state; *Sarvasaakshee*: witness of all these; *Parah*: one that is beyond also.

Translation

Vishva, the ruler of the conscious state, is always the enjoyer of the gross dimension also. Tejasa, the ruler of the subconscious, enjoys the subtle dimension. And Prajna, the ruler of the unconscious, enjoys the blissful dimension. Sarvasakshi is the witness of all these and beyond them as well.

Commentary

From this mantra, concepts that are more vedantic in nature are being introduced into the text. In Vedanta, the consciousness is divided into four states or dimensions. The seers of these states are described here as follows: *Vishva*, ruler of the conscious state; *Tejasa*, ruler of the subconscious; *Prajna*, ruler of the unconscious; and *Sarvasakshi*, witness of all the states. In yogic terminology these four states correspond with *jagrit* (wakefulness), *swapna* (dream), *nidra* (deep sleep) and *turiya* (transcendence). This mantra thus depicts the entire range of human experience from waking consciousness to the super-conscious state.

The state of wakefulness relates to the conscious mental perceptions. The dream state relates to the subconscious subtle perceptions. Deep sleep relates to the unconscious where the conscious and subconscious remain inactive in their potential state. The transcendental state of inner awareness corresponds to the super-conscious, which experiences the conscious, subconscious and unconscious dimensions, and is beyond them as well.

In the conscious or jagrit state, one is aware of the concrete evidence and existence of name, form, and idea within the realm of time, space and object. The enjoyer and controller of this state are Vishva or *Vaishvanara*. The word *vishva* means 'universe' and *nara* means 'the changing or decaying principle'. The term indicates the range of consciousness subject to change, transformation and decay which is inherent in the world.

According to *Mandukyopanishad*: "The external awareness is the realm of Vishva. He enjoys the visible objects of the world through his seven limbs and nineteen mouths." (v. 3) The seven limbs of Vishva are the seven chakras, or psychic energy centres: mooladhara, swadhisthana, manipura, anahata, vishuddhi, ajna and sahasrara. These centres provide the energy necessary for the development, functioning and experiences of the physical body and mind in relation to the material world.

Vishva experiences the external dimension through his nineteen mouths, which represent the four aspects of mind (*manas* – rational mind, *buddhi* – higher intellect, *chitta* – memory, and *ahamkara* – ego or I-ness, the five *tanmatras*, or subtle senses (hearing, feeling, seeing, tasting, smelling), the five *jnanendriyas* or organs of knowledge (eyes, ears, tongue, nose and skin), and the five *karmendriyas* or organs of action (hands, feet, vocal organ, excretory organ, reproductive organ). Vishva is the master of these nineteen mouths. He receives information through them from the material world, and then makes appropriate decisions on how to respond in order to enjoy and evolve in the external dimension.

In the subconscious or swapna state, the awareness of concrete, material evidence recedes into dreaming and imaginary recognition of name, form and idea. The ruler of this state is Tejasa, the subtle, hidden, luminous principle of consciousness. In yogic terminology this dimension is described as *hiranyagarbha*, the golden womb, and Tejasa also means the 'golden light'. Gold is the colour attributed to this state due to its pure and luminous nature. Swapna is also known as the golden womb, because it is here that the sense of individuality is first conceived in a state of pure, radiant light.

In *Mandukyopanishad*, Tejasa is described as "the ruler of the dream state, where he enjoys the invisible objects through his seven limbs and nineteen mouths." (v. 4) The objects enjoyed by Tejasa are immaterial and therefore subtle in nature. They do not have physical form or dimension as material objects do. They are expressions of the subconscious mind in the form of impressions, feelings, thoughts and desires. Tejasa experiences these invisible objects through his seven limbs, which represent the seven *lokas* or subtle planes of existence: *Bhu, Bhuvah, Swaha, Maha, Janah, Tapah* and *Satya*. These are the planes through which the subtle consciousness evolves beyond the material experiences.

The nineteen mouths by which Tejasa experiences these subtle planes are the same as described previously for Vishva. Here, however, they represent the inner essence or quality of these sensory modalities. Thus Tejasa receives information by direct cognition of the subconscious mind, rather than by contact with the external objects. In this way he creates his own world and acts within it according to his own dictates. In this way Tejasa experiences the invisible objects in the form of fantasy, inner vision or dream.

179

In the unconscious or nidra state, there is a conceptual loss of time, space and object. In this state inactivity of the conscious and subconscious states related to time, space and object sets in. *Shoonya,* or the state of nothingness, bordering between the cognitive and non-cognitive faculties, is experienced. Loss of individual perception is the indication of nidra and shoonya. Prajna, the all-knowing inner awareness, is the ruler of this state. External awareness and knowledge are related to the realm of time, space and object. In the absence of these an inner awareness combined with wisdom evolves, which is qualified by peace and equipoise. Nidra in this sense is not sleep as it is generally understood, but total absence of the conscious and subconscious cognitive faculties.

Prajna is the ruler of the causal dimension in which the seeds of all knowledge and existence remain in their potential state. *Mandukyopanishad* describes this state as follows: "Prajna abides in the dimension of deep, dreamless sleep, beyond desire, where all things have vanished. He enjoys bliss at the gateway to the dreaming and waking states." (v. 5). Prajna is thus the seer of the unconscious where the entire potentiality remains in total stillness. There is no subtle activity of thoughts, impressions or desires. This state is completely self-contained and free from any action related to the dimensions of Tejasa or Vishva.

Prajna, the seer of the unconscious state, beyond cognition of time, space and object, heralds the attainment of Turiya. Here all the dissipated and fragmented faculties of consciousness merge into one awareness in time and beyond time, in space and beyond space, in object and beyond object, in cognition and beyond cognition. Sarva-sakshi, the seer of the Atma or the Self, rules this dimension. Turiya relates to the super-conscious mind in yoga which is experienced in the final stage of samadhi or oneness with the Supreme Being.

This mantra thus describes the conscious principle of the entire cosmos which is objective, subtle, causal and supramental. This concept is also explained as bodies of experience. In relation to this mantra, it can also be seen that all beings have three bodies. The *sthoola sharira* or gross body is ruled by Vishva and experienced as motion and activity of the physical body and its organs. The *sukshma sharira* or subtle body is ruled by Tejasa and experienced as the four faculties of manifest consciousness, because of the subtle and unseen nature of their activity and performance. The *karana sharira* or causal body is ruled by Prajna and experienced as a potential state in which the gunas, qualities of nature, remain in total stillness. Apart from these three, there is a fourth known as Atman, which is the pure spirit or transcendental body. This is the spiritual dimension of Sarvasakshi, the seer of all the three, and that which is also beyond.

Mantra 73: Pranava

प्रणव: सर्वदा तिष्ठेत्सर्वजीवेषु भोगत: ।
अभिरामस्तु सर्वासु ह्यवस्थासु ह्यधोमुख: ॥ 73 ॥

Pranavah Sarvadaa Tishthet Sarvajeeveshu Bhogatah;
Abhiraamastu Sarvaasu Hyavasthaasu Hyadhomukhah. (73)

Anvay

Pranavah: Aum mantra; *Sarvadaa*: always; *Bhogatah*: enjoying;
Sarvajeeveshu: in all living beings; *Sarvaasu*: all; *Hi avasthaasu*:
in states also; *Abhiraamah tu*: enjoying the world; *Hi
adhomukhah*: having the mouth downward; *Tishthet*: resides.

Translation

The Pranava resides in all living beings ever enjoying. It
resides in all states also with the mouth downward, enjoying
the world.

Commentary

Pranava is a term used interchangeably in yogic philosophy
with Aum, the primal sound vibration. According to yogic
philosophy, the entire creation, including all the diverse
forms, originally emanated from Aum, the cosmic sound.
Therefore, Aum or Pranava is the object of contemplation
and meditation as the source of all existence. Aum is also
described as Brahman, Shakti, the created worlds, the three
bodies, and the gross and subtle aspects of consciousness.
Aum is the Om-nipresent, Om-nipotent and Om-niscient
spirit, whose realization leads to *kaivalya* or *moksha*.

The Pranava or Aum is spoken of in all scriptures. Even
in the Bible we find the statement: "In the beginning was the
word and the word was with God." In Christianity, Aum is
pronounced *Amen*, and in Islam, *Amin*. Aum is described as
eternal, pure, omniscient, beyond the mind, untainted,

indescribable, without beginning, the sole source of all life, and the transcendental reality. Aum is the vibrational experience of the absolute reality existing beyond the phenomenal plane, which is perceived as real by the lower mind.

The phenomenal plane is transitory; therefore, all human experiences are also transitory and changeable. The finite exists in infinity and that infinity is eternal, having no beginning and no end. It is pure for it is beyond the fold of duality and, therefore, untainted by any form of gross, subtle or causal knowledge. It is omniscient for all the wisdom of the entire manifest and unmanifest cosmos is contained within it for eternity. It is indescribable for its experience is beyond the reach of speech, cognition and intellect. It is the source of creation from which all life is generated, by which all is sustained and into which all merges at the time of dissolution.

Aum is beyond the three divisions of time: past, present and future. Therefore, it is known as *Shabdha Brahman*, the word of Brahman, which is Brahman itself. Here we can understand Brahman in terms of pure consciousness, which is free from all associations with maya, illusion or limitation, and the gunas or qualities of nature which comprise all aspects of phenomenal reality. All phenomenal experience is confined to cognition of time, space and object. Time is understood as having three divisions, known as past, present and future. In this sense time is limited and finite, but in the cosmic sense it is an unending continuum, representing eternity. The cosmic continuum in which reality is always present is *Brahman*, the ever-expansive awareness.

The word Brahman is derived from the Sanskrit root *brih*, which means 'continuously expanding'. *Parambrahman* is the supreme cosmic consciousness from which *Paramshakti*, its self-luminous, great power emanates. Paramshakti is the supreme cosmic energy, the power of action. Parabrahman is the eternal consciousness of the cosmos and Paramshakti is his creative power. This cosmic consciousness and cosmic energy are known by many names. In Samkhya philosophy, they are known as Purusha and Prakriti, in Tantra as Shiva and Shakti, and in Vedanta as Brahman and Maya. These terms represent the same source from which all creation and individual beings originally evolved.

The Pranava or Aum is described as having all the attributes of Brahman or the supreme consciousness from which Paramshakti, the supreme power or creator, has emanated. The terms Brahman and Atman are also used synonymously to express the level of absolute reality. The only difference is that Brahman is used objectively and Atman subjectively. Brahman refers to the cosmic reality and Atman to the individual reality. Therefore, the Pranava is equated with Brahman on the cosmic plane, and with Atman, the spirit or pure consciousness which dwells within each being, at the individual level. Brahman is considered to be the enjoyer of the universal creation manifested by Paramshakti and Atma is the enjoyer within the individual beings.

Pranava is the luminosity of each Atma and thus represents Turiya, the transcendental state of consciousness which is beyond and, therefore, unlimited by the three states: nidra (unconscious, deep sleep), swapna (subconscious, dream) and jagrit (conscious, waking). The mantra states that Pranava resides within all beings as the enjoyer. What does this principle of pure consciousness enjoy? It enjoys the interactions of the mind and senses with the world. In the absence of a conscious principle to observe and enjoy the creation, there would be no purpose in creating it.

The mantra further states that Pranava resides with its mouth turned downwards, ever enjoying the world in all states. Here, 'with the mouth turned downward' implies that, rather than experiencing its pure and unlimited state, the consciousness is directed downward towards the enjoyment of the three limited states, where it experiences interactions with the objects of the gross and subtle worlds. In this way the consciousness feeds on these interactions and becomes identified and bound to the limited states, instead of realizing itself as the totality.

Mantra 74: Aum matras

अकारो जाग्रति नेत्रे वर्तते सर्वजन्तुषु ।
उकार: कण्ठत: स्वप्ने मकारो हृदि सुप्तित: ॥ 74 ॥

Akaaro Jaagrati Netre Vartate Sarvajantushu;
Ukaarah Kanthatah Swapne Makaaro Hridi Suptitah. (74)

Anvay

Akaarah: 'A' letter; *Jaagrati*: in the waking state; *Netre*: in the eyes; *Vartate*: is located; *Sarva*: all; *Jantushu*: in living beings; *Ukaarah*: 'U' letter; *Kanthatah*: in the throat; *Swapne*: in the dreaming state; *Makaarah*: 'M' letter; *Hridi*: in the heart; *Suptitah*: in the sleeping state.

Translation

The 'A' letter corresponds to the waking state and is located in the eyes. The 'U' letter corresponds to the dream state and is located at the throat. The 'M' letter corresponds to the deep sleep state and is located in the heart.

Commentary

Pranava represents the totality of consciousness in its unlimited or turiya state. At the same time, as a sound form, the syllable Aum is comprised of three *matras,* or letters 'A', 'U' and 'M'. The mantra states that each of these letters has a correlation in the three states of consciousness and is situated in a particular area of the body accordingly.

The 'A' sound form relates to *jagrit*, the waking or conscious state. It is thus said to be located in the eyes, which facilitate awareness of the external world and one's role and interactions within it. The 'U' sound form relates to *swapna*, the dreaming or subconscious state, where one is neither awake nor asleep. It is located in the throat where there is no direct sensory awareness or contact with the

186

material world, but still the consciousness functions on the subtle plane through dream imagery. The 'M' sound form relates to *nidra*, the sleeping or unconscious state, where there is no awareness of the senses or the world. It is located in the heart, which is completely surrounded and protected by the ribcage. Being totally removed from sensory awareness and contact, the heart is said to be the seat of the soul, or atma, where the external and internal awareness merge.

Mantras 75, 76a: Attributes of the aum matras

अकारो राजसो रक्तो ब्रह्मा चेतन उच्यते ।
उकार: सात्त्विक: शुक्लो विष्णुरित्यभिधीयते ॥ 75 ॥
मकारस्तामस: कृष्णो रुद्रश्चेति तथोच्यते ॥ 76a ॥

Akaaro Raajaso Rakto Brahmaa Chetana Uchyate;
Ukaarah Saattvikah Shuklo Vishnurityabhidheeyate. (75)
Makaarastaamasah Krishno Rudrascheti Tathochyate. (76a)

Anvay

Akaarah: 'A' sound form; *Raajasah*: rajasic; *Raktah*: red;
Brahmaa: of Brahma; *Chetanah*: consciousness; *Uchyate*: has
been called; *Ukaarah*: 'U' sound form; *Saattvikah*: sattvic;
Shuklah: white; *Vishnuh*: Vishnu; *Iti abhideeyate*: (like this) is
called; *Makaarah*: 'M' sound form; *Taamasah*: tamasic; *Cha*:
and; *Krishnah*: black; *Rudrah*: Rudra; *Iti tathaa uchyate*: it has
been said like this.

Translation

The 'A' sound form, which is rajasic and red, has been
called the consciousness of Brahma. Similarly, the 'U' sound
form, which is sattwic and white, is called Vishnu. Like this,
it has been said that the 'M' sound form, which is tamasic
and black, is called Rudra.

Commentary

The Pranava or Aum, comprising the three letters 'A', 'U' and
'M', is said to represent the vedic trinity – *Brahma, Vishnu* and
Rudra, representing the powers of creation, preservation and
dissolution respectively. The three syllables of Aum also
represent the three gunas, or qualities of nature, as well as the
three primal colours, which represent the forms of nature. In
this way, the Pranava, which combines the three *aksharas,* or
eternal sound vibrations, is said to be illumined in all beings,

because it represents the three powers, aspects and forms of nature, which are divine as well as terrestrial and are responsible for the entire cycle of evolution.

The 'A' sound form represents Brahma, the Creator, who brings all the worlds into existence. He was the first *deva* or illumined being. Brahma corresponds to the manifest consciousness and rules over matter or the earth element. Matter is the element which supports all forms of life and gives birth to the knowledge of objects. The majority of life forms are dependent on matter for production and multiplicity. Samkhya philosophy understands matter as the basis of physical nature. The whole universe and all its objects must have some material form into which they evolve and from which they return after dissolution. It is further stated that Brahma is born from rajas, because creation requires the energy of dynamism. *Rajoguna* is the dynamic attribute of nature, characterized by restlessness, activity and ambition. Rajas is also associated with the colour red, which symbolizes passion, fertility and procreation.

The 'U' sound form relates to Vishnu, the Preserver, who organizes and maintains the entire manifest existence. Vishnu represents the subtle consciousness which rules over the water element. In yogic mysticism, water represents the subconscious dimension which is the basis of the individual mind and the storehouse of mental impressions, samskaras and karmas. Individual being is shaped by the subconscious mind, and many instinctive drives that are experienced in life come up from the depths of the subconscious. The subconscious state should never be considered as inactive or dormant; rather it is far more dynamic and powerful than the conscious state.

In the subconscious state, the samskaras and karmas are stored in the form of long-term memories. A painful or pleasant experience of yesterday becomes a process or force which acts, colouring the conscious awareness today. In this

189

way, there are many experiences from the past which one does not consciously recall, but nevertheless they play a part in determining the daily behaviour, attitude and reactions. There are many karmas and samskaras which influence us in this way, but we remain completely unaware of them. All such significant and insignificant, impressive and unimpressive karmas and samskaras which have been registered in the field of consciousness are stored in deeper layers of the subconscious.

It is further stated that Vishnu is born out of sattwa because maintenance requires the energy of balance and stability. Sattoguna is the attribute of nature representing the balanced and harmonized state of being. Sattwa is thus associated with the colour white, which is pure and not mixed with any other colour. White is also the colour of pure light and the subconscious is associated with consciousness in the form of luminosity.

The 'M' sound form represents Rudra, the Destroyer, who is responsible for the dissolution of all the worlds at the time of *Pralaya*. Rudra represents the unconscious, where all the karmas and samskaras reside in their seed or potential state. There is no vision, no dream, no desire and no thought. The consciousness rests within itself in a state of total stillness, undisturbed by any activity or outward motion. Rudra is one of the many names of Shiva, who governs the fire element. Fire represents prana and the source of dynamism, energy, will and achievement. Just as fire has the ability to burn and destroy everything, Rudra has the ability to break down the combination of the elements, transmuting them into their original, pure form.

It is stated that Rudra is born out of tamas. Tamoguna is the third quality of nature, representing inertia after fullfledged activity. Tamas is associated with the colour black, representing the dissolution, or void, wherein all forms return to the source. Black is the colour into which all the

190

other colours of the spectrum are merged and lose their separate identity.

The original idea of the trinity, represented by the three letters of the Pranava, can be seen in this concept of Brahma, Vishnu and Rudra, which existed long before any of the religions and philosophies known today. Brahma, the Creator, plays the part of the regenerating principle at all times. Vishnu, the Preserver, plays the role of the stabilizing entity, and Rudra, the Dissolver, is constantly breaking down the combination of the elements and their attributes. Brahma, Vishnu and Rudra are the trinity with the potential to create, sustain and dissolve the creation, worlds, dimensions, life forms and so on.

Even at a practical level, while chanting the Aum mantra, it can be experienced that the 'A' sound is the most dynamic and externalized vibration. Therefore, this letter is described as rajasic in nature and red in colour, both of which indicate dynamism and activity. Similarly, the 'U' syllable is the balance of sound between the 'A' and the 'M'. Thus it relates to the subtle state of consciousness which is in-between the gross and the causal. While chanting Aum, the 'U' sound merges with the 'A' forming the sound 'Au' or 'O'. The final 'M' sound is also clear and distinct, while the 'U' sound is not distinct in itself but merges the 'A' and the 'M'. Thus the 'U' sound, which is subtle, balancing and harmonizing, is said to be sattwic in quality and white in colour.

The 'M' sound, which creates a humming vibration at the end of the Aum mantra, induces a state of introversion and detachment. Thus it corresponds to the unconscious principle which relates to the concept of dissolution, wherein the mind and senses again return to their source. The 'M' sound subsides into a long buzzing sound, which has an introverting effect on the mind. So it is said to be tamasic in nature, producing stillness and therefore characterized by the colour black, which relates to space, shoonya, the void.

Mantras 76b, 77: Creation and dissolution

प्रणवात्प्रभवो ब्रह्मा प्रणवात्प्रभवो हरि: ॥ 76b ॥
प्रणवात्प्रभवो रुद्र: प्रणवो हि परो भवेत् ।
अकारे लीयते ब्रह्मा उकारे लीयते हरि: ॥ 77 ॥

Pranavaatprabhavo Brahmaa Pranavaatprabhavo Harih. (76b)
Pranavaatprabhavo Rudrah Pranavo Hi Paro Bhavet;
Akaare Leeyate Brahmaa Ukaare Leeyate Harih. (77)

Anvay

Pranavaat: from Pranava; *Brahmaa*: Brahma; *Prabhavah*: emanates; *Pranavaat*: from Pranava; *Harih*: Vishnu; *Prabhavah*: emanates; *Pranavaat*: from Pranava; *Prabhavah*: emanates; *Rudrah*: Rudra; *Pranavah hi*: that Pranava; *Parah*: supreme; *Bhavet*: originates; *Akaare*: in 'A' sound form; *Leeyate*: merges; *Brahmaa*: Brahma; *Ukaare*: in 'U' sound form; *Leeyate*: merges; *Harih*: Vishnu.

Translation

From the Pranava emanate Brahma, Vishnu and Rudra. That Pranava originates from the supreme reality. Brahma merges in the 'A' sound form, Vishnu merges in the 'U' sound form.

Commentary

In the Upanishads, Pranava is spoken of as Shabdha Brahman, the word or vibration emanating from the absolute reality. This vibration is the subtlest aspect of creation which is still connected to the original source in the unmanifest Brahman. Therefore, from the Pranava, or primal vibration of the unmanifest dimension, all of the manifest qualities of nature have evolved. Hence, the mantra states that Brahma, the universal Creator, and Vishnu, the universal Preserver, emanate from Pranava, and again Rudra, the universal

Destroyer, also emanates from Pranava. These are the three powers of Pranava or the universal consciousness by which all the worlds, universes and galaxies are constantly being born, evolving and dissolving.

Just as Brahma and Vishnu emanate from Pranava for the purpose of creation and evolution, each merges back into it at the time of *Pralaya*, or universal dissolution. When the entire manifest creation is dissolved back into its source, the process of evolution ceases along with the need to sustain it. Therefore, it is said that Brahma merges back into the 'A' sound form and Vishnu merges back into the 'U' sound form. As long as these cosmic principles are merged back into their point of origin, the process of creation and evolution will not take place. At the individual level this can be understood as the reunion of the gross and subtle aspects of consciousness with the self or atma.

Mantra 78: Illumination

मकारे लीयते रुद्र: प्रणवो हि प्रका॒ते ।
ज्ञानिनामूर्ध्वगो   भूयादज्ञानीनामधोमुख: ॥ 78 ॥

Makaare Leeyate Rudrah Pranavo Hi Prakaashate;
Jnaaninaamoordhvago Bhooyaad Ajnaaneenaam Adhomukhah. (78)

Anvay

Makaare: in 'M' sound form; *Leeyate*: merges; *Rudrah*: Rudra; *Pranavah hi*: then only the Pranava; *Prakaasha te*: continues to illumine; *Jnaaninaam*: in the realized ones; *Oordhvagah*: facing upward; *Bhooyaat*: is; *Ajnaaneenaam*: in the ignorant people; *Adhomukhah*: facing downward.

Translation

Rudra merges in the 'M' sound. Then only the Pranava continues to illumine. In the realized ones (this Pranava) faces upward, (whereas) in the ignorant it faces downward.

Commentary

Here the mantra states that when the unconscious aspect of consciousness also merges back into the self or atma, then only the Pranava remains. This is the transitional point between the manifest and the unmanifest, between Shabdha Brahman and Brahman. It is the dimension of total darkness which has been spoken of as 'the dark night of the soul', where there is no experience of any movement or fluctuation, whether gross or subtle – only impenetrable darkness.

With the merging of Rudra into the 'M' sound, the last vestiges of unconsciousness are removed, then only the Pranava continues to illumine. This means that the Pranava ceases to manifest as word, sound form or vibration, because it no longer relates to the conscious, subconscious or unconscious dimensions. However, it continues to illumine the pure consciousness in the transcendental dimension. Therefore, the sound vibration of Aum ceases, but the Pranava continues to illumine.

The text further states that in the realized or wise ones, Pranava faces upward, denoting liberation through realization of the transcendental, unmanifest dimensions. In the ignorant, however, it faces downward, indicating bondage to the lower manifest realms. By merging the three matras, 'A', 'U' and 'M', and thus the three dimensions of consciousness: jagrit, swapna and nidra, or conscious, subconscious and unconscious, into the Pranava, the yogi enters the fourth dimension of turiya or super-consciousness, which is illumined by the Pranava.

The mantra speaks of Pranava facing upward to describe the path of liberation which is known by the wise. Whereas, for the ignorant, who are not able to transcend the three dimensions of consciousness and realize the absolute, the Pranava faces downward. They are unenlightened who acknowledge the manifest realms as reality. The projection of consciousness down into the lower states represents attachment to the material world of name and form, and thus bondage to the wheel of birth and death.

Therefore, the goal of yoga is to transcend the modifications and associations of the mind. This can only be achieved through realization that the entire manifest existence, in all of its change and complexity, is the projection of the unmanifest reality. Behind the world of name and form there abides one eternal reality, symbolized by Aum. Meditation on the Pranava brings liberation to the wise, who understand this truth. However, for the ignorant, who see the phenomenal world as real, bondage continues until Pranava is experienced as the absolute reality in the highest dimension of consciousness.

Mantra 79: Anahad nada

एवं वै प्रणवस्तिठेद्यस्तं वेद स वेदवित् ।
अनाहतस्वरूपेण ज्ञानिनामूर्ध्वगो भवेत् ॥ 79 ॥

Evam Vai Pranavastishthet Yastam Veda Sa Vedavit;
Anaahatasvaroopena Jnaaninaam Oordhvago Bhavet. (79)

Anvay

Evam: thus; *Vai*: certainly; *Pranavah*: Pranava; *Tishthet*: resides; *Yah*: one who; *Tam*: that, this; *Veda*: knows; *Sah*: he; *Vedavit*: realized, knowledgeable; *Anaahata swaroopena*: in the form of anahata; *Jnaaninaam*: for the wise or realized ones; *Oordhvagah*: going upward, ascending; *Bhavet*: becomes.

Translation

Thus resides the Pranava. One who knows this is certainly realized or knowledgeable. In its anahata form (the Pranava) becomes an ascending (path) for the wise.

Commentary

Here, Pranava is said to abide within itself, as the light of the soul or the atma. This is the transcendental state which is beyond the three states, as well as the source from which they emanate. This is the highest knowledge and the one who attains it is said to be truly knowledgeable. All other forms of knowledge are accessible to him; just as from the mountaintop all the surrounding areas can easily be seen and recognized. One who is established in Pranava abides in the *avyakta* or unmanifest dimension and thus attains moksha or liberation from all bondage.

The mantra also refers to Pranava in the anahata form as an ascending path for the wise. The experience of Aum in the heart, which is described in nada yoga as the anahad nada or unstruck sound, is said to lead the yogi upward to the unmanifest dimension. In the system of nada yoga, there are four classifications of sound: *baikari* (audible), *upanshu* (whispered), *manasi* (mental) and *para* (supreme or transcendental). When Pranava is repeated verbally, whispering or mentally, it can be heard as the sound of Aum in the stages of baikari, upanshu and manasi. Here, the syllables 'A', 'U' and 'M' are experienced as sound vibration which has been struck or produced by an agent, i.e., the vocal cords, lips or mind.

Ultimately, however, the Pranava is experienced as unstruck sound vibration, which has no manifest cause or source as it originates from the unmanifest. Hence Pranava in the anahata form is that pure sound vibration which represents the first emanation from the unmanifest or transcendental plane into the causal dimension, where it can be experienced internally as unstruck sound, having no objective source or cause. This pure vibration is heard at anahata chakra because the heart is the location for the unconscious (which was stated in Mantra 75, in relation to the 'M' matra) as well as for the soul or atma.

This unstruck sound forms a link or an opening between the manifest and unmanifest, just like the black hole in space which takes one from the plane of material existence into the void. In this sense, the yogi who experiences Pranava in its anahata form is said to be truly knowledgeable, having realized the cause or origin of the self and of all manifest creation. This is the highest knowledge, which few seekers ever attain.

Mantra 80: Pranava and nada yoga

तैलधारामिवाच्छिन्नम् दीर्घघण्टानिनादवत् ।
प्रणवस्य ध्वनिस्तद्वत्तदग्रं ब्रह्म चोच्यते ॥ 80 ॥

Tailadhaaraamiva Achchinnam Deerghaghantaa Ninaadavat;
Pranavasya Dhvanistadvat Tadagram Brahma Chochyate. (80)

Anvay

Tailadhaaraamiva: like the flow of oil; *Achchhinnam*: constant
and unbroken; *Deergha ghantaa*: very heavy bell; *Ninaadavat*:
like the sound of; *Pranavasya*: of Pranava; *Dhvanih*: sound;
Tadvat: thus; *Tadagram*: its front portion; *Brahma*: Brahma;
Cha: and; *Uchyate*: is called.

Translation

The Pranava flows like oil, constant, unbroken, like the sound
of a very big bell. Thus its front portion is called Brahma.

Commentary

This mantra refers to the Pranava as a spontaneous form of
japa, where the sound flows like a stream of oil, constant
and unbroken. This is the highest form of japa, called ajapa
japa, where the vibration of the mantra becomes internalized
and repeats itself continuously, from moment to moment,
without any interruption or gap. This ajapa form of the
Pranava is attained after mastering the lower meditative
stages of *pratyahara* (sensory withdrawal) and *dharana* (one-
pointed concentration). When the subjective and objective
awareness merge into Pranava, the higher states of *dhyana*
dawn, wherein Aum is experienced as a constant, unbroken
flow of vibration at the heart.

Next the mantra describes the inner sound vibration of
the Pranava, which is like the ringing of a very large, heavy
bell. This refers to the meditative system of nada yoga,

which is based on sound vibration produced entirely from within. All manifest or external sounds are caused by friction of one object striking another. The internal sounds which can be heard in deep states of meditation arise in the absence of any objective cause or friction. Furthermore, manifest or 'struck' sounds have a limitation in time; they begin at one point and end at another. Whereas the Pranava is described here as unbroken and continuous, like the flow of oil.

In the yogic texts, different nadas or inner sounds are described, such as a bell, flute, veena, conch, symbols, drums and thunder. So, here the sound of a large bell, attributed to the Pranava, is in direct association with nada yoga. This means that Pranava is intimately linked with nada and kundalini yogas. The different nadas are said to manifest one by one, and sometimes in great profusion, with the rising of kundalini through the sushumna nadi, which is located at the centre of the spinal column. This is the ascending path of the Pranava in its anahata form which was spoken of in the previous mantra. By merging the awareness with the internal sound of Pranava, the consciousness is drawn upward into higher, transcendental realms with the rising of the kundalini, like a kite born up into the sky by a strong breeze.

The mantra then states that the front portion of the Pranava is called Brahma. The front portion here refers to the first *matra* or letter of the Pranava, 'A'. Here the 'A' matra is associated with Brahma, the creative principle, which is responsible for the manifest world of name and form. Although Brahma is responsible for creation, he still exists within the formless dimension of luminosity or pure vibration, also known as Hiranyagarbha, the golden womb of creation. Brahma is the source of creation or manifestation but not creation itself. So, Brahma is a divine being or principle of light because he remains unmanifest but is responsible for the manifest creation. This is the subtle aspect attributed to the first letter or matra 'A' of the Pranava.

199

Mantra 81: Qualities of the 'A' matra

ज्योतिर्मयं तदग्रं स्यादवाच्यं बुद्धिसूक्ष्मतः ।
दद्गुर्ये महात्मानो यस्तं वेद स वेदवित् ॥ 81 ॥

Jyotirmayam Tadagram Syaadavaachyam Buddhisookshmatah;
Dadrishurye Mahaatmaano Yastam Veda Sa Vedavit. (81)

Anvay

Jyotirmayam: luminous; *Tat agram*: that front portion; *Syaat*: is; *Avaachyam*: beyond speech; *Buddhisookshmatah*: because of subtle intelligence; *Dadrishuh*: can visualize; *Ye*: who; *Mahaatmaanah*: the wise; *Yah*: who; *Tam*: that, this; *Veda*: knows; *Sah*: he; *Vedavit*: real knower.

Translation

That front portion is luminous and beyond speech. The wise can visualize this by subtle intelligence. He who knows that is the real knower.

Commentary

This mantra is a continuation of the previous one, where it was said that the front portion is called Brahma. The front portion refers to the first matra or letter of the Pranava, which is 'A'. According to yogic philosophy, all the fifty Sanskrit matras are considered as divine and indestructible, and so beyond speech in their subtlest form. Furthermore, 'A' is not an ordinary letter but the first of the vowels, so it is given even greater importance. Every matra or letter is always followed by 'A', either short or long, unless otherwise designated. Here the 'A' matra is described as luminous in nature and beyond speech. Luminosity is the quality of sound vibration in its subtle state. Beyond speech refers to the source of the matra, which is the causal dimension beyond produced or audible sound.

The mantra continues to say that the wise can visualize this matra by subtle intelligence. The wise are those who have expanded their conscious awareness beyond the manifest dimension, allowing them to experience the subtle realms of consciousness. Thus subtle intelligence implies knowledge of the unseen reality which is beyond duality, name and form, time and space. This is the realm from which sound can be experienced as pure vibration or emanation of light. Finally, the text says that he who knows this, who experiences this matra as luminosity, beyond speech, is the real knower. He knows that all sound vibration in the form of letters, words and speech are manifestations of the Pranava. This is the source of the objective world and exists beyond it, but is accessible only to those who have the eyes to perceive it. Others see only the outer appearance of name and form and think that to be the ultimate reality.

Mantras 82, 83: Hamsa

जाग्रन्नेत्रद्वयोर्मध्ये हंस एव प्रकाशते ।
सकार: खेचरी प्रोक्तस्त्वंपदं चेति निश्चितम् ॥ 82 ॥
हकार: परमेश: स्यात्तत्पदं चेति निश्चितम् ।
सकारो ध्यायते जन्तुर्हकारो हि भवेद् ध्रुवम् ॥ 83 ॥

Jaagrannetradvayormadhye Hamsa Eva Prakaashate;
Sakaarah Khecharee Proktastvam Padam Cheti Nishchitam. (82)
Hakaarah Parameshah Syaattatpadam Cheti Nishchitam;
Sakaaro Dhyaayate Janturhakaaro Hi Bhaved Dhruvam. (83)

Anvay

Jagrat: in the waking state; *Netradvayoh*: of both eyes; *Madhye*: in the middle; *Hamsa eva*: Hamsa; *Prakaashate*: shines; *Sakaarah*: form of Sa; *Khecharee*: khechari; *Proktah*: has been called; *Nishchitam*: certainly; *Twam padam*: of 'Twam'; *Cha iti*: is indicative of; *Hakaarah*: form of Ha; *Parameshah*: Supreme Lord; *Syaat*: is; *Nishchitam*: certainly; *Tatpadam*: of That; *Cha iti*: is indicative of; *Sakaarah*: letter Sa; *Dhyaayate*: contemplating; *Jantuh*: soul, person; *Dhruvam*: surely; *Hakaarah hi*: that form Ha; *Bhavet*: becomes, identifies.

Translation

In the waking state Hamsa shines at the eyebrow centre. Of these (two syllables), the 'Sa' has been called khechari, and is certainly indicative of 'Twam'. The letter 'Ha' is of the form of the Supreme Lord, and is certainly indicative of 'Tat' (That). The person who contemplates on 'Sa', i.e. 'Twam', surely becomes identified with the 'Ha' letter, i.e. 'Tat'.

Commentary

Here the text shifts from Pranava to Hamsa. Both of these mantras, Aum and Hamsa, form the basis of meditation in the Yoga Upanishads. Hamsa is a mantra composed of two

202

syllables, *Ham* and *Sah*. In other yogic texts, the mantra Hamsa has been literally translated as Ham or *Aham*, meaning 'I', and Sah, 'That'. Here, however, the definition of the two syllables is given a different context. Thus the letter Sa is indicative of *twam*, meaning 'thou' or 'you', which implies the individual consciousness, and the letter Ha or Ham is analogous with the Supreme Lord, or absolute consciousness. Accordingly, Ha is indicative of *Tat* or 'That', referring to the highest state of consciousness, which is beyond words and, therefore, inferred by 'That'.

Furthermore, Sa, which is indicative of *twam*, or the individual consciousness, has been called khechari. The practice of khechari mudra was described earlier in Mantras 52–55. The word khechari is derived from two roots: *khe* meaning 'in the sky' or 'in the cosmic space', and *chari* 'one who wanders'. The association of Sa with khechari and also with twam or thou thus indicates the path or practice by which the individual consciousness is drawn up to the higher centres of luminosity and merged with the infinite space. Hence the mantra also states that Hamsa shines between the eyebrows in the waking state, where the mind is conscious of the external world. The psychic centre known as bhrumadhya, which is the trigger point for ajna chakra, is located at the eyebrow centre and has important associations with the frontal brain as well. Ajna controls the subtle mental faculties and is the threshold to higher conscious experiences, while bhrumadhya, being the outer contact point, is associated more with the conscious state of awareness. Bhrumadhya is awakened by constant repetition of Hamsa in the conscious state, and light is perceived there.

Hamsa thus implies the process and the journey of the jiva or individual consciousness to meet and merge within the absolute consciousness described here as the Supreme Lord. By attuning the individual consciousness to the infinite reality, the jiva, or individual soul, becomes the pure

203

consciousness itself. Thus the mantra finally states that one who contemplates on Sa or Twam, the manifest, eternal reality, becomes identified with Ha or Tat, the unmanifest eternal reality. In this way the individual soul is liberated from the associations with the material and psychic planes, which result in the continuous cycle of birth and death, and attains the highest goal of yoga.

The Hamsa mantra is also linked with the breath, which is the source of life. Concentration on Hamsa as the inherent sound vibration repeated by each breath in turn is described as Ajapa Gayatri in Mantras 31–35 of this text.

Mantra 84: Jiva and atma

इन्द्रियैर्बध्यते जीव आत्मा चैवन बध्यते।
ममत्वेन भवेज्जीवो निर्ममत्वेन केवल: ॥ 84 ॥

Indriyairbadhyate Jeeva Aatmaa Chaivana Badhyate;
Mamatvena Bhavejjeevo Nirmamatvena Kevalah. (84)

Anvay

Indriyaih: by the senses; *Jeevah*: individual soul; *Aatmaa*: pure soul; *Cha*: but; *Eva*: so; *Na*: never; *Badhyate*: bound; *Mamatvena*: from attachment; *Bhavet*: becomes; *Jeevah*: individual soul; *Nirmamatvena*: with freedom from attachment; *Kevalah*: pure consciousness is attained.

Translation

The individual soul is bound by the senses, but the pure soul is never so bound. The individual soul is born of attachment and self-realization is attained by freedom from attachment.

Commentary

When the individual soul becomes manifest in the body, it passes through five stages of limitation, which have been described by Sage Patanjali in the *Yoga Sutras* as the five *kleshas*. The first of these limitations is *avidya* or ignorance, which signifies that the individual consciousness loses sight of the absolute reality and sees itself as a separate entity. Avidya has thus been described as a curtain or veil which comes down between the unmanifest and manifest reality, concealing the one from the other.

When the individual soul experiences itself as separate from the whole, it then requires an identity in order to relate with other manifest entities. So, from avidya, or ignorance of the unmanifest reality, *asmita*, the sense of 'I-ness' or the

205

individual ego, is born. Through the sense of I-ness the individual soul relates with the external world of time, space and object in terms of 'I and other', and thus the experience of duality arises. Hence, asmita or I-ness, gives birth to *raga*, attraction, and *dwesha*, repulsion. The ego is attracted to those objects which are perceived through the senses as pleasant and repulsed by those which are painful or unpleasant.

Finally, the individual consciousness, having lost sight of the absolute reality, becomes totally identified with the manifest world and the objects of experience which are of a pleasant or painful nature. Hence, *abhinivesha* or insecurity and fear arise because there is no permanence at this level of existence. What is born will die; what is gained will be lost. In this way, the individual soul, limited by the influence of ignorance and I-ness, loses sight of reality and takes the unreal to be real. Thus it becomes attached and bound to the objects, relationships and situations which it experiences through the senses in the material world.

The mantra states that the pure soul is never bound in this way because it has been liberated from the limitations, and is able to perceive the absolute reality directly. This form of direct perception is called self-realization. When the soul experiences its true nature, which is eternal, unqualified and unbound, all mundane associations and attachments fall away. So while the *jiva*, or individual soul, is born of attachment, the *jivanmukta*, or liberated soul, attains self-realization through freedom from attachment.

Mantra 85: Lokas and deities of aum

भूर्भुवः स्वरिमे लोकाः सोमसूर्याग्निदेवताः ।
यस्य मात्रासु तिष्ठन्ति तत्परं ज्योतिरोमिति ॥ 85 ॥

Bhoorbhuvah Swarime Lokaah Somasooryaagnidevataah;
Yasya Maatraasu Tishthanti Tatparam Jyotiromiti. (85)

Anvay

Bhooh: Earth; *Bhuvah*: Intermediate; *Swah*: Heaven; *Eme*: these; *Lokah*: all the planes; *Soma*: Moon; *Soorya*: Sun; *Agni*: Fire; *Devataah*: all these deities; *Yasya*: of which; *Maatraasu*: in the letters; *Tishthanti*: are established; *Tat*: that; *Paramjyoti*: supreme light; *Aum iti*: it is Aum.

Translation

All the planes, Earth, Intermediate and Heaven, and all the deities, Sun, Moon and Fire, are established in the (three) letters, of that supreme light which is Aum.

Commentary

Pranava or Aum is the sound vibration or the luminosity, representing Atman as well as Brahman, the individual and the universal pure consciousness. The *lokas* are planes or dimensions of consciousness. *Bhuh* loka or Earth is the plane where consciousness is influenced by the material world and its associations. This relates to *jagrit*, the waking dimension of consciousness, where the mind is totally absorbed and identified with the external forms and experiences. Bhuh or the earthly dimension corresponds to the 'A' matra of the Aum syllable.

Bhuvah is the Intermediate plane where the consciousness enters a kind of purgatory state, in between the earthly and heavenly existence. Here the consciousness is freed from the physical body, but is still influenced by the samskaras and karmas, accumulated impressions which are carried within the causal body. This plane relates with *swapna*, the dreaming or subconscious dimension of consciousness, which can be experienced consciously in deeper meditative states. It is also the dimension of purgatory for disembodied souls whose karmic associations are very strong, even after death, thus preventing them from ascending to the higher dimensions. Bhuvah or the Intermediate plane corresponds to the 'U' matra of the Aum syllable.

Swaha or *Swarga* is the heavenly plane, where the consciousness is freed from both the material and karmic associations. Although the karmas still remain here in seed form, they lie dormant, awaiting further expression at some later time. This plane relates with *nidra* or *sushupti*, the deep sleep or unconscious dimension, which is beyond all activity of thoughts, desires and impressions. Here, all associations related with name, form and idea have disappeared, and unity or oneness with the individual soul is experienced in a state of total stillness. This dimension is known as Swarga or Heaven because it is free from the dualities of life, and thus from all the negative propensities associated with it. However, the unconscious plane still contains all the karmic seeds which are the source of life, so rebirth is always imminent. Thus Swarga is not considered to be a liberated plane, as are the planes above it. This loka corresponds with the 'M' matra of the Aum syllable.

The mantra further discusses the deities, or luminous aspects of divinity, which correspond with the three letters of the Aum syllable. The Pranava is considered to be the source of light which manifests in every plane of existence. Fire, the moon and the sun are mediums through which that pure luminosity can be experienced in the different lokas or dimensions of consciousness. Fire is thus the symbol of this luminosity at the earthly level or conscious plane of existence. Fire blazes forth on the earth itself and is fed by

208

earthly substances or fuels, such as wood, coal, oil, gas and so on. Fire represents the luminosity of Pranava, which can be experienced through the five senses and known by the conscious mind. So, fire relates with the 'A' matra of the Aum syllable.

The moon is the symbol of pure luminosity on the Intermediate plane or Bhuvah loka. The moon casts a reflected light into the darkness of night, just as fabrications of the mind are reflected in the dream world. Moonlight is also associated with fantasy, imagination and other purely mental constructions. Thus it represents the source of light which can be known and experienced on the Intermediate plane by the subconscious mind. In this way the moon relates with the 'U' matra of the Aum syllable.

The sun is considered to be the source of light which is closest to the Pranava. Thus it is the symbol of pure luminosity on the heavenly plane. Just as the Pranava is the source of all radiance, the sun is the second manifestation of this pure energy principle. The sun can be regarded as the lens through which the luminosity of Pranava is seen most directly. Just as the eyes see by the light of the sun, so the individual soul sees by the light of the atman or the Pranava. In this way, the sun represents the source of light which can be experienced by the unconscious mind. Again, this does not refer to the physical sun only, but to the elemental sun and the pure energy source from which its radiance is derived. Thus, the sun corresponds with the 'M' matra of the Aum syllable.

In this way, the mantra has related the existence of the three planes, Earth, Intermediate and Heaven, as well as the three deities, or divine forms of luminosity, Fire, Moon and Sun, with the three letters of the Pranava.

Mantra 86: Powers of aum

इच्छा क्रिया तथा ज्ञानं ब्राह्मी रौद्री च वैष्णवी ।
त्रिधा मात्रा स्थितिर्यत्र तत्परं ज्योतिरोमिति ॥ 86 ॥

Ichchhaa Kriyaa Tathaa Jnaanam Braahmee Raudree Cha Vaishnavee;
Tridhaa Maatraa Sthitiryatra Tatparam Jyotiromiti. (86)

Anvay

Ichchhaa: power of willing; *Kriyaa*: power of action; *Tathaa*: and; *Jnaanam*: power of knowledge; *Braahmee*: power of creation; *Raudree*: power of destruction; *Cha*: and; *Vaishnavee*: power of maintenance; *Tridhaa*: of three; *Maatraa*: letters; *Sthitih*: established; *Yatra*: is where; *Tat*: that; *Param*: supreme; *Jyotih*: light; *Aum iti*: it is Aum.

Translation

Ichcha, the power of willing, Kriya, the power of action, and Jnana, the power of knowledge, as well as Brahmi, the power of creation, Vaishnavi, the power of maintenance, and Raudri, the power of destruction, are established in that supreme light which is Aum.

Commentary

Pranava or Aum is the supreme light of the cosmic energy principle, which pervades and is inseparable from the cosmic consciousness. In this sense it is the pure consciousness itself, and so it is also known as Shabdha Brahman, the word or cosmic vibration of God. Cosmic energy, being the pure creative principle, is also comprised of the three gunas or creative qualities: *sattwa* (luminosity), *rajas* (dynamism) and *tamas* (stability). From pure rajas arises *Ichchha Shakti*, the power of willing, which corresponds with the 'A' matra of the Aum syllable. From pure sattwa issues *Jnana Shakti*, the

210

power of knowing, which corresponds with the 'U' matra of the Aum syllable. From pure tamas emerges *Kriya Shakti*, the power of action, which corresponds with the 'M' matra of the Aum syllable.

When the cosmic energy rests in its pure luminous state, which is completely merged in the pure consciousness, these three creative aspects remain in total equilibrium. They are the unconditioned, pure elements which are the first emanations of the supreme light of the Pranava. These three shaktis or powers remain in their potential state within the cosmic energy, and thus are unlimited and unaffected by other elemental forms. Therefore, the mantra states that these three powers are established in the supreme light, which is Aum.

Similarly, the mantra speaks of Brahmi, Vaishnavi and Raudri, the three shaktis or powers of creation, maintenance and destruction. These are the consorts of the trinity: Brahma, Vishnu and Rudra or Shiva, responsible for the manifestation, organization and dissolution of all beings, universes and galaxies, for all time and throughout all space. As such, Brahmi corresponds with the pure quality of rajas that relates with the power of willing and therefore the creative energy. Vaishnavi corresponds with the pure quality of sattwa that relates with the power of organizing and sustaining, which requires knowledge and discernment. Raudri corresponds with the pure quality of tamas that relates with the destructive power, leading to dissolution and stillness.

In this way, the three devis, or cosmic consorts, Brahmi, Vaishnavi and Raudri, are also said to be established in the supreme light of Aum. Each represents the individual matras: Brahmi corresponds to the 'A' matra, Vaishnavi to the 'U' matra, and Raudri to the 'M' matra.

211

Mantra 87: Aum gayatri

वचसा तज्जपेन्नित्यं वपुषा तत्समभ्यसेत् ।
मनसा तज्जपेन्नित्यं तत्परं ज्योतिरोमिति ॥ 87 ॥

Vachasaa Tajjapennityam Vapushaa Tatsamabhyaset;
Manasaa Tajjapennityam Tatparam Jyotiromiti. (87)

Anvay

Vachasaa: verbally; *Tat*: that; *Japet*: should repeat; *Nityam*: always; *Vapushaa*: with the body; *Tat*: that; *Samabhyaset*: should practise regularly; *Manasaa*: mentally; *Tat*: that; *Japet*: should repeat; *Nityam*: always; *Tat*: that; *Param*: supreme; *Jyotih*: light; *Aum iti*: it is Aum.

Translation

That supreme light is Aum. One should always repeat that verbally, should practise that regularly within the body, and should repeat that mentally.

Commentary

Aum is the supreme light, the cosmic energy merged with cosmic consciousness. Although we may understand this intellectually, we still cannot experience this state directly because our awareness is mundane, conditioned and limited by its material associations. In order go from the mundane to the spiritual dimension, we must travel from point A to point B and so on. It is not possible to arrive at any goal simply by wishful thinking, imagining or fantasizing. Even as the traveller requires a destination, a vehicle and a chosen route, the serious yogic practitioner also requires a goal, a vehicle or object of meditation, and a route or method of practice. These three are absolutely necessary in order to transcend the lower dimensions of consciousness and reach the supreme light.

This mantra is very precise and in a few words it supplies the three requirements for the spiritual journey. First, it gives the destination, which is the supreme light. Second it gives the vehicle or object of meditation, which is the mantra Aum. Third, it gives the route or method of practice to be followed in three stages. The mantra states that one should always repeat Aum verbally. Audible repetition of the mantra is called *baikari* japa. By continuous chanting of the mantra aloud, the conscious mind is attuned to the Aum vibration and thus brought under control.

Next the mantra states that one should practise Aum within the body, which implies internalization of the sound vibration. This stage is known as *madhyama* or whispering japa, where only the lips move and little or no audible sound is produced. The sound is heard within the body rather than outside. By internalizing the mantra repetition, the subconscious mind is attuned to the Aum vibration. Thus the awareness is able to traverse this previously obscure dimension without obstruction.

Finally the mantra states that one should repeat Aum mentally. This form of practice is called *manasi,* or mental japa, whereby the mantra is produced within the mind, by the mind. This form of japa has no audible or verbal sound which can be heard by the ears, rather it can be seen by the inner vision in the form of colour or light. By repetition of the mantra in the deeper levels of the mind, the unconscious also becomes attuned and directed by the Aum vibration.

Hence, the yogi who follows this designated route or method of practice as described in the mantra transcends the lower dimensions of consciousness and experiences the Pranava as supreme light. Thus he arrives at his spiritual destination in good time, without losing his way.

Mantra 88: Benefit of the pranava

शुचिर्वाप्यशुचिर्वापि यो जपेत्प्रणवं सदा ।
न स लिप्यति पापेन पद्मपत्रमिवाम्भसा ॥ 88 ॥

Shuchirvaapyashuchirvaapi Yo Japetpranavam Sadaa;
Na Sa Lipyati Paapena Padmapatramivaambhasaa. (88)

Anvay

Shuchih: pure; *Vaapi*: whether; *Ashuchih*: impure; *Vaapi*: whether; *Yah*: one who; *Japet*: repeats; *Pranavam*: Aum mantra; *Sadaa*: always; *Na*: not; *Sah*: he; *Lipyati*: touched; *Paapena*: by sin; *Padma*: lotus; *Patra*: leaf; *Eva*: just as; *Ambhasaa*: by water.

Translation

Whether pure or impure, one who always repeats the Pranava remains untouched by sin, just as the lotus leaf (remains untouched) by water.

Commentary

Satsang or positive associations have always been given great importance in all the yogic and scriptural texts. Mental conditioning is formed to a large extent by associations. By remaining for some time in the company of yogis and saints, a little of their spiritual vibration naturally rubs off. This helps to neutralize the negative vibrations which may have accumulated due to worldly habits and associations. However, by giving oneself entirely to service and the company of saints, one becomes a saint. Such is the power of positive associations. In the *Bhagavad Gita* (Ch. 9) Lord Krishna has also said that, 'Even if a man is sinful and wicked, but he worships me continuously, he should be regarded as a saint.'

Here the mantra states that one who continually repeats the Pranava, be he pure or impure, remains untouched by negativity or sin, like a lotus leaf on water. This is because Pranava is the word of God which is even more powerful than the presence or darshan of a saint. One who repeats Aum constantly is attuned to the luminosity and vibration of God from within, which is the highest form of darshan. In this way purity and impurity are transcended and all negative or sinful propensities are transformed into light. Thus one who ever remains absorbed in the Pranava remains free from all mundane associations, just as the lotus leaf remains dry, even though it rests directly upon the water.

Mantra 89: Control of prana

चले वाते चलो बिन्दुर्निश्चले निश्चलो भवेत् ।
योगी स्थाणुत्त्वमाप्नोति ततो वायुं निरुन्धयेत् ॥ 89 ॥

Chale Vaate Chalo Binduh Nishchale Nishchalo Bhavet;
Yogee Sthaanuttvamaapnoti Tato Vayum Nirundhayet. (89)

Anvay

Chale: with movement; *Vaate*: of prana; *Chalah*: (also) moves; *Binduh*: point; *Nishchale*: (when prana) remains steady; *Nishchalah*: (then bindu) is also steady; *Bhavet*: becomes; *Yogee*: adept in yoga; *Sthaanutwam aapnoti*: steadfast and firm; *Tatah*: therefore; *Vayum*: the prana; *Nirundhayet*: should be controlled.

Translation

When the prana moves, the bindu also moves. When the prana remains steady, then the bindu is also steady. Thus the yogi becomes steadfast and firm. Therefore, the prana should be controlled.

Commentary

From this mantra the focus of the text shifts again from vedantic theory and practice to the mastery of prana and pranayama, and its relevance in yoga.

Prana is the universal energy which is unmanifest in itself, but is responsible for all manifest existence, macrocosmic as well as microcosmic. At the universal level this energy is known as *Mahashakti* or *Mahaprana*. At the individual level it can be designated as Prana with a capital 'P'. This individual Prana is the actual source of our embodied existence, and contains within it the potential of both the conscious energy (*chitta shakti*) as well as the vital energy (*prana shakti*).

The word *bindu* means 'point', and in this sense it refers to the first point of manifestation of the Prana or individual energy. As such, bindu is the nucleus of consciousness and energy from which our individual being is formed. From bindu the individual mind emerges, and from mind, the five pranas, which will be referred to as prana with a small 'p', and the five elements, comprising the body. In its original state, the bindu is ensconced at the top back of the head where the consciousness remains aloof from all the associations and attractions of the mind and body in the material world.

However, the consciousness does not remain in this lofty state because, as the mantra asserts, the bindu moves when the prana moves. The prana moves in and out with every breath we breathe, and normally we breathe about twenty-one thousand six hundred times per day. This means that the bindu moves constantly, and the only direction in which it can move is downward. The downward flow of the bindu is said to be responsible for the dissipation of this subtle, life-giving essence, thus initiating the process of degeneration, followed by suffering, disease, old age and death.

Again the mantra states that the bindu remains steady only when the prana remains steady. However, the prana remains steady only when the breathing process stops. The breathing stops by itself only occasionally when we are asleep or in shock. Otherwise it continues lifelong, from birth to death. Therefore, it was deemed necessary to adopt a method for stopping the breath which can be performed consciously. This is the actual meaning of yogic pranayama: to retain the breath after inhalation or exhalation or both for a specific period of time. All other techniques of pranayama are preparations for or adjuncts to this practice.

The technique of *kumbhaka*, or breath retention, is thus an important component of kundalini yoga because it provides a means of stabilizing the prana and the bindu so that the mind remains fixed in the higher centres. Breath retention is an important method of awakening sushumna and thus of attaining deep states of concentration and meditation. Hence, the mantra continues, when the prana and bindu are steady, the yogi becomes steadfast and firm. This means that the mind is withdrawn from the external world and established in the higher realm of consciousness at bindu. Therefore, the mantra states that prana should be controlled, and this is achieved by retention of the breath.

Mantra 90: Retention of prana

यावद्वायुः स्थितो देहे तावज्जीवो न मुञ्चति ।
मरणं तस्य निष्क्रान्तिस्ततो वायुं निरुन्धयेत् ॥ 90 ॥

Yaavadvaayuh Sthito Dehe Taavajjeevo Na Munchati;
Maranam Tasya Nishkraantistato Vayum Nirundhayet. (90)

Anvay

Yaavat: as long as; *Vaayuh*: prana; *Sthitah*: is retained; *Dehe*: in the body; *Taavat*: until then; *Jeevah*: individual soul; *Na*: not; *Munchati*: leave; *Maranam*: death; *Tasya*: of that; *Nishkraantih*: departure; *Tatah*: therefore; *Vayum*: prana; *Nirundhayet*: should be controlled.

Translation

As long as the prana is retained in the body, the individual soul does not leave. The departure of that (force) is death. Therefore, the prana should be controlled.

Commentary

Prana is the universal source of life and light. In the absence of prana no being can exist, sentient or insentient. This includes the multiplicity of animate and inanimate forms on earth, as well as planets, stars, galaxies and universes within the cosmos. The physical body, an animate life form, is comprised of five pranas: udana, prana, samana, apana, vyana, and five elements: space, air, fire, water, earth. Each prana represents a different direction and function of energy, and taken altogether they are responsible for the vital function and dynamism of the body. Similarly, each element represents a particular density of prana which, when combined with the other elements, produces a material form.

Thus, although the body appears to be solid and permanent, it is actually a mass of interpenetrating energy

219

fields which are in constant flux and change. As long as these energies comprising the body and mind remain intact, there is life. At the time of death, the individual soul leaves the body along with the pranas, after which the five elemental energies disintegrate and return to their source. In this way, prana can be understood as the basic constituent of all life, as well as the binding force which holds all corporate beings together. Generally, at the time of death, the breath and the heart stop, followed by a quickening of the pranas as they leave the body along with the soul. However, the yogi who has mastery over the breath is able to avert death by retaining the prana.

Therefore, it is said that the yogi is never overtaken by death, but is able to choose the time and manner of his passing. The *Mahabharata* tells of Bhishma Pitama, who lay on the battlefield of Kurukshetra upon a bed of arrows waiting for the sun to enter the Northern Hemisphere, before he would succumb to death. Normally, the breath, prana and consciousness are linked in the living, and when they are separated, death occurs. The only way they can be separated and still maintain life is by retention of the prana and the breath. When the breath is held, the prana does not move in or out, but becomes stabilized and absorbed within. As long as the prana is retained the soul does not leave the body, and thus death is avoided. So, the mantra states that the prana should be controlled because the departure of that force is death.

Mantra 91: Fear of death

यावद्बद्धो मरुत् देहे तावज्जीवो न मुञ्चति ।
यावद्दृष्टिर्भुवोर्मध्ये तावत्कालभयं कुत: ॥ 91 ॥

Yaavadbaddho Marut Dehe Taavajjeevo Na Munchati;
Yaavaddrishthi Bhruvormadhye Taavatkaalabhayam Kutah. (91)

Anvay

Yaavat: as long as; *Baddhah*: is tied down; *Marut*: prana;
Dehe: in the body; *Taavat*: until then; *Jeevah*: individual
soul; *Na*: not; *Munchati*: leave; *Yaavat*: as long as; *Drishthi*:
vision; *Bhruvormadhye*: eyebrow centre; *Taavat*: until then;
Kaalabhayam: fear of death; *Kutah*: from where.

Translation

As long as the prana is tied down in the body, the individual
soul does not leave it. As long as the vision is fixed on the
eyebrow centre, from where is the fear of death?

Commentary

Again the mantra affirms that as long as the prana is contained in the body, the soul cannot leave it. The prana is
initially tied down by retention of the breath. Here the
method of concentration is given to further bind the prana,
for the mantra states that as long as the vision is fixed at the
eyebrow centre, the fear of death does not arise. The eyebrow
centre, which is known as bhrumadhya, functions as the
trigger point for ajna chakra. Yogis traditionally use this
centre for concentration and meditation, due to its inherent
luminosity as well as its proximity to ajna.

In India, it is not uncommon to find yogis who enter
samadhi by restraining the breath and concentrating on
prana as a point of light at the eyebrow centre until the
consciousness becomes totally absorbed in that light. In this

way, the consciousness is merged in prana, and the prana thus remains fixed in the body as long as the breath is retained. Throughout the duration of this samadhi, there is no absorption of prana (inhalation) and no elimination of prana (exhalation). There is no functioning of the five pranas or of the bodily systems. Even the heart stops beating, and the body and mind remain absolutely still.

However, the moment the consciousness is withdrawn from the point of light at the eyebrow centre, the breathing process is resumed. Thus the movement of prana is resumed and the yogi comes out of samadhi. So, the mantra asks, as long as the consciousness is absorbed within the light at the eyebrow centre, where is the fear of death? The answer is that the fear of death is thereby transcended and left behind, like so many other worldly accoutrements. Even when the yogi returns to the normal state, he will never be afflicted by the fear of death again, for he has mastered the prana and is thus able to control the time of death and go beyond death at will.

Mantra 92: Pranayama and longevity

अल्पकालभयाद्ब्रह्मा प्राणायामपरो भवेत् ।
योगिनो मुनयश्चैव ततः प्राणान्निरोधयेत् ॥ 92 ॥

Alpakaalabhayaadbrahmaa Praanaayaamaparo Bhavet;
Yogino Munayashchaiva Tatah Praanaannirodhayet. (92)

Anvay

Alpakaala: short life span; *Bhayaat*: fear; *Brahmaa*: Lord of creation also; *Pranaayaamaparah*: practitioner of pranayama; *Bhavet*: become; *Tatah*: therefore; *Yoginah*: adepts of yoga; *Cha*: and; *Munayah*: sages; *Eva*: also; *Praanaan*: pranas; *Nirodhayet*: should control.

Translation

Even Brahma, fearing a short life span, became a practitioner of pranayama. Therefore, yogis and munis should also control the prana.

Commentary

Even Brahma, the universal creator, practised pranayama due to fear of a short life span, so what to speak of us poor mortals with an expected life span of seventy to eighty years. Of course, the pranayama that he practised must have been different to the pranayama we know. Perhaps it was some cosmic form of kumbhaka, between creation (inhalation) and dissolution (exhalation). The idea here is that breath is life and long life is desirable in order to achieve the aim of self-realization or illumination. Therefore, Brahma practised pranayama, not because he was attached to life, but in order to live long enough to complete his cycle of evolution.

Therefore, yogis and munis should also gain control over the prana by performing pranayama in order to achieve their purpose in life. Control of prana results in mastery of

223

the mind. This enables the yogi to attain the state of samadhi, where fear is transcended. Fear of death is the last limitation or *klesha* to be transcended at the time of samadhi. It is said in Patanjali's *Yoga Sutras* that *abhinivesha,* or fear of death, dominates even the learned and is very difficult to root out. The mantra implies that fear is overcome by pranayama, and thus yogis and munis should also control the prana by this means.

Mantra 93: Preparation for pranayama

षड्विंशदङ्गुलीहंस: प्रयाणं कुरुते बहि:।
वामदक्षिणमार्गेण प्राणायामो विधीयते ॥ 93 ॥

Shadvinshad Anguleerhamsah Prayaanam Kurute Bahiha;
Vaamadakshina Maargena Praanaayaamo Vidheeyate. (93)

Anvay

Shad vinshat: twenty-six; *Anguleeh*: anguls or finger-widths;
Hamsah: Hamsa; *Prayaanam kurute*: goes; *Bahih*: out; *Vaama
dakshina*: left and right; *Maargena*: through the paths;
Praanaayaamah: pranayama; *Vidheeyate*: is to be practised.

Translation

Hamsa (the exhaled breath) goes out for twenty-six anguls
or finger-widths. Pranayama is to be practised through the
left and right paths.

Commentary

Hamsa here represents the exhalation because *Ham* is the
sound vibration produced by the exhaled breath. Twenty-
six anguls or finger-widths are the length of the expiration
required to empty the lungs completely. This distance can
be measured easily by raising both hands in front of the face
so that the palms face downward with the fingers straight.
Place the middle joint of the right index finger in contact
with the nose tip and count eight anguls. Then remove the
right hand, leaving the left hand in place. Place the right
hand outside the left in the same way, so that the right index
finger aligns with the left little finger, and count twelve
anguls. Continue in this way until you have found the
distance of twenty-six anguls.

The exhaled breath should go out for a distance of
twenty-six anguls, before kumbhaka can be practised. In

normal exhalation the lungs are not emptied fully and a large residue of carbon dioxide remains. The following inhalation cannot fill the lungs properly due to the build-up of carbon. Before kumbhaka can be started, the lungs must be emptied and the build-up of carbon removed. This should be achieved slowly and systematically, allowing the lungs to strengthen as the breath is lengthened.

The mantra further states that this pranayama practice is to be performed through the left and right nostrils. The left nostril is the physical termination point of *chandra* or ida nadi, which is the flow of lunar or mental energy (chitta shakti). The right nostril is the physical termination point of *surya* or pingala nadi, which is the flow of solar or vital energy (prana shakti). By systematically moving the breath through these two paths alternately, the pranas are purified and balanced. This practice can be performed in the following way:

Raise the right hand so that the palm is in front of the face. Place the index and middle finger tips at the eyebrow centre. Using the remaining fingers of the raised hand to control the nasal passages, gently close the right nostril with the thumb and inhale through the left nostril. Then release the right nostril, close the left nostril with the ring and little fingers and exhale through the right nostril. Keeping the fingers in the same position, inhale again through the right nostril. Release the left nostril, close the right nostril with the thumb and exhale through the left nostril. This makes one round.

When the practice becomes natural and effortless, apply the ratio. Start with a comfortable count, such as 3:3, 4:4 or 5:5, and gradually increase the duration of the breath. At first the inhalation and exhalation should be elongated equally in a 1:1 ratio up to the count of 10:10. Then a 1:2 ratio should be applied, so that the exhalation becomes double the length of inhalation. In this way the breath should be elongated up to the count of 10:20, 15:30, 20:40, until the exhaled breath reaches the distance of twenty-six anguls.

The practice referred to in this mantra corresponds to nadi shodhana pranayama, technique 2, which can be referred to in *Asana Pranayama Mudra Bandha*, published by Yoga Publications Trust.

Mantra 94: Purification of nadis and chakras

शुद्धिमेति यदा सर्व नाडीचक्रं मलाकुलम् ।
तदैव जायते योगी प्राणसंग्रहणक्षमः ॥ 94 ॥

Shuddhimeti Yadaa Sarva Naadeechakram Malaakulam;
Tadaiva Jaayate Yogee Praanasangrahanakshamah. (94)

Anvay

Shuddhim eti: become pure, free; *Yadaa*: when; *Sarva*: all; *Naadee*: pranic energy channels; *Chakram*: psychic energy centres; *Mala*: impurities; *Aakulam*: accumulation; *Tadaa eva*: only then; *Jaayate*: becomes; *Yogee*: adept in yoga; *Praana*: breath; *Sangrahana*: of controlling; *Kshamah*: capable.

Translation

When all the nadis and chakras become free from accumulation of impurities, then only the yogi becomes capable of controlling the breath.

Commentary

In pranayama, we are working with the two major nadis, ida and pingala, as well as with the third major nadi, sushumna, which is the spiritual channel. Ida and pingala relate with the separate flows of breath through the left and right nostrils respectively. Sushumna corresponds with the equalized flow of breath through both nostrils simultaneously, or with the retention of both flows as in kumbhaka. In order to understand the interrelationship of these three major energy flows, we must see their point of origin and then observe how they connect with the chakra or psychic energy centres at the centre of the spinal column.

These three major energy pathways issue from mooladhara chakra, the root centre below the coccyx at the pelvic floor. Sushumna flows straight up from mooladhara through

228

the very centre of the spinal column, piercing all of the psychic centres in turn. Ida and pingala issue from the left and right sides of mooladhara and form spiralling pathways, criss-crossing at each chakra junction. Ida and pingala terminate at ajna, where they unite with sushumna. From there these energies rise as one channel to the subtle energy centres of bindu and sahasrara, which are beyond duality and all physical and mental association.

Ajna chakra is the psychic termination point for ida and pingala nadis, but the nostrils represent their physical termination. Therefore, the nadis as well as the chakras are influenced and controlled by the breath. And likewise, the nadis and chakras must be purified before the yogi becomes capable of controlling or retaining the breath. Impurities in the nadi and chakra system create obstructions which cause imbalance in the energy flows and hence in the breath. Sushumna, the spiritual channel symbolizing unity and transcendence, can open only when the nadis and chakras are unobstructed and balanced. Furthermore, kumbhaka or breath retention opens and awakens sushumna. Therefore, the nadis and chakras must be completely free from impurities before the yogi becomes capable of controlling the breath.

Mantra 95: Chandra Bheda Pranayama

बद्धपद्मासनो योगी प्राणं चन्द्रेण पूरयेत् ।
धारयेद्वा यथाशक्त्या भूय: सूर्येण रेचयेत् ॥ 95 ॥

Baddhapadmaasano Yogee Praanam Chandrena Poorayet;
Dhaarayedvaa Yathaashaktyaa Bhooyah Sooryena Rechayet. (95)

Anvay

Baddhapadmaasanah: in the variation of lotus posture; *Yogee*: adept in yoga; *Praanam*: the breath; *Poorayet*: should inhale; *Chandrena*: through the left nostril; *Dhaarayet vaa*: retain it; *Yathaa shaktyaa*: to the best of his ability; *Bhooyah*: again; *Sooryena*: through the right nostril; *Rechayet*: exhale.

Translation

(Sitting) in baddhapadmasana, the yogi should inhale the breath through the left nostril, retain it for as long as possible, and exhale again through the right nostril.

Commentary

Chandra bheda pranayama is the method of breathing which 'pierces the moon', or activates the mental energy. The yogi is recommended to sit in baddha padmasana to perform the practice. This is a variation of padmasana with the arms crossed behind the back so that the fingers of the opposite hands grasp the toes. The position of the arms in this posture stretches the shoulders back and opens the chest and lungs. It also stimulates an important marma, or energy point, just under the shoulders in front, which activates the lungs. This is a very stable and balanced posture that allows the practitioner to enter into meditative states directly from the pranayama practice.

The mantra next says to inhale through the left nostril. Inhalation is the active breath, so this pranayama stimulates chandra or ida nadi, the mental force. Breath retention is then performed for as long as is comfortably possible. Internal breath retention activates the region of prana in the chest, as well as the sushumna nadi. Then the exhalation or passive breath is taken out through the right nostril associated with pingala or surya nadi, the vital force. So this practice activates chandra nadi, the mental energy, and pacifies surya nadi, the vital energy, which makes it ideal as a prelude to yogic meditation.

Chandra bheda pranayama is considered to be a highly volatile practice, as it brings about an awakening of the mental energy. There are two aspects of the moon, or mind, represented in the chakra system. The higher mind is represented by the moon at bindu visarga and the lower mind by the moon at swadhisthana. One should have an understanding of the mind and its propensities before attempting this practice. For the experienced practitioner, however, this method may be very effective for inducing deep meditative states associated with the awakening of the vijnanamaya kosha and its psychic faculties.

Mantra 96: Moon at bindu

अमृतोदधिसंकाशं गोक्षीरधवलोपमम् ।
ध्यात्वा चन्द्रमसं बिम्बं प्राणायामे सुखी भवेत् ॥ 96 ॥

Amritodadhisankaasham Goksheeradhavalopamam;
Dhyaatvaa Chandramasam Bimbam Praanaayaame Sukhee
Bhavet. (96)

Anvay

Amritah: of nectar; *Udadhi*: ocean; *Sankaasham*: like;
Goksheera: cow's milk; *Dhavala*: white; *Upamam*: like;
Dhyaatvaa: meditate on; *Chandramasam*: of the moon;
Bimbam: halo of light; *Praanaayaame*: at the time of prana-
yama; *Sukhee*: pleasant; *Bhavet*: should become.

Translation

At the time of pranayama one should meditate on the
luminous disc of the moon, which is like the ocean of nectar
and white like the milk of cows.

Commentary

This mantra is a continuation of the last. 'At the time of
pranayama' means in between each round of chandra bheda
pranayama, after performing the inhalation, retention and
exhalation, as described in the previous mantra. Each round
of pranayama, especially as it is performed with kumbhaka or
breath retention, induces a state of deep concentration. So,
before beginning the next round the practitioner should
remain in the posture without moving and meditate for three
to five minutes or for as long as the meditative state lasts. The
object of concentration at this time is described next.

The mantra states that one should meditate on the
luminous disc of the moon, which is at bindu visarga, the
psychic centre at the top back of the head. In fact, bindu is

232

often represented as a moon, which is the source of amrita, the immortal nectar, or essence of energy responsible for individual consciousness and evolution. The moon is further described as an ocean of nectar which is white like milk. The moon is also associated with the pranayama practice itself, chandra bheda, or 'moon piercing'. By meditating on the moon at bindu in between each round of pranayama, the energy activated in the chandra and sushumna nadis by the practice is directed upward and restored to this centre, rather than being dissipated through the lower mental processes.

Mantra 97: Surya bheda pranayama

स्फुरत्प्रज्वलसज्ज्वालापूज्यमादित्यमण्डलम्   ।
ध्यात्वा हृदि स्थितं योगी प्राणायामे सुखीभवेत् ॥ 97 ॥

Sphuratprajvala Sajjvaalaa Poojyam Aadityamandalam;
Dhyaatvaa Hridi Sthitam Yogee Praanaayaame Sukhee Bhavet. (97)

Anvay

Sphurat: shining, bright; *Prajvala*: blazing fast; *Sajjvaalaa*: having very bright blaze; *Poojyam*: worshipful, prescribed; *Aaditya*: Sun; *Mandalam*: zone, area; *Dhyaatvaa*: meditating on; *Hridi*: in the heart; *Sthitam*: having established; *Yogee*: adept in yoga; *Praanaayaame*: at the time of pranayama; *Sukhee*: happy; *Bhavet*: should be.

Translation

At the time of pranayama, the yogi should meditate in the heart on the prescribed zone of the Sun, which is blazing brightly. Having established this state, he should be happy.

Commentary

Here 'at the time of pranayama' refers to the practice of surya bheda, 'piercing the sun', which is the reverse rotation of the breathing that was described in the previous mantra. In chandra bheda the breath is taken in through the left nostril, retained and taken out through the right nostril, which activates the lunar or mental energy. The visualization prescribed for this practice was the moon, which relates with the aspect of chandra nadi. This mantra, however, describes the visualization of the sun, and thus refers to surya bheda pranayama, where the breath is inhaled through the right nostril, thus activating surya or pingala nadi, retained for as long as is comfortable and then exhaled through the left nostril, chandra or ida nadi.

234

Surya bheda pranayama thus activates the vital energy and pacifies the mental energy. In between each round, the mantra states that the yogi should meditate in the heart on the prescribed zone of the Sun. Inhalation through the right nostril results in activation of the surya nadi. The seat of the solar or vital energies is at manipura chakra, behind the navel. Again, after inhalation, the breath is retained, so there follows an activation of sushumna nadi, through which the vital energies are drawn up from manipura to the region of the heart, or anahata chakra, where the Sun is seen to be blazing brightly.

Furthermore, activation of the vital or solar energy is said to produce a blissful experience. Thus the mantra continues, having established this state, the yogi should enjoy bliss and be happy.

Mantra 98: Nadi shodhana pranayama

प्राणं चेदिडया पिबेन्नियमितं भूयोऽन्यथा रेचयेत्
पीत्वा पिङ्गलया समीरणमथो बद्ध्वा त्यजेद्वामया ।
सूर्याचन्द्रमसोरनेन विधिना बिन्दुद्वयं ध्यायतः
शुद्धा नाडिगणा भवन्ति यमिनो मासद्वयादूर्ध्वतः ॥ 98 ॥

Praanam Chedidayaa Pibenniyamitam Bhooyoh Anyathaa Rechayet;
Peetvaa Pingalayaa Sameeranamatho Baddhvaa Tyajedvaamayaa;
Sooryaachandramasoranena Vidhinaa Bindudvayam Dhyaayatah;
Shuddhaa Naadiganaa Bhavanti Yamino Maasadvayaadoordhvatah.
(98)

Anvay

Praanam: breath; *Chet*: if; *Idayaa*: through the left nostril; *Pibet*: be drawn in; *Niyamitam*: regularly; *Bhooyah*: again; *Anyathaa*: through the other; *Rechayet*: taken out; *Peetvaa*: drawn in; *Pingalayaa*: through the right nostril; *Sameeranam*: breath; *Atho baddhvaa*: and retaining; *Tyajet*: drawn out; *Vaamayaa*: through the left nostril; *Sooryaa*: the sun or left; *Chandramasah*: and the moon or right; *Anena*: through this; *Vidhinaa*: method; *Bindudvayam*: both points; *Dhyaayatah*: by practising; *Oordhvatah*: regularly; *Shuddhaah*: purified; *Naadiganaah*: network of energy channels; *Bhavanti*: becomes; *Yaminah*: control; *Maasadvayaat*: within two months.

Translation

The breath should be drawn in through the left nostril, retained and taken out through the right. Again, the breath should be drawn in through the right and retained, then taken out through the left. By practising this method regularly, one gains control over both points of sun and moon, and the energy channels become purified within two months.

236

Commentary

Nadi shodhana pranayama was dealt with previously in Mantra 93 as a preparatory practice. Here the practice is described with internal kumbhaka. Nadi shodhana combines both chandra bheda and surya bheda pranayamas into one practice. The mantra describes this technique without naming it. The breath is to be inhaled through the left nostril, retained and exhaled through the right nostril, then it is again inhaled through the right nostril, retained and exhaled through the left nostril. The two complete rotations, from left to right and again from right to left, make one round of this pranayama.

The mantra further describes the results of this pranayama. By regularity of practice one gains control over both points of sun and moon, and the energy channels become purified within two months. The first thing to note here is regularity of practice. Pranayama activates the subtle energy infrastructure and, therefore, it is must be performed regularly and systematically, otherwise pranic imbalances may arise which cannot be corrected by external means. Regularity in pranayama refers to the time and place of practice each day, the number of rounds, and the ratio or counting of the breath.

By regular practice of this pranayama the yogi gains control over the points of the sun and moon, which correspond to manipura and bindu chakras respectively. These are two important psychic energy centres in kundalini yoga. The ongoing awakening of kundalini is said to take place from manipura. Bindu is the seat of the cosmic point as well as the nectar of life, which may be considered as the source or origin point of kundalini at the time of individual manifestation. This also relates with the meditations described in the previous mantras for chandra bheda and surya bheda.

Furthermore, the mantra states that the ida and pingala energy channels become purified within two months. Hence the practice referred to here is *nadi shodhana,* which means 'purification of the energy channels'. Of course, we must remember that the concept of yoga practice at the time when this text was written was very different to what it is today. Here two months means systematic, intensive practice of pranayama during two-hour sessions, four to five times each day. By practising regularly in this way, every day, the energy channels are purified in two months. Today, however, one may practise for fifteen minutes and then go off to work. So, the time required to achieve the same results may be much longer.

Mantra 99: Mastery of nadi shodhana

यथेष्ट धारणं वायोरनलस्य प्रदीपनम् ।
नादाभिव्यक्तिरारोग्यं जायते नाडिशोधनात् ॥ 99 ॥

Yatheshta Dhaaranam Vaayoranalasya Pradeepanam;
Naadaabhivyaktih Aarogyam Jaayate Naadishodhanaat. (99)

Anvay

Yathaa ishta: full; *Dhaaranam*: retention; *Vaayoh*: breath; *Analasya*: of the fire; *Pradeepanam*: activation; *Naada*: inner sound; *Abhivyaktih*: is heard; *Aarogyam*: good health; *Jaayate*: is gained; *Naadishodhanaat*: by purification of the nadis.

Translation

With full retention of the breath, there is activation of the fire and inner sound is heard. Good health is gained by purification of the nadis.

Commentary

This is a continuation of the previous mantra. Full retention of the breath here does not mean to hold the breath for as long as possible as was described earlier. It implies a certain mastery of the breathing ratios, which takes months or even years to perfect. Usually one begins with the ratio of 1:1:1 and after some time works up to 1:1:2, 1:2:2 and then 1:4:2. These are the four basic ratios by which the breath is slowly extended. For example, one may begin with the count of 5:5:5, and gradually increase by one count up at a time to 10:10:10. Then the second ratio can be taken up, gradually working up to a count of 10:10:20. Then the third ratio may be applied, gradually working up 10:20:20, and then to 20:40:40. At this point the final ratio can be attempted, working up to 20:80:40. This is considered to be the full form of retention.

Next the mantra states that with full retention of the breath, there is activation of the fire and inner sound is heard. Activation of the fire refers to the awakening of kundalini shakti at manipura and its ascent through sushumna nadi. At this time psychic sounds begin to manifest, according to the level of inner awakening, as the ascending spiritual force pierces anahata and the higher chakras one by one. These *nada* or inner sounds which accompany the awakening of kundalini draw the awareness into sushumna and raise it up to the crown of the head. This ascent culminates in the union of the kundalini energy with pure consciousness in samadhi.

Furthermore, the mantra states that good health is gained by purification of the nadis. The body and mind are maintained and controlled by the vital and mental energies, which are transmitted by the nadis. These energy flows directly influence the nervous and glandular systems, as well as all the systems of the body, including the brain and mind. When the nadis are impure they become blocked and unbalanced. This results in low energy levels and ill health, especially in those areas most affected by the blockages. By purification of the nadis, the body and mind are harmonized and balanced, which results in efficient functioning, good health and long life.

Mantra 100: Method of retention

प्राणो देहस्थितो यावदपानं तु निरुन्धयेत् ।
एकश्वासमयी मात्रा ऊर्ध्वाधो गगने स्थिति: ॥ 100 ॥

Praano Dehasthito Yaavadapaanam Tu Nirundhayet;
Ekashvaasamayee Maatraa Oordhvaadho Gagane Sthitih. (100)

Anvay

Praanah: vital ascending energy; *Deha sthitah*: remains in the
body; *Yaavat*: as long as; *Apaanam tu*: vital descending energy;
Nirundhayet: should be retained; *Ekashvaasamayee*: drawn in
one breath; *Maatraa*: quantity; *Oordhva adhah*: up and down;
Gagane: in hridayakasha; *Sthitih*: should remain.

Translation

As long as prana remains in the body, apana should be
retained, so that the quantity drawn in one breath remains
and moves up and down in hridayakasha.

Commentary

This mantra alludes to kumbhaka and how it is to be
performed. 'As long as prana remains in the body' means as
long as the inhaled breath is retained, apana should be
retained. Apana pertains to exhalation as well as to the
downward flow of energy between the navel and the pelvic
floor. By retaining apana, this quantum of energy which
would normally pass out of the body either through the
exhalation or through the lower orifices can be drawn upward
in one breath to *hridayakasha*, the 'heart space'. Hridayakasha
is also synonymous with the region of prana between the
shoulders and the diaphragm.

It is important to note that the energy which is stored in
the region of prana or hridayakasha does not dissipate or
get burned up, as it would in the other pranic regions.

241

Hridayakasha is a completely protected and isolated area surrounded by the rib cage. There are no metabolic processes here to burn up the energy or external orifices from which it can flow out of the body. Therefore, the mantra recommends that the apana breath and energy be drawn up to the region of prana, or hridayakasha, where the energy can be stored. While retaining the breath, the energy is then moved up and down in the space of the heart, which is also the seat of the soul, thus activating and awakening this subtle dimension.

Mantras 101, 102: Omkara pranayama

रेचक: पूरकश्चैव कुम्भक: प्रणवात्मक: ।
प्राणायामो भवेदेवं मात्राद्वादशसंयुत: ॥ 101 ॥
मात्राद्वादशसंयुक्तौ निशाकरदिवाकरौ ।
दोषजालमबध्नन्तौ ज्ञातव्यौ योगिभि: सदा ॥ 102 ॥

Rechakah Poorakashchaiva Kumbhakah Pranava Aatmakah;
Praanaayaamo Bhavedevam Maatraadvaadashasamyutah. (101)
Maatraadvaadashasamyuktau Nishaakara Divaakarau;
Doshajaalam Abadhnantau Jnaatavyau Yogibhih Sadaa. (102)

Anvay

Rechakah: exhalation; *Poorakah*: inhalation; *Cha eva*: and;
Kumbhakah: breath retention; *Pranava*: Aum; *Aatmakah*: itself;
Praanaayaamah: pranayama; *Bhavet*: should be; *Evam*: like
this; *Maatraa*: its number; *Dvaadasha*: twelve; *Samyutah*:
times; *Maatraa*: number; *Dvaadasha*: twelve; *Samyuktau*:
times; *Nishaakara*: through ida nadi; *Divaakarau*: through
pingala nadi; *Dosha*: impurities; *Jaalam*: net; *Abadhnantau*:
unfastens; *Jnaatavyau*: should be known; *Yogibhih*: by the
yogis; *Sadaa*: always.

Translation

The inhalation, retention and exhalation are the Pranava
itself. Pranayama should be practised like this for a number
of twelve rounds. Twelve rounds through the ida and pingala
nadis unfastens the net of impurities. The yogis should
know this always.

Commentary

Here the three types of breath – inhalation, retention and
exhalation, are synchronized with the three matras of Pranava,
'A', 'U' and 'M', in order to align the breath, prana and
consciousness and experience their interrelationship. Thus

243

while inhaling, the 'A' sound should be drawn up the ida passage or left nostril, along with the breath. During this time the 'A' sound should be contemplated along with all of its associations, i.e., the conscious state and rajo guna. While retaining the breath, the 'U' sound is contemplated in relation to the subconscious state and sattwa guna. While exhaling, the 'M' sound is directed out through the pingala passage or right nostril, along with the breath. During this time, the 'M' sound is contemplated in relation to the unconscious state and tamo guna. The same process is followed on the other side in order to make one round.

This practice is known as *Omkara pranayama*. It should be performed for twelve rounds in order to balance the body and mind, and as a preparation for meditation on the Pranava. This pranayama can also be performed through both nostrils together, as in *sama vritti pranayama*, for meditative purposes. However, in order to purify the nadi or energy channels it should be done through the alternate nostrils, as in nadi shodhana pranayama. Twelve rounds performed through the alternate nostrils will remove all the accumulated blockages and impurities in the ida and pingala nadis, ensuring health, harmony and longevity. Therefore, the mantra states that yogis should always know this practice, so that they may perform it regularly and thus derive the benefits.

Mantra 103: Ratio of the breath

पूरकं द्वादशं कुर्यात्कुम्भकं षोडशं भवेत् ।
रेचकं दश चोंकारः प्राणायामः स उच्यते ॥ 103 ॥

Poorakam Dvaadasham Kuryaat Kumbhakam Shodasham Bhavet;
Rechakam Dasha Chomkaarah Praanaayaamah Sa Uchyate. (103)

Anvay

Poorakam: inhalation; *Dvaadasham*: twelve; *Kuryaat*: should
be practised; *Kumbhakam*: retention; *Shodasham*: sixteen;
Bhavet: should be done; *Rechakam*: exhalation; *Dasha*: ten;
Cha: and; *Omkaarah*: Aum; *Praanaayaamah*: pranayama; *Sah*:
like this; *Uchyate*: is called.

Translation

The inhalation should be practised to the count of twelve,
retention to the count of sixteen and exhalation to the
count of ten. This is called the Omkara pranayama.

Commentary

This mantra deals specifically with the ratio of the breath for
Omkara pranayama, described in the previous mantras.
The ratio given here differs from the ratio generally
recommended for pranayama, which is 1:4:2. However, the
instruction is very precise. While inhaling, the duration of
the breath should be counted slowly and rhythmically up to
12. Then, while retaining, the duration should be counted
with the same uniform rhythm to 16. And while exhaling,
the duration of the breath should be counted up to 10. This
ratio should be performed without straining the lungs, so
that the attention can be focused on the Omkara.

Mantra 104: Levels of pranayama

अधमे द्वादशा मात्रा मध्यमे द्विगुणा मता ।
उत्तमे त्रिगुणा प्रोक्ता प्राणायामस्य निर्णय: ॥ 104 ॥

Adhame Dvaadashaa Maatraa Madhyame Dvigunaa Mataa;
Uttame Trigunaa Proktaa Pranaayaamasya Nirnayah. (104)

Anvay

Adhame: lowest level; *Dvaadashaa*: twelve; *Maatraa*: letters or counts; *Madhyame*: middle level; *Dvigunaa*: double or twenty-four; *Mataa*: letters or counts; *Uttame*: highest level; *Trigunaa*: triple or thirty-six; *Proktaa*: has been said; *Praanaayaamasya*: about pranayama; *Nirnayah*: it has been said.

Translation

About pranayama it has been said that the lowest level is twelve counts, the middle level is double that or twenty-four counts, and the highest level is triple or thirty-six counts.

Commentary

The three levels of pranayama are described here. The ratio given in the previous mantra, 12:16:10, is thus regarded as the lowest level of proficiency. In the middle level this ratio is doubled, making it 24:32:20. It should also be understood that the practitioner does not jump from the first level of practice to the second. The lowest ratio should be extended slowly, one count at a time over a period of months, and perhaps even years, depending on the regularity and duration of practice as well as on the lung capacity of the practitioner. It is never beneficial to force the lungs beyond their capacity.

The highest level is triple the initial ratio, which makes it 36:48:30. The same slow and methodical procedure of extending the breath applies in order to reach this level of

246

pranayama. Each of these levels induces a corresponding shift of consciousness in the practitioner, leading him into progressively deeper meditative states. This occurs spontaneously due to the Omkara vibration as well as activation and awakening of sushumna nadi during the extended periods of breath retention. This is why pranayama is considered to be an important adjunct to kundalini yoga.

Mantra 105: Effects of pranayama

अधमे स्वेदजननं कम्पो भवति मध्यमे ।
उत्तमे स्थानमाप्नोति ततो वायुं निरुन्धयेत् ॥ 105 ॥

Adhame Swedajananam Kampo Bhavati Madhyame;
Uttame Sthaanamaapnoti Tato Vayum Nirundhayet. (105)

Anvay

Adhame: lowest level; *Swedajananam*: causes perspiration; *Kampah*: trembling of the body; *Bhavati*: results in; *Madhyame*: middle level; *Uttame*: highest level; *Sthaanam*: stability; *Aapnoti*: achieved; *Tatah*: therefore; *Vayum*: the breath; *Nirundhayet*: should be retained.

Translation

The lowest level causes perspiration. The middle level results in trembling of the body. At the highest level stability is achieved. Therefore, the breath should be retained.

Commentary

Here the effects of pranayama are described in relation to the ratios of breathing given in the previous mantra. This mantra is also found almost word for word in *Hatha Yoga Pradipika* (2:12) and *Gherand Samhita* (5:56). The lowest level of pranayama gives rise to perspiration. The middle level, where the initial ratio is doubled, results in trembling of the body. The highest level, where the ratio is tripled, produces stability. These are the signs which occur at the different levels of pranayama to indicate the activation and purification of prana.

At the lowest level, the pranas are stimulated, creating heat in the body and thus causing perspiration. Regardless of the weather, the body will perspire copiously when this level has been mastered. At the middle level, the pranas are awakened, which gives rise to tremor and trembling of the body, especially in the vacinity of the spine. The awakening of the pranas at this stage is known as *prannothana,* or 'rising of the pranas'. Initially different sensations such as twitching, itching, vibrating or tingling may also be experienced in the peripheral parts as well as in the internal organs and parts. This indicates that the pranas are activated, but not yet balanced.

The final stage of stability is achieved when the third level of ratio is mastered. Stability arises as the awakening of the pranic field becomes established and balanced. This experience of stability that arises with the awakening of the pranas is the main requisite for attaining deep meditative states as well as for the arousal and ascent of the kundalini shakti. Therefore, the mantra states that the breath should be retained.

Mantra 106: Guidelines for pranayama

बद्धपद्मासनो योगी नमस्कृत्य गुरुं शिवम्।
नासाग्रदृष्टिरेकाकी प्राणायामं समभ्यसेत् ॥ 106 ॥

Baddhapadmaasano Yogee Namaskritya Gurum Shivam;
Naasaagra Drishtirekaakee Praanaayaamam Samabhyaset. (106)

Anvay

Baddhapadmaasanah: sitting in a variation of padmasana; *Yogee*: yogic adept; *Namaskritya*: pay homage to; *Gurum*: spiritual master; *Shivam*: Shiva; *Naasaagra*: on the nose tip; *Drishtih*: fixed gaze; *Ekaakee*: solitary place; *Praanaayaamam*: pranayama; *Sam abhyaset*: should practise properly.

Translation

Retiring to a solitary place, the yogi should sit in baddha padmasana, with the gaze fixed on the nose tip. Paying homage to the Guru, who is Shiva, he should practise pranayama properly.

Commentary

Here the mantra gives some practical guidelines for the practice of pranayama. First the yogi should retire to a solitary place. In previous times, yogis used to set aside some time in the year for intensive practice of yogic methods, such as pranayama. To avoid all kinds of social disturbance during their retreat, they would leave their family and community and retire to a solitary place, perhaps nearby, preferably in a forest, by a riverbank, near the sea or in the mountains. They could devote themselves solely to practice throughout the day and for intervals in the night.

The recommended sitting position for the intensive practice of pranayama is said to be baddha padmasana, which was mentioned previously in Mantra 95, also in relation to the practice of pranayama. This posture is a variation of padmasana with the arms stretched behind the back, so that the fingers of each hand grasp the toes of the opposite foot. This is a very stable position which also opens the lungs and chest and so is favourable for the practice of pranayama.

Furthermore, while seated in baddha padmasana, *nasikagra drishti* is performed so that the gaze is fixed at the nose tip. This has a dual effect, which makes it an important adjunct to the practice of pranayama. First, it provides a focus for awareness of the breath which flows in and out at the nose tip. Second, the nose tip is a psychic point associated with mooladhara chakra, so nasikagra drishti also helps indirectly to activate this centre along with the latent kundalini force residing therein.

Before any sadhana is undertaken, one should always remember the master, or Guru, who is considered to be God incarnate, with respect, gratitude and humility in order to attain perfection in the practice. In all the higher yogas, it is not by effort alone that the fruit of the practice is attained. There is also some element of grace by which the highest experience of the practice is finally bestowed by the divine. Without this grace, the spiritual outcome of the practice is never assured. Therefore, the mantra says to pay homage to the Guru, who is Shiva. The name of Shiva is given because this Upanishad deals with kundalini yoga, which is a tantric tradition, and Shiva is the allegorical God of Tantra, as well as the *Adi yogi*, the first practitioner and teacher of yoga.

Finally, the mantra says to practise pranayama properly. This can be understood in different contexts. Of course, one should practise the technique correctly as taught by the master. The practice should also be performed regularly at the correct times of the day, i.e. early morning, mid morning, afternoon, early evening and mid night.

By observing all of these guidelines, the yogi is assured of maximum success in the practice within the shortest duration of time.

251

Mantra 107: Naumukhi and shaktichalini

द्वाराणां नव संनिरुध्य मरुतं बद्ध्वा दृढां धारणां
नीत्वा कालमपानवह्निसहितं शक्त्या समं चालितम् ।
आत्मध्यानयुतस्त्वनेन विधिना विन्यस्य मूर्ध्नि स्थिरं
यावत्तिष्ठति तावदेव महतां सङ्गो न संस्तूयते ॥ 107 ॥

Dvaaraanaam Nava Samnirudhya Marutam Baddhvaa Dridhaam Dhaaranaam; Neetvaa Kaalam Apaanavahni Sahitam Shaktyaa Samam Chaalitam; Aatmadhyaanayutastvanena Vidhinaa Vinyasya Moordhni Sthiram; Yaavattishthati Taavadeva Mahataam Sango Na Sanstooyate. (107)

Anvay

Dvaaraanaam: gates; *Nava*: nine; *Samnirudhya*: closing properly; *Marutam*: breath; *Baddhvaa*: retain; *Dridhaam*: making strong; *Dhaaranaam*: concentration; *Neetvaa*: taking; *Kaalam*: divine element, kundalini; *Apaana*: apana vayu; *Vahni*: fire (samana vayu); *Sahitam*: with; *Shaktyaa*: shakti-chalini mudra; *Samam*: correctly; *Chaalitam*: performing; *Aatmadhyaana yutah tu*: absorbed in meditation on the Self; *Anena*: through; *Vidhinaa*: the method; *Vinyasya*: taking to; *Moordhni*: the head; *Sthiram*: steady; *Yaavat*: when; *Tishthati*: becomes still; *Taavat eva*: only then; *Mahataam*: superior, great; *Sangah*: company, association; *Na sanstooyate*: does not praise.

Translation

Closing the nine gates properly and retaining the breath, intensify the concentration. Performing shaktichalini mudra correctly, take the divine element, kundalini, along with apana vayu and fire (samana vayu) to the (crown of the) head. By this method become absorbed in meditation on the Self. When steadiness and stillness (are achieved), only then he does not praise the company of the great ones.

Commentary

Shaktichalini is an important practice of kundalini and kriya yoga. Closing the nine gates refers to naumukhi mudra, which is the basis of shaktichalini. *Nau* or *nava* means 'nine', *mukhi* 'gates' or 'doors' and *mudra* 'psychic energy gesture'. The seven orifices in the head, the ears, eyes, nostrils and mouth, as well as the two orifices of elimination, anal sphincter and urinary passage, located below are closed. This is done by raising both hands in front of the head. The ears are closed with the thumbs, the eyes with the index fingers, the nostrils with the middle fingers and the lips with the ring fingers above and the little fingers below. Simultaneously, moola bandha (contraction of the perineal body) and vajroli mudra (contraction of the urinary passage) are applied to close the two lower orifices.

All of the nine orifices are closed after inhalation is completed and remain closed during the period of breath retention. Normally, the prana is constantly flowing out of these nine gates throughout the waking state, and it is also flowing in and out with the breath. The combination of closing these nine apertures, along with retention of the breath, blocks this outflow and creates an internal build-up of energy, which in turn intensifies the concentration. Furthermore, the locks placed on the lower apertures activate mooladhara and swadhisthana chakras, where the kundalini shakti lies asleep.

Naumukhi mudra is an independent practice, but it can also be performed in combination with shaktichalini mudra, which is the method instructed by the mantra. Shaktichalini is the essence of kundalini yoga and means 'moving the kundalini energy'. According to the instructions given in the mantra, naumukhi and shaktichalini are combined in the following way: after closing the nine gates, while retaining the breath, intensify the concentration and perform shaktichalini. The kundalini energy, visualized in the form

253

of a serpent at mooladhara, should thus be raised through sushumna, along with the energies of apana and fire (samana), up to the crown of the head. This is the culmination of yoga, the merging of consciousness and energy, Shiva and Shakti, at sahasrara chakra.

The mantra continues that by this method the yogi becomes absorbed in meditation on the Self. When the highest degree of steadiness and stillness are achieved, only then he does not praise the company of the great ones. Absorbed in meditation on the Self refers to the conscious experience of the atman, the pure, unlimited, transcendental dimension of consciousness and energy. This is self-realization in the ultimate sense. The realization of Self is attained in a state of absolute steadiness and stillness which is impenetrable by any external or internal sources, because it is beyond the body, mind and psyche. When this state is experienced, the yogi has no need to praise the realized masters, as he has become one of them himself.

Mantra 108: Pranayama and karma

प्राणायामो भवेदेवं पातकेन्धनपावक: ।
भवोदधिमहासेतु: प्रोच्यते योगिभि: सदा ॥ 108 ॥

Praanaayaamo Bhavedevam Paatakendhanapaavakaha;
Bhavodadhimahaasetuh Prochyate Yogibhih Sadaa. (108)

Anvay

Praanaayaamah: pranayama; *Bhavet*: become; *Evam*: like this; *Paataka*: of sin; *Indhana*: for the fuel; *Paavakah*: fire; *Bhava udadhi*: for crossing the worldly ocean; *Mahaa*: great; *Setuh*: bridge; *Prochyate*: has been regarded; *Yogibhih*: by the yogis; *Sadaa*: always.

Translation

In this way, pranayama becomes fire for the fuel of sin, and has always been regarded by the yogis as a great bridge for crossing the ocean of the world.

Commentary

When pranayama is used as an adjunct to kundalini yoga, as described in the previous mantras, then it becomes a method of great significance. The most insurmountable obstacle to spiritual attainment is the blockage of the karmas, samskaras or subliminal impressions which are stored within the deepest strata of the consciousness. These karmas do not die with the body at the time of death, but pass on with the psyche and the soul from birth to birth. In each successive lifetime, the individual works through some of these karmas and creates many more in the process.

Negative actions and reactions continuously create negative impressions, and similarly, negative impressions invariably produce negative actions and reactions. This vicious cycle of negativity clouds the inner vision and causes

255

untold suffering for oneself as well as for others. This is the source of all sinful thoughts, behaviour, characteristics and nature. Almost everyone, with the exception of saints and realized souls, has this dark, negative side embedded in their consciousness, and it is very difficult to remove it. In fact, most spiritual teachings and methods deal with this very theme.

The mantra states that pranayama performed as an accessory to kundalini yoga becomes a fire for the fuel of sins and thus burns them up, along with all the other karmas. Breath retention is a requisite to kundalini awakening because it builds up the quantum of prana and intensifies the concentration. In this way, the kundalini shakti is quickly aroused from its dormant state at mooladhara chakra and raised through the sushumna pathway. Thus, when pranayama is practised in order to awaken the kundalini energy, it leads to the meditative state of samadhi where all the karmas are finally burnt and thus cannot be regenerated.

Karmas are the invisible cords which bind all individual souls to the world. No one has ever been free from the worldly tendencies and drives as long as the karmas remain active within. Pranayama is a method of de-activating or burning the karmas. Therefore, the yogis have always regarded it as a great bridge for crossing the ocean of samsara, or the world.

Mantra 109: Asana, pranayama and pratyahara

आसनेन रुजं हन्ति प्राणायामेन पातकम् ।
विकारं मानसं योगी प्रत्याहारेण मुञ्चति ॥ 109 ॥

Aasanena Rujam Hanti Praanaayaamena Paatakam;
Vikaaram Maanasam Yogee Pratyaahaarena Munchati. (109)

Anvay

Aasanena: by yogic posture; *Rujam*: diseases; *Hanti*: are destroyed; *Praanaayaamena*: by pranayama; *Paatakam*: the sins; *Vikaaram*: impurities; *Maanasam*: of the mind; *Yogee*: yogic adept; *Pratyaahaarena*: sensory withdrawal; *Munchati*: removes.

Translation

Diseases are destroyed by asana and sins by pranayama. By pratyahara, the yogi removes the impurities of the mind.

Commentary

Now the text focuses on the benefits of *shatanga* (six limbed) *yoga*, which was described in Mantra 2 at the beginning of the text. Asana, pranayama and pratyahara are included in this verse, and dharana, dhyana and samadhi in the next.

Asanas remove disease because they rebalance and regulate the pranas, nadis and chakras. Different diseases arise due to imbalances in the pranic infrastructure which are relayed to the nervous system, glandular system and then to all the bodily systems, their organs and parts. Each asana is designed to remove pranic blockages from the nadis, or subtle energy flows, thus allowing the energy to flow throughout the body in a regulated manner. The asanas also stimulate and regulate particular chakras, or psychic energy centres, thus rebalancing the energy of the pranas and nadis within those areas. In this way regular practice of

257

asana harmonizes and regulates all the energy fields within the body, which results in freedom from disease.

The previous mantra has discussed how the sins or negative tendencies are removed by pranayama. Next the mantra takes up the topic of pratyahara, by which impurities of the mind are removed. Pratyahara is the first stage of meditation in which the senses are withdrawn from the external objects and associations and focused within the mind. In many yogic texts the analogy of a tortoise is given to explain pratyahara. When the tortoise withdraws its four limbs and tail inside the shell, the head is withdrawn also. The five senses function as the external sensors for the mind, providing it with all kinds of information about the outer situations and conditions. As long as the senses are attached to outside objects, the mind is focused outside also. However, when the senses are withdrawn, the mind also withdraws and becomes focused within. This is the state of pratyahara.

The *vikara* or mental impurities referred to in this mantra are inherent in all thoughts, memories, ideas, desires and aversions. They continually arise and associate the mind to the objects and relationships of the world, rather than to the atman or spirit within. Vikara can also be understood as the mental expression of the karmas, or subliminal impressions. These mental impurities cannot be removed or cleared until they are seen and recognized for what they are. This requires a meditative process as the vikara are very subtle as well as prolific. They go on creating and recreating themselves within the mind in association with each and every experience and identification in life.

The vikara are not recognized as long as the mind and senses are focused outside, creating further associations and impressions. So, it is necessary to stop this process by withdrawing the senses and the mind from the external world of objects back into the mental dimension. Then the mental energy which would normally be dissipated by the mind and senses in the outside world can be redirected to observe the inner thoughts and impressions as they arise within the conscious mind from the deeper levels of consciousness. In this way, the awareness is trained to function attentively within the mind, just as it would if it were outside.

The awareness must be trained to perceive the mental field and all the thought patterns arising within it. As the mind learns to recognize the different impressions or vikara, without associating or identifying itself with them, the process of mental clearing begins. This is a slow and methodical process, known as *chitta shuddhi*, or mental purification. Gradually, the awareness observes and discards each thought pattern and impression as it arises until the mind becomes empty and quiet. This is the way yogis remove mental impurity by the practice of pratyahara, which is the third limb of shatanga yoga.

Mantra 110: Dharana and samadhi

धारणाभिर्मनोधैर्यं याति चैतन्यमद्भुतम् ।
समाधौ मोक्षमाप्नोति त्यक्त्वा कर्म शुभाशुभम् ॥ 110 ॥

Dhaaranaabhirmanodhairyam Yaati Chaitanyamadbhutam;
Samaadhau Mokshamaapnoti Tyaktvaa Karma Shubhaashubham.
(110)

Anvay

Dhaaranaabhih: by concentration; *Manodhairyam*: steadiness
of mind; *Yaati*: is acquired; *Chaitanyam*: consciousness;
Adbhutam: wonderful; *Samaadhau*: in samadhi; *Moksham*:
liberation; *Aapnoti*: achieves; *Tyaktvaa*: giving up; *Karma*:
action; *Shubha*: auspicious; *Ashubham*: inauspicious.

Translation

By concentration, steadiness of mind is acquired. In samadhi
a wonderful state of consciousness (unfolds). The auspicious
and inauspicious actions are given up and liberation is
achieved.

Commentary

Dharana means one-pointed concentration. This stage of
meditation cannot be experienced by the dissipated and
fragmented mind. Therefore, dharana must be undertaken
after pratyahara has been mastered. The mental impurities
that disturb the mind must be removed so that the mind
becomes calm and still. Then one-pointed concentration
can be practised whereby steadiness of mind is acquired.
There are many stages of dharana before concentration is
perfected. At first, the awareness fluctuates or oscillates
while concentrating on the object of meditation. Gradually,
the periods between oscillation become longer and the
awareness fluctuates less and less.

In this way, the mind becomes capable of sustained concentration on one object of meditation for prolonged periods of time. During these periods of concentration, which are free from fluctuation or oscillation, steadiness of mind intervenes and the awareness becomes more powerful. As the mind is periodically freed from physical and mundane associations, it undergoes certain changes and refinement. With the development of concentration, the awareness gradually merges with the object of meditation. The stage of perfected concentration, where the awareness of the object remains constant and unbroken, is known as dhyana. So, it can be inferred that perfection of concentration culminates in dhyana. Although the stage of dhyana is omitted in this mantra, it is mentioned in the next.

With perfection of concentration, meditation becomes a spontaneous, ongoing process. This ultimately leads to samadhi where a wonderful and luminous state of consciousness unfolds. Even in samadhi, there are many stages wherein the last vestiges or traces of mental associations are removed. Finally, in the highest state of samadhi, the consciousness soars free of all individual association and experiences itself in its own glory, as one with the spirit or atman. In this transcendent state the yogi is freed from all the karmas, good and bad. Karmas bind the soul to the body and are the causes of birth and death. In samadhi the karmic bondage is removed and liberation is thus attained.

Mantras 111, 112: Progression of yoga

प्राणायामद्विषट्केन प्रत्याहार: प्रकीर्तित: ।
प्रत्याहारद्विषट्केन जायते धारणा शुभा ॥ 111 ॥
धारणा द्वादश प्रोक्तं ध्यानं योगविशारदै: ।
ध्यानद्वादशकेनैव समाधिरभिधीयते ॥ 112 ॥

Praanaayaama Dvishatkena Pratyaahaarah Prakeertitah;
Pratyaahaara Dvishatkena Jaayate Dhaaranaa Shubhaa. (111)
Dhaaranaa Dvaadasha Proktam Dhyaanam Yogavishaaradaih;
Dhyaanadvaadashakenaiva Samaadhirabhidheeyate. (112)

Anvay

Praanaayaama: by pranayama; *Dvishatkena*: twelve; *Pratyaa-haarah*: pratyahara results; *Prakeertitah*: has been said; *Pratyaahaara*: by pratyahara; *Dvishatkena*: twelve; *Jaayate*: results; *Dhaaranaa*: concentration; *Shubhaa*: auspicious; *Dhaaranaa*: by dharana; *Dvaadasha*: twelve; *Proktam*: it has been said; *Dhyaanam*: spontaneous meditation results; *Yoga vishaaradaih*: by people well-versed in yoga; *Dhyaana*: dhyana; *Dvaadashakena*: by twelve; *Eva*: and; *Samaadhih*: transcendental meditation; *Abhidheeyate*: is attained.

Translation

People who are well-versed in yoga have said that by twelve pranayamas, pratyahara results. Twelve pratyaharas result in the auspicious state of dharana. By twelve dharanas, dhyana results and by twelve dhyanas, samadhi is attained.

Commentary

Twelve pranayamas means twelve units or rounds of the practice, such as described previously, with mastery over the three levels of breathing and retention. Twelve rounds of pranayama performed in this way will induce the state of pratyahara in which the senses are withdrawn and the awareness is focused totally within the mind. Again the mantra says that twelve units of pratyahara lead to the auspicious state of dharana. Here a unit of pratyahara implies not merely a practice session, but mastery over the senses and the ability to focus them within at will. Pratyahara is the state of pure, controlled and quiet mind, free from vikara or impurities. Twelve units of this state would naturally result in dharana or concentration. This is an auspicious state because it signifies the beginning of in-depth meditation.

There are many stages of concentration also. Dharana means concentration with breaks. With mastery of this stage, however, the mind fluctuates less and less. So dharana here means the level of concentration with few breaks. Twelve units of the perfected state of dharana lead to dhyana, which is unbroken concentration. In dhyana, the mind remains totally merged in the object of concentration, without any fluctuation or break. Of course, in the beginning the awareness may flow from dharana into dhyana for a few moments, and then back into dharana or even pratyahara again. With mastery of dhyana, however, the awareness remains merged in the object of concentration for longer periods without any break or fluctuation.

Again the mantra states that twelve such dhyanas lead to samadhi. Twelve units of unbroken concentration with no fluctuation result in the state of luminosity where the awareness transcends the mind and all of its limitations. Even in samadhi, however, the awareness progresses through states in which the remaining traces of the mind are discarded one by one until the pure transcendental state of consciousness is experienced.

Mantra 113: Culmination of yoga

समाधौ परमं ज्योतिरनन्तं विश्वतोमुखम् ।
तस्मिन्दृष्टे क्रियाकर्म यातायातो न विद्यते ॥ 113 ॥

Samaadhau Paramam Jyotiranantam Vishvatomukham;
Tasmindrishte Kriyaakarma Yaataayaato Na Vidyate. (113)

Anvay

Samaadhau: in samadhi; *Paramam*: supreme; *Jyotih*: light;
Anantam: infinite; *Vishvatomukham*: in all directions; *Tasmindrishte*: having seen this; *Kriyaakarma*: all actions; *Yaata ayaata*:
coming and going; *Na vidyate*: do not remain.

Translation

In samadhi, (there is) supreme, infinite illumination in all
directions. Having seen this, neither karmas nor birth and
death remain.

Commentary

This mantra describes the final state of samadhi, which is
the apex of yoga, in terms of absolute and limitless illumination or enlightenment. The atman or pure consciousness is
said to have no comparison or equivalent in words or material
associations. However, the scriptures have used the analogy
of light to describe this ultimate experience. That light
which is without beginning or end, which is unqualified by
any name, form or description, and unbounded by any
direction, is said to be the nature of the supreme
consciousness. Thus, in samadhi, when individual consciousness merges with the supreme consciousness, infinite
luminosity is experienced. In this sense, samadhi represents
that expanded field of awareness known as super-consciousness, which is unbound by any individual field or perception
and encompasses the total field of consciousness.

The word samadhi comes from two roots: *sama*, 'equal' and *dhi*, 'reflection'. So, *samadhi* means equal awareness of all the states of consciousness. This is the undivided or unified state in which consciousness is perceived as One without a second. Even in samadhi, however, there are distinct stages which lead to this final state. The two basic states of samadhi are known as *sabija* (with seed) and *nirbija* (without seed). Nirbija is the final state of samadhi, which is free from all traces or remnants of individuation. Sabija comprises the stages of samadhi in which the last vestiges of the individual mind are transcended.

Within sabija, there are six progressive stages of samadhi: savitarka, nirvitarka, savichara, nirvichara, ananda and asmita. In *savitarka*, the last traces of conceptualized thought in the form of language or words are eliminated, thus culminating in *nirvitarka*, awareness which is free of objective ideation. In *savichara*, the last traces of reflection or subjective thinking are removed, culminating in *nirvichara*, awareness which is free from all subtle thought in the form of mental imagery, colors, lights and symbols. At this point the intellectual process ceases to operate and *ananda* samadhi intervenes. Here consciousness is experienced in the form of absolute bliss. From ananda samadhi, *asmita* samadhi dawns, where the last vestiges of ego association are removed.

As the awareness passes progressively through these six stages of samadhi, the last traces of individual mind are removed until the yogi enters nirbija, the final state of samadhi, which is without seed, or free from all impression or association. Samskaras and karmas arise due to identification of the consciousness with the individual self and association of the self with the world. Birth and death are the outcome of this association of consciousness with the self and the world. In the final state of samadhi, where all the traces of this association are transcended, neither karmas nor the cycle of birth and death remain.

Just as the ocean is the source of all the waves which emerge from the surface and again subside back into it, so the cosmic mind gives birth to the individual mind, which is ultimately reabsorbed back into it. Thus, having attained unity with the pure consciousness, the yogi remains attuned with the absolute reality and is no longer subject to the relative laws of karma or birth and death.

Mantra 114: Union of prana and apana

संबद्धवाऽऽसनमेढ्रमङ्घ्रियुगलं   कर्णाक्षिनासापुट-
द्वारानङ्गुलिभिर्नियम्य पवनं वक्त्रेण वा पूरितम् ।
बद्ध्वा वक्षसि बह्वपानसहितं मूर्ध्नि स्थितं धारये
देवं याति विशेषतत्त्वसमतां योगीश्वरस्तन्मनाः ॥ 114 ॥

*Sambaddhvaa   Aasanamedramanghriyugalam   Karnaakshi
Naasaaputa Dvaaraanangulibhirniyamya Pavanam Vaktrena Vaa
Pooritam; Badhvaa Vakshasi Bahvapaanasahitam Moordhni
Sthitam Dhaaraye Devam Yaati Visheshatattvasamataam
Yogeeshwarastanmanaah.* (114)

Anvay

Sambaddhvaa: perfectly locked; *Aasana*: posture; *Medram*:
nadi plexus above mooladhara; *Anghriyugalam*: with both
feet; *Karna*: ears; *Akshi*: *eyes; Naasaaputa*: nasal passages;
Dvaaraan: gates; *Angulibhih*: with fingers; *Niyamya*: controlling, closing; *Pavanam*: breath; *Vaktrena*: with the mouth;
Va: and; *Pooritam*: filling, drawing in; *Badhvaa*: retaining;
Vakshasi: in the chest; *Bahu*: enough; *Apaana*: apana; *Sahitam*:
with; *Moordhni*: in the head; *Sthitam*: retaining; *Dhaarayet*:
hold, fix; *Evam*: like this; *Yaati*: gains; *Vishesha*: special,
supreme; *Tattva*: element; *Samataam*: experiences; *Yogee*:
yogic adept; *Ishwarah*: God; *Tat manaah*: in his mind.

Translation

Sit in sambaddhvasana, with both feet pressing the medhra.
Close the gates of the ears, eyes and nasal passages with the
fingers. Drawing the breath in through the mouth, retain it
in the region of the chest, along with the apana vayu. Then
raise (the vital air) up to the head and fix it there. Like this,
the yogi gains the supreme element and experiences God in
his mind.

Commentary

This mantra describes a unique and effective practice which includes instructions for the merging of prana and apana vayus and the establishing of kundalini shakti in the higher chakras of the head region. The recommended posture, *sambaddhvasana*, meaning 'perfectly locked', is a variation of padmasana where the heels are firmly pressed against the pelvis, just above the pubic bone. The pressure of the heels stimulates the *medhra*, a complex of major nadis or energy channels just above swadhisthana. This posture is used in kundalini yoga because it directs the flow of apana from the lower region upward to the higher centres. Being a perfectly locked posture, the body and mind also remain balanced and unaffected by this major shift in the vital energy currents.

While sitting in sambaddhvasana, the gates of the major senses: eyes, ears and nose, are closed with the fingers, as in shanmukhi mudra. This is accomplished by raising the hands in front of the face and closing the ears with the thumbs, the eyes with the index fingers and the nostrils with the middle fingers. In this variation, however, the mouth is not closed with the remaining two fingers, as described previously.

The inspired breath is drawn in through the mouth and directed downward to the chest, which is the area of prana vayu. Simultaneously, the apana vayu is drawn upward from the pelvic region to the chest. At the end of inhalation, the breath is retained inside with awareness of the union of prana and apana at the chest. While exhaling, slowly draw the breath together with the vayus upward to the higher centres in the head. Again retaining the breath outside, focus the awareness and establish the pranas there.

Relax and breathe normally in between rounds. Experience increasing luminosity within the headspace and the absence of all thought. By practising in this way, the yogi raises the supreme element, the kundalini shakti, and thus experiences God within the transcendent state of mind.

Mantra 115: Nada yoga

गगनं पवने प्राप्ते ध्वनिरुत्पद्यते महान् ।
घण्टाऽऽदीनां प्रवाद्यानां नादसिद्धिरुदीरिता ॥ 115 ॥

Gaganam Pavane Praapte Dhvanirutpadyate Mahaan;
Ghantaa Adeenaam Pravaadyaanaam Naadasiddhirudeeritaa. (115)

Anvay

Gaganam: in the sky; *Pavane*: prana; *Praapte*: when; *Dhvanih*: inner sounds; *Utpadyate*: are produced; *Mahaan*: great; *Ghantaadeenaam*: bell and so on; *Pravaadyaanaam*: of musical instruments; *Naadasiddhih*: power or perfection of sound; *Udeeritaa*: is achieved.

Translation

When the prana rises into the sky, inner sounds of musical instruments are produced, like the bell and so on, and the perfection of inner sound is achieved.

Commentary

The union of prana and apana is an important threshold in yoga which leads to the awakening of kundalini. This mantra describes the arising of kundalini shakti through the sushumna pathway and its most prominent accompanying experience, the awareness of inner sounds. Nada yoga is meditation on these internal sounds which manifest from the causal dimension. These sounds are produced within the subtle vibratory field as the kundalini shakti ascends the sushumna pathway. The origin of these sounds has no other cause or explanation.

'When the prana rises into the sky' is a poetic description of this process. Here prana refers to kundalini, which is also known as mahaprana, and the sky to unlimited and therefore infinite conscious potential. Prana rises into the sky through the sushumna pathway. Sushumna is the psychic passage situated at the centre of the spinal column, which connects the individual consciousness with its worldly, manifest attributes and associations, as well as with its highest cosmic potential. The individuation and manifestation of pure consciousness at the level of the material world is represented by the six major chakras from ajna to mooladhara, which are connected to sushumna.

The descent of individual consciousness from sahasrara, where it was originally vast and unlimited like the sky, to mooladhara, where it is totally ensconced in the world of matter, is the story of man's manifest evolution. The reversal of this process takes place when 'prana flies up into the sky' and man's consciousness is liberated from its confining, individual associations and again experiences its unity with the source, which is pure consciousness, infinite and immeasurable, like the sky.

The reverberations which are heard internally on this return journey of the prana or kundalini to its consort in the sky are described as the sounds of different musical instruments, such as the bell, gong, conch, veena, flute, cymbals and drum. Other sounds of nature are also heard, such as the rumbling of thunder, ocean waves, rain, wind, and many others. In the process of nada yoga, the aspirant focuses his awareness on each of these sounds, one by one. In this way, the consciousness is slowly pulled upward through the sushumna by the sound vibration to subtler and subtler dimensions of perception.

Ultimately, perfection of inner sound is achieved when the awareness reaches sahasrara chakra at the crown of the head. Here, all the chakras along with their manifest associations are transcended and the awareness merges in the unqualified dimension of pure consciousness. As such, nada yoga can be understood as a component of kundalini yoga. The manifestation of inner sound is the natural outcome of the ascension of kundalini shakti through the sushumna passage. As the kundalini rises through each psychic centre in turn, these sounds become subtler and subtler until the awareness transcends even this form of vibratory association and is united with its source.

Mantra 116: Pranayama prevents disease

प्राणायामेन युक्तेन सर्वरोगक्षयो भवेत् ।
प्राणायामवियुक्तैभ्य: सर्वरोगसमुद्भव: ॥ 116 ॥

Praanaayaamena Yuktena Sarvarogakshayo Bhavet;
Praanaayaamaviyuktaibhyah Sarvarogasamudbhavah. (116)

Anvay

Praanaayaamena: by pranayama; *Yuktena*: being yoked, practised; *Sarva*: all; *Roga*: diseases; *Kshayah*: removed; *Bhavet*: are; *Praanaayaama*: by pranayama; *Viyuktaibhyah*: indifference to, not practised; *Sarva*: all; *Roga*: diseases; *Samudbhavah*: arise.

Translation

By the practice of pranayama, all diseases are removed. By not practising pranayama, all diseases arise.

Commentary

Pranayama refers to those practices which balance and expand the quantum of prana. The body and mind are manifestations of vital and mental energy. According to yoga, disease is said to have its origins in the mind but is then deflected down through the body. As long as the vital energies are balanced and maintained at a high level, the individual will not succumb to disease even though the seeds of disease are inherent in the mind and deflect down into the body at all times. However, when any disturbance or crisis arises, whether physiological or psychological, the pranas are affected. The pranas act like a bridge between the body and mind, so that the pranas are affected by the body and mind and vice versa.

When the body or mind is positively or adversely affected, the pranas are also likewise affected. If a stressful or adverse

272

habit or situation is not resolved and continues on for some time, a pranic imbalance will set in. At this point, disease can take hold in some area or areas of the body where the material constituents or organic functions are weakest. The duration of time which may elapse before the disease becomes evident depends upon the level of *vyana vayu*, the vital air responsible for overall pranic balance and, therefore, resistance. The level of vyana determines the course of the disease and how fast it will set in. Vyana flows throughout the system and its function is to regulate the other pranas as and when they become excessive or deficient.

When pranayama is practised regularly and appropriately, the level of vyana vayu is maintained, ensuring a constant balance within the pranic system, even in the face of disturbing factors. The practices of pranayama are furthermore divided into four categories: balancing, relaxing, heating and cooling. So, when selected and combined according to the individual nature and needs as well as climate and season, pranayama establishes a balance within the pranic system and expands the dimension of prana within the individual. In this way, the pranas receive regular support and so are unlikely to be extremely affected even in the face of internal or external crises. Therefore, the mantra states that the practice of pranayama removes disease, and by not practising pranayama all diseases arise.

Mantra 117: Diseases managed by pranayama

हिक्का कासस्तथा श्वास: शिर:कर्णाक्षिवेदना।
भवन्ति विविधा रोगा: पवनव्यत्ययक्रमात् ॥ 117 ॥

Hikkaa Kaasastathaa Shvaasah Shirah Karnaakshivedanaa;
Bhavanti Vividhaa Rogaah Pavanavyatyayakramaat. (117)

Anvay

Hikkaa: hiccups; *Kaasah*: bronchitis; *Tathaa*: and; *Shvaasah*: asthma; *Shirah*: head; *Karna*: ear; *Akshi*: eye; *Vedanaa*: afflictions; *Bhavanti*: accrue; *Vividhaa*: of different types; *Rogaah*: diseases; *Pavanavyatyayakramaat*: by not practising pranayama.

Translation

Various types of diseases like hiccups, bronchitis, asthma and afflictions of the head, ear and eye accrue when pranayama is not practised.

Commentary

The diseases that are manageable by pranayama are given in the mantra. These include respiratory diseases such as bronchitis, asthma and hiccups, as well as disorders of the head, i.e. eyes and ears. Pranayama practices regulate and balance the pranas by controlling and manipulating the breath. Sometimes the two terms, prana and breath, are used synonymously. Although the breath is not prana, it is the closest physical correlation to prana. The breath, therefore, influences the prana directly and vice-versa. When the breath is regulated and controlled in specific ways, as in the practices of pranayama, the pranas are balanced, activated and expanded.

In the case of respiratory diseases, there are major pranic imbalances in the body which can be rectified by the practice

274

of pranayama. Due to the close association of breath and prana, respiratory diseases can be managed more easily by pranayama than by other modalities. Nadi shodhana, the balancing pranayama, performed by alternate nostril breathing, corrects imbalance in the two major nadis, ida and pingala, which have their physical termination points at the nostrils. Bhastrika, the activating pranayama, or bellows breathing, deals with imbalances in the vayus, or vital airs, especially samana and prana, flowing in the abdomen and chest region, which are generally deficient in respiratory disorders. Ujjayi pranayama, or psychic breathing, activates ida nadi and hence the parasympathetic nervous system, thereby releasing lung spasm and opening the respiratory tract.

In this way, regular practice of pranayama balances the flow of energy in the nadis and restores the level of prana vayus, thereby alleviating and removing diseases of the respiratory tract. Disorders that arise in the region of the head, such as eyes, ears, nose and throat, can also be managed by the practice of pranayama. The head and neck are the region of udana vayu. When this vital air becomes deficient, different problems arise in the brain and the senses, each of which utilize large amounts of energy to perform their various functions. Brahmari, the humming pranayama, relaxes the brain and mind and is beneficial for problems of the ears. Kapalbhati, the head purification pranayama, activates the brain, removing mental dissipation, and benefits the eyes. Nadi shodhana, the balancing pranayama, regulates the left and right hemispheres of the brain as well as the sympathetic and parasympathetic nervous systems, and is beneficial for the eyes.

These are some disorders which are amenable to pranayama. However, pranayama forms an integral part of yogic management for all diseases.

Mantra 118: Pranic control

यथा सिंहो गजो व्याघ्रो भवेद्वश्यः शनैः शनैः।
तथैव सेवितो वायुरन्यथा हन्ति साधकम् ॥ 118 ॥

Yathaa Simho Gajo Vyaaghro Bhavedvashyah Shanaih Shanaih;
Tathaiva Sevito Vaayuranyathaa Hanti Saadhakam. (118)

Anvay

Yathaa: just as; *Simhah*: lion; *Gajah*: elephant; *Vyaaghrah*: tiger; *Bhavet vashyah*: are controlled; *Shanaih shanaih*: slowly and steadily; *Tathaa eva*: similarly; *Sevitah*: should be controlled; *Vaayuh*: prana; *Anyathaa*: otherwise; *Hanti*: becomes destructive; *Saadhakam*: to practitioners.

Translation

Just as the lion, elephant and tiger are brought under control slowly and steadily, similarly the prana should be controlled, otherwise it becomes destructive to the practitioner.

Commentary

Here prana is likened to the lion, tiger and elephant, which were regarded as the mightiest animals of the jungle. All the other animals would immediately defer to the lion and tiger because of their great strength and ferocity, as well as to the elephant because of its enormous size and power. Similarly, prana is the most powerful principle of life. It is prana alone which gives life to the body, senses and mind. Death ensues the moment prana leaves the body. When the pranas are sublimated and redirected to the brain, enlightenment occurs. When the pranas are allowed to dissipate and flow out of the body in the course of life's interactions, disease and old age occur. Therefore, the yogic texts advise that the pranas should be controlled and retained, and this is the basic principle of yoga from ancient times.

276

However, the mantra gives a warning in relation to controlling the pranas. Just as the taming of a lion, tiger or elephant requires great skill and is only accomplished over a long period of time; similarly the pranas must be controlled slowly, steadily and skillfully. Otherwise harm can come to the practitioner, just as harm may come to the trainer who carelessly mishandles a powerful lion, tiger or elephant. Therefore, yogic practices that work directly with the pranas, such as pranayama, mudra, bandha and kriya, must be undertaken cautiously and under expert guidance.

Proper preparation must be done before the practitioner is able to safely take up these practices and progress through them successfully. It is imperative that the nadis and chakras should be purified, balanced and activated slowly and systematically, so that the awakened flow of pranas can be channelled through them. When the nadis and chakras are full of toxins, the energies activated by strong yogic practices become blocked in those areas, causing further irregularities. The damming up of energy in one area creates excess energy there and deficiencies of energy in adjacent areas. Over time this results in serious energy imbalances, destabilizing the body, mind or both.

When the body and mind are imbalanced, diseases of many kinds find an easy entry. Furthermore, such diseases are not easily treated by medical modalities, especially as doctors do not understand the nature of their cause. Therefore, the mantra rightly states that prana is very powerful and must be handled with great care and controlled slowly and steadily.

Mantra 119: Perfection in pranayama

युक्तं युक्तं त्यजेद्वायुं युक्तं युक्तं प्रपूरयेत् ।
युक्तं युक्तं प्रबध्नीयादेवं सिद्धिमवाप्नुयात् ॥ 119 ॥

Yuktam Yuktam Tyajedvaayum Yuktam Yuktam Prapoorayet;
Yuktam Yuktam Prabadhneeyaadevam Siddhimavaapnuyaat. (119)

Anvay

Yuktam yuktam: slowly with awareness; *Tyajet*: should exhale;
Vaayum: the breath; *Yuktam yuktam*: slowly with awareness;
Prapoorayet: should inhale; *Yuktam yuktam*: slowly with
awareness; *Prabadhneeyaat*: should retain; *Evam*: thus;
Siddhim: perfection; *Avaapnuyaat*: is attained.

Translation

The breath should be inhaled slowly with awareness. The
breath should be retained properly with awareness. The
breath should be exhaled slowly and carefully. Thus
perfection is attained.

Commentary

The correct method of practice is most important in
pranayama, because of its subtle effects on the nerves and
nadis. This mantra is also found almost word for word in
Hatha Yoga Pradipika (2:18). Although the ratio of the breath
is not given here, the emphasis on *yuktam*, *yuktam*, meaning
'slowly', 'carefully', 'properly', 'with awareness', alludes to
the ratio that must be maintained throughout the practice,
be it 1:1:1, 1:2:2, or 1:4:2. The ratio is a factor, which varies
from individual to individual and from season to season.
Therefore, it is usually fixed and modified from time to time
by the preceptor or guide.

The mantra further states that by performing pranayama
skillfully, perfection or *siddhi* is attained. Perfection in

278

pranayama does not refer to the careful manipulation of inhalation and exhalation, but to retention of the breath or *kumbhaka*. There are two types of kumbhaka: one is *sahita*, meaning 'performed by practice', and the other is *kevala*, meaning 'spontaneous', or beyond practice. The practice of pranayama involving breath retention is sahita kumbhaka. Perfection in pranayama, however, is kevala kumbhaka, where the breath stops spontaneously and the mind soars into superconscious states.

Ultimately, all practices of pranayama are mainly concerned with kumbhaka, which has very powerful effects on the prana and consciousness. Kumbhaka activates the central nervous system, opens the sushumna nadi and stills the mind. Regular and sustained practice purifies the nadis and chakras, and awakens the perception of inner sound or *nada*. Therefore, pranayama is considered to be an important aspect of kundalini yoga.

Mantra 120: Pratyahara

चरतां चक्षुरादीनां विषयेषु यथाक्रमम् ।
तत्प्रत्याहरणं तेषां प्रत्याहारः स उच्यते ॥ 120 ॥

Charataam Chakshuraadeenaam Vishayeshu Yathaakramam;
Tatpratyaaharanam Teshaam Pratyaahaarah Sa Uchyate. (120)

Anvay

Charataam: involvement, wandering; *Chakshuh*: eyes;
Aadeenaam: and so on; *Vishayeshu*: with sensory objects;
Yathaa kramam: in a systematic way; *Tatpratyaaharanam*:
withdrawal of senses; *Teshaam*: them; *Pratyaahaarah*:
pratyahara; *Sah*: that; *Uchyate*: is called.

Translation

Withdrawal of the senses, such as the eyes and so on, in a
systematic way, from involvement with the sensory objects,
that is called pratyahara.

Commentary

Systematic withdrawal of the awareness from the senses and
their associated objects constitutes pratyahara, which is the
first stage of meditation. Normally the awareness is directed
outward through the five senses: eyes, ears, nose, tongue
and skin, in order to perceive the external world and its
objects. The senses then convey information to the brain of
the various sights, sounds, smells, tastes and touch that they
pick up in the surrounding environment. While the awareness operates through the five senses, the mind is activated
by the external stimuli that it constantly receives.

When the mind receives too many stimuli for too long, it
becomes excited, stressed and ultimately exhausted.
However, when the stimuli are too few the mind becomes
bored, disinterested and dull. The exhausted mind seeks

rest while the bored mind seeks further diversion, entertainment or work to occupy it. This process is known as externalization of the mind through the senses, which most people experience every day of their lives. In yogic meditation, however, there is a second process which involves internalization of the mind and senses, known as *pratyahara*.

When the senses are withdrawn from their external associations, the awareness remains inside the mind watching the mental patterns which arise from within. The state of pratyahara leads to mastery over the senses. The awareness which seeks association with the sensory objects must be established in the mental field. In this way, the senses learn to follow the mind, rather than the mind following the senses. The state of pratyahara is symbolized in many yogic texts by the turtle, which has the ability to withdraw its two legs, two arms and tail (five senses) along with its head (mind) into the shell for long periods of time.

Pratyahara is a process of involution. The external sensory contact is cut in order to enter the depths of the mind. When the senses are withdrawn, the awareness remains inside. When the sense organs are attached to particular objects, the mind receives experiences which may be pleasant or unpleasant. In pratyahara the senses are withdrawn from the external objects and forms, but the mind continues to function internally through idea and name. Idea is active as long as mind is active, and name or identification is active as long as idea is active. So, in the state of pratyahara, even though the senses are withdrawn, the mind continues to function through idea and name.

Mantra 121: Mental purification

यथा तृतीयकाले तु रवि: प्रत्याहरेत्प्रभाम् ।
तृतीयाङ्गस्थितो योगी विकारं मानसं हरेत् ॥ 121 ॥
इत्युपनिषत् ॥

Yathaa Triteeyakaale Tu Ravih Pratyaaharetprabhaam;
Triteeyaangasthito Yogee Vikaaram Maanasam Haret. (121)
Ityupanishat.

Anvay

Yathaa: just as; *Triteeya kaale*: third quarter of the day; *Tu ravih*: sun; *Pratyaaharet*: begins to withdraw; *Prabhaam*: glory, heat and light; *Triteeya*: third; *Anga*: limb; *Sthitah*: established; *Yogee*: yogic adept; *Vikaaram*: impurities; *Maanasam*: of the mind; *Haret*: should remove; *Ityupanishat*: thus ends the Upanishad.

Translation

Just as the sun begins to withdraw its heat and light in the third quarter of the day, the yogic adept, established in the third limb, should remove the impurities of the mind. Thus ends the Upanishad.

Commentary

In this Upanishad, asana and pranayama are considered to be the first two limbs of yoga (mantra 2) and the third limb is pratyahara. The image of the sun which has passed the zenith and begins to withdraw its heat and light in third quarter of the day represents the process of pratyahara. The rising sun represents the mental energy which is dispersed in the world to establish external associations and position. In the third quarter of the day, the sun starts its downward journey towards the horizon, and gradually its heat and light are withdrawn from the world. Similarly, pratyahara

282

represents the stage in life where man's external evolution has reached its peak and his inner evolution or the awakening of awareness within begins.

In this sense, pratyahara is a process of re-education whereby the mind learns to observe itself rather than the world outside. By observing the mental patterns, the practitioner realizes how far the senses and their impressions influence the mind and personality. The aim of pratyahara is to analyze the mental processes and achieve a state of mental purification, or chitta shuddhi. Purification of mind takes place gradually by eliminating the accumulation of mental toxins in the form of stored sensory impressions. As the excess mental patterns and impressions are released, the mind becomes calm and quiet. At this stage of pratyahara it becomes possible to control the mental activity by directing the mind rather than allowing it to direct itself. This leads to further states of concentration and creative thinking.

In kundalini yoga, pratyahara arises as a natural outcome of the practices of pranayama, mudra, bandha and kriya which regulate, balance and awaken the energies in the nadis and chakras. It is also achieved by dynamic meditation practices which rotate the breath, pranas and mantras through the sushumna nadi.

Thus ends *Yoga Chudamani Upanishad*, a vedantic treatise on kundalini yoga.

Appendices

Appendices

Sanskrit Text

योगचूडामण्युपनिषत्

1. योगचूडामणिं वक्ष्ये योगिनां हितकाम्यया।
   कैवल्यसिद्धिदं गूढं सेवितं योगवित्तमैः ॥

2. आसनं प्राणसंरोधः प्रत्याहारश्च धारणा।
   ध्यानं समाधिरेतानि योगाङ्गानि भवन्ति षट् ॥

3. एकं सिद्धासनं प्रोक्तं द्वितीयं कमलासनम्।
   षट्चक्रं षोडशाधारं त्रिलक्ष्यं व्योमपञ्चकम् ॥

4. स्वदेहे यो न जानाति तस्य सिद्धिः कथं भवेत्।
   चतुर्दलं स्यादाधारं स्वाधिष्ठानं च षड्दलम् ॥

5. नाभौ दशदलं पद्मम् हृदयं द्वादशारकम्।
   षोडशारं विशुद्धाख्यं भ्रूमध्ये द्विदलं तथा ॥

6. सहस्रदलसंख्यातं ब्रह्मरन्ध्रे महापथि।
   आधारं प्रथमं चक्रं स्वाधिष्ठानं द्वितीयकम् ॥

7. योनिस्थानं द्वयोर्मध्ये कामरूपं निगद्यते।
   कामाख्यं तु गुदस्थाने पंकजं तु चतुर्दलम् ॥

8. तन्मध्ये प्रोच्यते योनिः कामाख्या सिद्धवन्दिता।
   तस्य मध्ये महालिङ्गं पश्चिमाभिमुखम् स्थितम् ॥

9. नाभौ तु मणिवद्बिम्बं यो जानाति स योगवित् ।
तप्तचामीकराभासं तडिल्लेखेव विस्फुरत् ॥

10. त्रिकोणं तत्पुरं वह्नेरधोमेढ्रात्प्रतिष्ठितम् ।
समाधौ परमं ज्योतिरनन्तं विश्वतोमुखम् ॥

11. तस्मिन्दृष्टे महायोगे यातायातो न विद्यतेब ।
स्वशब्देन भवेत्प्राणः स्वाधिष्ठानं तदाश्रयम् ॥

12. स्वाधिष्ठानाश्रयादस्मान्मेढ्रमेवाभिधीयते ।
तन्तुना मणिवत्प्रोतो योऽत्र कन्दः सुषुम्नया ॥

13. तन्नाभिमण्डले चक्रं प्रोच्यते मणिपूरकम् ।
द्वादशारे महाचक्रे पुण्यपापविवर्जिते ॥

14. तावज्जीवो भ्रमत्येवं यावत्तत्त्वं न विन्दति ।
ऊर्ध्वं मेढ्रादधोनाभेः कन्दयोनिः खगाण्डवत् ॥

15. तत्र नाडचः समुत्पन्नाः सहस्राणिः द्विसप्ततिः ।
तेषु नाडीसहस्रेषु द्विसप्ततिरुदाहता ॥

16. प्रधानाः प्राणवाहिन्यो भूयस्तासु दश स्मृताः ।
इडा च पिङ्गला चैव सुषुम्ना च तृतीयगा ॥

17. गान्धारी हस्तिजिह्वा च पूषा चैव यशस्विनी ।
अलम्बुसा कुहूश्चैव शङ्खिनी दशमी स्मृता ॥

18. एतन्नाडीमहाचक्रं ज्ञातव्यं योगिभिः सदा ।
इडा वामे स्थिता भागे दक्षिणे पिङ्गला स्थिता ॥

19. सुषुम्ना मध्यदेशे तु गान्धारी वामचक्षुषि ।
दक्षिणे हस्तिजिह्वा च पूषा कर्णे तु दक्षिणे ॥

२०. यशस्विनी वामकर्णे चानने चाप्यलम्बुसा।
कुहूश्च लिङ्गदेशे तु मूलस्थाने तु शङ्खिनी ॥

२१. एवं द्वार समाश्रित्य तिष्ठन्ते नाडय: क्रमात्।
इडापिङ्गलसौषुम्ना: प्राणमार्गे च संस्थिता: ॥

२२. सततं प्राणवाहिन्य: सोमसूर्याग्निदेवता:।
प्राणापानसमानाख्या व्यानोदानौ च वायव: ॥

२३. नाग: कूर्मोऽथ कृकरो देवदत्तो धनंजय:।
हृदि प्राण: स्थितो नित्यमपानो गुदमण्डले ॥

२४. समानो नाभिदेशे तु उदान: कण्ठमध्यग:।
व्यान: सर्वशरीरे तु प्रधाना: पञ्च वायव: ॥

२५. उद्गारे नाग आख्यात: कूर्म उन्मीलने तथा।
कृकर: क्षुत्करो ज्ञेयो देवदत्तो विजृम्भणे ॥

२६. न जहाति मृतं वापि सर्वव्यापी धनंजय:।
एते नाडीषु सर्वासु भ्रमन्ते जीवजन्तव: ॥

२७. आक्षिप्तो भुजदण्डेन तथा यथोच्चलति कन्दुक:।
प्राणापानसमाक्षिप्तस्तथा जीवो न तिष्ठति ॥

२८. प्राणापानवशो जीवो ह्यधश्चोर्ध्वं च धावति।
वामदक्षिणमार्गाभ्यां चञ्चलत्वान्न दृश्यते ॥

२९. रज्जुबद्धो यथा श्येनो गतोऽप्याकृष्यते पुन:।
गुणबद्धस्तथा जीव: प्राणापानेन कर्षति ॥

३०. प्राणापानवशो जीवो ह्यधश्चोर्ध्वं च गच्छति।
अपान: कर्षति प्राणं प्राणोऽपानेन कर्षति ॥

31. ऊर्ध्वाध: संस्थितावेतौ यो जानाति स योगवित्।
हकारेण बहिर्याति सकारेण विशेत्पुन: ॥

32. हंसहंसेत्यमुं मन्त्रम् जीवो जपति सर्वदा।
षट्शतानि दिवारात्रौ सहस्राण्येकविंशति: ॥

33. एतत्संख्यान्वितं मन्त्रम् जीवो जपति सर्वदा।
अजपानाम गायत्री योगिनां मोक्षदा सदा ॥

34. अस्या: संकल्पमात्रेण सर्वपापै: प्रमुच्यते।
अनया सदृशी विद्या अनया सदृशो जप: ॥

35. अनया सदृशं ज्ञानं न भूतं न भविष्यति।
कुण्डलिन्यां समुद्भूता गायत्री प्राणधारिणी ॥

36. प्राणविद्या महाविद्या यस्तां वेत्ति स वेदवित्।
कन्दोर्ध्वे कुण्डलीशक्तिरष्टधा कुण्डलाकृति: ॥

37. ब्रह्मद्वारमुखं नित्यं मुखेनाच्छाद्य तिष्ठति।
येन द्वारेण गन्तव्यं ब्रह्मद्वारमनामयम् ॥

38. मुखेनाच्छाद्य तद्द्वारं प्रसुप्ता परमेश्वरी।
प्रबुद्धा वह्नियोगेन मनसा मरुता सह ॥

39. सूचीवद्गात्रमादाय व्रजत्यूर्ध्वं सुषुम्नया।
उद्घाटयेत्कवाटं तु यथाकुञ्चिकया गृहम्।
कुण्डलिन्या तथा योगी मोक्षद्वारं प्रभेदयेत् ॥

40. कृत्वा संपुटितौ करौ दृढतरं बध्वाऽथ पद्मासनं
गाढं वक्षसि संनिधाय चुबुकम् ध्यानं च तच्चेष्टितम्।
वारंवारमपानमूर्ध्वमनिलं प्रोच्चारयेत्पूरितं
मुञ्चन्प्राणमुपैति बोधमतुलं शक्तिप्रभावान्नर: ॥

41. अज्ञानां मर्दनं कृत्वा श्रमसंजातवारिणा।
कट्वम्ललवणत्यागी क्षीरभोजनमाचरेत् ॥

42. ब्रह्मचारी मिताहारी योगी योगपरायणः।
अब्दादूर्ध्वं भवेत्सिद्धो नात्र कार्या विचारणा ॥

43. सुस्निग्धमधुराहारश्चतुर्थांशावशेषितः।
भुङ्क्ते शिवसंप्रीत्या मिताहारी स उच्यते ॥

44. कन्दोर्ध्वे कुण्डलीशक्तिरष्टधा कुण्डलाकृतिः।
बन्धनाय च मूढानां योगिनां मोक्षदा सदा ॥

45. महामुद्रा नभोमुद्रा ओडच्याणं च जलन्धरम्।
मूलबन्धं च यो वेत्ति स योगी मुक्तिभाजनम् ॥

46. पार्ष्णिघातेन संपीडच्च योनिमाकुञ्चयेद्दृढम्।
अपानमूर्ध्वमाकृष्य मूलबन्धो यमुच्यते ॥

47. अपानप्राणयोरैवं क्षयान्मूत्रपुरीषयोः।
युवा भवति वृद्धोऽपि सततं मूलबन्धनात् ॥

48. ओडच्याणं कुरुते यस्मादविश्रान्तम् महाखगः।
ओड्डियाणं तदेव स्यान्मृत्युमातङ्गकेसरी ॥

49. उदरात्पश्चिमं ताणमधोनाभेर्निगद्यते।
ओडच्याणमुदरे बन्धस्तत्र बन्धो विधीयते ॥

50. बध्नाति हि शिरोजातमधोगामि नभोजलम्।
ततो जालन्धरो बन्धः कण्ठदुःखौघनाशनः ॥

51. जालन्धरे कृते बन्धे कण्ठ दुःखौघनाशने।
न पीयूषं पतत्यग्नौ न च वायुः प्रधावति ॥

52. कपालकुहरे जिह्वा प्रविष्टा विपरीतगा।
भ्रुवोरन्तर्गता दृष्टिर्मुद्रा भवति खेचरी ॥

53. न रोगो मरणं तस्य न निद्रा न क्षुधा तृषा।
न च मूर्छा भवेत्तस्य यो मुद्रां वेत्ति खेचरीम् ॥

54. पीड्यते न च रोगेण लिप्यते न स कर्मभिः।
बध्यते न च केनापि यो मुद्रां वेत्ति खेचरीम् ॥

55. चित्तं चरति खे यस्माज्जिह्वा चरति खे यतः।
तेनेयं खेचरी मुद्रा सर्वसिद्धनमस्कृता ॥

56. बिन्दुमूलशरीराणि सिरा यत्र प्रतिष्ठिताः।
भावयन्ति शरीराणि आपादतलमस्तकम् ॥

57. खेचर्या मुद्रितं येन विवरं लम्बिकोर्ध्वतः।
न तस्य क्षीयते बिन्दुः कामिन्यालिङ्गितस्य च ॥

58. यावद्बिन्दुः स्थितो देहे तावन्मृत्युभयं कुतः।
यावद्बद्धा नभोमुद्रा तावद्बिन्दुर्न गच्छति ॥

59. ज्वलितोऽपि यथा बिन्दुः संप्राप्तश्च हुताशनम्।
व्रजत्यूर्ध्वं गतः शक्त्या निरुद्धो योनिमुद्रया ॥

60. स पुनर्द्विविधो बिन्दुः पाण्डरो लोहितस्तथा।
पाण्डरं शुक्लमित्याहुर्लोहिताख्यं महारजः ॥

61. सिन्दूरव्रातसंकाशं रविस्थानस्थितं रजः।
शशिस्थानस्थितम् शुक्लं तयोरैक्यं सुदुर्लभम् ॥

62. बिन्दुर्ब्रह्मा रजः शक्तिर्बिन्दुरिन्दू रजो रविः।
उभयोः सङ्गमादेव प्राप्यते परमं पदम् ॥

63. वायुना शक्तिचालेन प्रेरितं च यथा रज:।
यादि बिन्दु: सदैकत्वं भवेद्दिव्यवपुस्तदा ॥

64. शुक्लं चन्द्रेण संयुक्तं रज: सूर्यसमन्वितम्।
तयो: समरसैकत्वं यो जानाति स योगवित् ॥

65. शोधनं नाडिजालस्य चालनं चन्द्रसूर्ययो:।
रसानां शोषणं चैव महामुद्राऽभिधीयते ॥

66. वक्षोन्यस्तहनु: प्रपीडच सुचिरं योनिं च वामाङ्घ्रिणा
हस्ताभ्यामनुधारयन्नसरितं पादम् तथा दक्षिणम्।
आपूर्य श्वसनेन कुक्षियुगलम् बद्ध्वा शनै रेचये-
देतद्व्याधिविनाशिनी सुमहती मुद्रा नृणां प्रोच्यते ॥

67. चन्द्रांशेन समभ्यस्य सूर्यांशेनाभ्यसेत्पुन:।
या तुल्या तु भवेत्संख्या ततो मुद्रां विसर्जयेत् ॥

68. नहि पथ्यमपथ्यं वा रसा: सर्वेऽपि नीरसा:।
अतिभुक्तं विषं घोरं पीयूषमिव जीर्यति ॥

69. क्षयकुष्ठगुदावर्तगुल्माजीर्णपुरोगमा:।
तस्य रोगा: क्षयं यान्ति महामुद्रां तु योऽभ्यसेत् ॥

70. कथितेयं महामुद्रा महासिद्धिकरी नृणाम्।
गोपनीया प्रयत्नेन न देया यस्य कस्यचित् ॥

71. पद्मासनं समारुह्य समकायशिरोधर:।
नासाग्रदृष्टिरेकान्ते जपेदोंकारमव्ययम् ॥

72. विश्वो हि स्थूलभुङ्नित्यं तैजस: प्रविविक्तभुक्।
आनन्दभुक्तथा प्राज्ञ: सर्वसाक्षीत्यत: पर: ॥

73. प्रणव: सर्वदा तिष्ठेत्सर्वजीवेषु भोगत:।
अभिरामस्तु सर्वासु ह्यवस्थासु ह्यधोमुख: ॥

74. अकारो जाग्रति नेत्रे वर्तते सर्वजन्तुषु।
उकार: कण्ठत: स्वप्ने मकारो हृदि सुप्तित: ॥

75. अकारो राजसो रक्तो ब्रह्मा चेतन उच्यते।
उकार: सात्त्विक: शुक्लो विष्णुरित्यभिधीयते ॥

76. मकारस्तामस: कृष्णो रुद्रश्चेति तथोच्यते।
प्रणवात्प्रभवो ब्रह्मा प्रणवात्प्रभवो हरि: ॥

77. प्रणवात्प्रभवो रुद्र: प्रणवो हि परो भवेत्।
अकारे लीयते ब्रह्मा उकारे लीयते हरि: ॥

78. मकारे लीयते रुद्र: प्रणवो हि प्रकाशते।
ज्ञानिनामूर्ध्वगो भूयादज्ञानीनामधोमुख: ॥

79. एवं वै प्रणवस्तिष्ठेद्यस्तं वेद स वेदवित्।
अनाहतस्वरूपेण ज्ञानिनामूर्ध्वगो भवेत् ॥

80. तैलधारामिवाच्छिन्नम् दीर्घघण्टानिनादवत्।
प्रणवस्य ध्वनिस्तद्वत्तदग्रं ब्रह्म चोच्यते ॥

81. ज्योतिर्मयं तदग्रं स्यादवाच्यं बुद्धिसूक्ष्मत:।
ददृशुर्ये महात्मानो यस्तं वेद स वेदवित् ॥

82. जाग्रन्नेत्रद्वयोर्मध्ये हंस एव प्रकाशते।
सकार: खेचरी प्रोक्तस्त्वंपदं चेति निश्चितम् ॥

83. हकार: परमेश: स्यात्तत्पदं चेति निश्चितम्।
सकारो ध्यायते जन्तुर्हकारो हि भवेद् ध्रुवम् ॥

84. इन्द्रियैर्बध्यते जीव आत्मा चैवन बध्यते।
ममत्वेन भवेज्जीवो निर्ममत्वेन केवल: ॥

85. भूर्भुव: स्वरिमे लोका: सोमसूर्याग्निदेवता:।
यस्य मात्रासु तिष्ठन्ति तत्परं ज्योतिरोमिति ॥

86. इच्छा क्रिया तथा ज्ञानं ब्राह्मी रौद्री च वैष्णवी।
त्रिधा मात्रा स्थितिर्यत्र तत्परं ज्योतिरोमिति ॥

87. वचसा तज्जपेन्नित्यं वपुषा तत्समभ्यसेत्।
मनसा तज्जपेन्नित्यं तत्परं ज्योतिरोमिति ॥

88. शुचिर्वाप्यशुचिर्वापि यो जपेत्प्रणवं सदा।
न स लिप्यति पापेन पद्मपत्रमिवाम्भसा ॥

89. चले वाते चलो बिन्दुर्निश्चले निश्चलो भवेत्।
योगी स्थाणुत्त्वमाप्नोति ततो वायुं निरुन्ध्येत् ॥

90. यावद्वायु: स्थितो देहे तावज्जीवो न मुञ्चति।
मरणं तस्य निष्क्रान्तिस्ततो वायुं निरुन्धयेत् ॥

91. यावद्बद्धो मरुत् देहे तावज्जीवो न मुञ्चति।
यावद्दृष्टिभ्रुवोर्मध्ये तावत्कालभयं कुत: ॥

92. अल्पकालभयाद्ब्रह्मा प्राणायामपरो भवेत्।
योगिनो मुनयश्चैव तत: प्राणान्निरोधयेत् ॥

93. षड्विंशदङ्गुलीहंस: प्रयाणं कुरुते बहि:।
वामदक्षिणमार्गेण प्राणायामो विधीयते ॥

94. शुद्धिमेति यदा सर्व नाडीचक्रं मलाकुलम्।
तदैव जायते योगी प्राणसंग्रहणक्षम: ॥

95. बद्धपद्मासनो योगी प्राणं चन्द्रेण पूरयेत्।
धारयेद्वा यथाशक्त्या भूयः सूर्येण रेचयेत् ॥

96. अमृतोदधिसंकाशं गोक्षीरधवलोपमम्।
ध्यात्वा चन्द्रमसं बिम्बं प्राणायामे सुखी भवेत् ॥

97. स्फुरत्प्रज्वलसज्ज्वालापूज्यमादित्यमण्डलम्।
ध्यात्वा हृदि स्थितं योगी प्राणायामे सुखीभवेत् ॥

98. प्राणं चेदिडया पिबेन्नियमितं भूयोऽन्यथा रेचयेत्
पीत्वा पिङ्गलया समीरणमथो बद्ध्वा त्यजेद्वामया।
सूर्याचन्द्रमसोरनेन विधिना बिन्दुद्वयं ध्यायतः
शुद्धा नाडिगणा भवन्ति यमिनो मासद्वयादूर्ध्वतः ॥

99. यथेष्ट धारणं वायोरनलस्य प्रदीपनम्।
नादाभिव्यक्तिरारोग्यं जायते नाडिशोधनात् ॥

100. प्राणो देहस्थितो यावदपानं तु निरुन्ध्येत्।
एकश्वासमयी मात्रा ऊर्ध्वाधो गगने स्थितिः ॥

101. रेचकः पूरकश्चैव कुम्भकः प्रणवात्मकः।
प्राणायामो भवेदेवं मात्राद्वादशसंयुतः ॥

102. मात्राद्वादशसंयुक्तौ निशाकरदिवाकरौ।
दोषजालमबध्नन्तौ ज्ञातव्यौ योगिभिः सदा ॥

103. पूरकं द्वादशं कुर्यात्कुम्भकं षोडशं भवेत्।
रेचकं दश चोंकारः प्राणायामः स उच्यते ॥

104. अधमे द्वादशा मात्रा मध्यमे द्विगुणा मता।
उत्तमे त्रिगुणा प्रोक्ता प्राणायामस्य निर्णयः ॥

105. अधमे स्वेदजननं कम्पो भवति मध्यमे।
उत्तमे स्थानमाप्नोति ततो वायुं निरुन्ध्येत् ॥

106. बद्धपद्मासनो योगी नमस्कृत्य गुरुं शिवम्।
नासाग्रदृष्टिरेकाकी प्राणायामं समभ्यसेत् ॥

107. द्वाराणां नव संनिरुध्य मरुतं बद्ध्वा दृढां धारणां
नीत्वा कालमपानवह्निसहितं शक्त्या समं चालितम्।
आत्ममध्यानयुतस्त्वनेन विधिना विन्यस्य मूर्ध्नि स्थिरं
यावत्तिष्ठति तावदेव महतां सङ्गो न संस्तूयते ॥

108. प्राणायामो भवेदेवं पातकेन्धनपावकः।
भवोदधिमहासेतुः प्रोच्यते योगिभिः सदा ॥

109. आसनने रुजं हन्ति प्राणायामेन पातकम्।
विकारं मानसं योगी प्रत्याहारेण मुञ्चति ॥

110. धारणाभिर्मनोधैर्यं याति चैतन्यमद्भुतम्।
समाधौ मोक्षमाप्नोति त्यक्त्वा कर्म शुभाशुभम् ॥

111. प्राणायामद्विषट्केन प्रत्याहारः प्रकीर्तितः।
प्रत्याहारद्विषट्केन जायते धारणा शुभा ॥

112. धारणा द्वादश प्रोक्तं ध्यानं योगविशारदैः।
ध्यानद्वादशकेनैव समाधिरभिधीयते ॥

113. समाधौ परमं ज्योतिरनन्तं विश्वतोमुखम्।
तस्मिन्दृष्टे क्रियाकर्म यातायातो न विद्यते ॥

114. संबद्ध्वाऽऽसनमेढ्रमङ्घ्रियुगलं कर्णाक्षिनासापुट-
द्वारानङ्गुलिभिर्नियम्य पवनं वक्त्रेण वा पूरितम्।
बद्ध्वा वक्षसि बह्रपानसहितं मूर्ध्नि स्थितं धारये
देवं याति विशेषतत्त्वसमतां योगीश्वरस्तन्मनाः ॥

115. गगनं पवने प्राप्ते ध्वनिरुत्पद्यते महान्।
घण्टाऽऽदीनां प्रवाद्यानां नादसिद्धिरुदीरिता ॥

116. प्राणायामेन युक्तेन सर्वरोगक्षयो भवेत्।
प्राणायामवियुक्तैभ्यः सर्वरोगसमुद्भवः ॥

117. हिक्का कासस्तथा श्वासः शिरःकर्णाक्षिवेदना।
भवन्ति विविधा रोगाः पवनव्यत्ययक्रमात् ॥

118. यथा सिंहो गजो व्याघ्रो भवेद्वश्यः शनैः शनैः।
तथैव सेवितो वायुरन्यथा हन्ति साधकम् ॥

119. युक्तं युक्तं त्यजेद्वायुं युक्तं युक्तं प्रपूरयेत्।
युक्तं युक्तं प्रबध्नीयादेवं सिद्धिमवाप्नुयात् ॥

120. चरतां चक्षुरादीनां विषयेषु यथाक्रमम्।
तत्प्रत्याहरणं तेषां प्रत्याहारः स उच्यते ॥

121. यथा तृतीयकाले तु रविः प्रत्याहरेत्प्रभाम्।
तृतीयाङ्गस्थितो योगी विकारं मानसं हरेत् ॥

इत्युपनिषत् ॥

Translation

Crown Jewel of Yoga

1. For the benefit of yogis, I give out the crown jewel of yoga. It is a secret (doctrine) which gives the power of emancipation and is worthy of practice by those who are well-versed in yoga.

2. Asana, pranayama, pratyahara, dharana, dhyana and samadhi are the six limbs of yoga.

3. The best asana is siddhasana (the adept's pose). The next is kamalasana (padmasana or the lotus pose).

4a. How can one attain perfection if one does not know the six psychic centres, the sixteen supports, the three aims and the five akashas within one's own body?

4b, 5, 6a. It has been said (of the six psychic centres), mooladhara, the base centre, has four petals. Swadhisthana, the centre of one's own self, has six petals. Manipura, the navel centre, has ten petals. Anahata, the heart centre, has twelve petals. Vishuddhi, the purification centre, has sixteen petals, and bhrumadhya, the eyebrow centre, has two petals. On the sublime path of Brahmarandhra (opening at the fontanel) is the thousand-petalled lotus (sahasrara chakra).

6b, 7, 8. First (in sequence) is the adhara (mooladhara) chakra and the second is swadhisthana. Between the two (mooladhara and swadhisthana) is the seat of the yoni called kamaroopa. The four-petalled lotus in the anal region is known by the name of Kama. In the centre of the lotus is the kamayoni, which is worshipped by siddhas. In the centre of this yoni, the westward facing mahalinga is situated.

9, 10. In the navel is the reflecting jewel-like (manipura). One who knows this is the real knower of yoga. This (centre) is lustrous like heated gold and iridescent like a streak of lightning. Therein is the triangle, the seat of fire, below which is the medhra. By meditating in samadhi (on this region) (the yogi) sees the all-pervading light which is eternal.

11, 12. By realizing that in the highest state of yoga, (no trace of) coming and going (the cycle of birth and death) remains. By the self (manifest) word the prana (life force) is generated and established in swadhisthana. Because of its location swadhisthana is also known as medhra. That point, which is the root of sushumna, is like gems strung together.

13, 14a. In the navel region is the centre known as manipura, which has twelve petals. As long as the individual does not realize the element of this great chakra, which is beyond virtue and vice (duality), he has to go through the cycles of birth and death.

14b, 15. From the medhra, (located) above the base of the womb and below the navel, which is the origin point of the nadis, and is shaped like an egg, seventy-two thousand energy channels emanate. From amongst these thousands of channels, seventy-two are considered to be principle.

16, 17. Again, among these (seventy-two), the principle nadis for the flow of prana are ten. These are known as: ida, pingala and the third sushumna, gandhari, hastijihva,

300

pusha, yashaswini, alambusa, kuhu and the tenth shankhini. So, they have been said.

18, 19, 20. The yogis should always be aware of this great nadi complex. Ida is on the left side and pingala on the right. Sushumna is in middle. Gandhari goes to the left eye and hastijihva to the right eye. Pusha goes to the right ear and Yashaswini to the left ear. Alambusa goes to the face region. Kuhu goes to genitals and Shankhini to the perineum.

21, 22a. Thus these nadis are dependent and located systematically in the (various) passages of the body. Ida, pingala and sushumna are the paths of prana located in soma (moon), surya (sun) and agni (fire) devatas (illumined divinities) which continue to move the prana.

22b, 23a. The vital airs are: prana, apana, samana, vyana, udana, and naga, kurma, krikara, devadatta, and dhananjaya.

23b, 24. Prana is located in the heart and apana is always in the lower regions. Samana is located in the navel region and udana in the throat region. Vyana moves in the entire body. These are the five principle vital airs.

25, 26. The energy which brings up as in belching, vomiting or spitting is named naga. That which controls the flickering of the eyelids is koorma. That which causes sneezing should be known as krikara, and yawning as devadatta. The all-pervading dhananjaya does not leave the body (immediately) even after death. All these (upa-pranas) move through the nadis in all the living beings.

27. Just as a ball goes up and down when thrown by hand, similarly, the individual soul is thrown up (and down) in the same way by the movement of prana and apana (and therefore) does not remain still.

28. Influenced by prana and apana, the individual soul ascends and descends. It also moves through the left and right passages, but cannot be perceived because of its rapid movement.

29. Just as a falcon tied by the string flies up and is drawn back down, similarly, the jiva, bound by the gunas, is attracted by prana and apana.

30, 31a. So the jiva, influenced by prana and apana, ascends and descends, for prana draws apana up and apana draws prana down. One who knows the significance of the ascending and descending of jiva is the knower of yoga.

31b, 32, 33. With the sound *Ha* (the breath) goes out and with the sound *Sa* it comes in again, making the sound *Hamsa, Hamsa.* Thus the individual soul continuously repeats the mantra. Day and night this mantra is being repeated twenty one thousand six hundred times. When the jiva ceaselessly continues to repeat this number of mantras, it is called the ajapa gayatri, which always brings liberation to the yogis.

34, 35. Such knowledge as this, such japa as this, removes all sins only by its awareness. Knowledge of this existed neither in the past nor will it be in the future. This (ajapa) gayatri, born of kundalini, is the sustainer of prana.

36. Knowledge of prana is the great knowledge. One who knows this knows the reality. Above the root is the kundalini shakti, a serpent of eight coils.

37. (The kundalini) lies eternally with its mouth closing the passage to the door of Brahman (all pervading consciousness). (By going) through that passage, one is freed from suffering when the door of Brahman is reached.

38. Parameshwari (kundalini) is at rest, closing that doorway with her mouth. She can be awakened (through) the mind along with the prana by the fire of yoga.

39. (When awakened) she goes straight up through sushumna passage, having a body like a needle. Just as a key opens the closed door of a house, similarly, the yogi opens the doors of liberation through (the awakening of) kundalini.

40. Sit in padmasana, crossing (the legs) with the hands pressed very firmly together (with the knees). Press the chin firmly against the chest and meditate on That (Brahman). Again and again breathe in and out, and raise the apana force to the region of prana, filling it fully. In this way, with the help of Shakti the practitioner acquires infinite knowledge.

41. Perspiration produced by the exertion of this practice should be rubbed into the body. Renounce pungent, sour and salty (foods). Milk based diet should be taken in proper and reasonable quantity.

42. The yogi who practises sexual abstinence, moderation in diet, and is a regular practitioner of yoga, should become an adept within one year. One need not have any doubt about it.

43. The diet (of a sadhaka) should be soft and sweet. One quarter of the stomach should remain empty. He who takes food (in this way) while remembering the name of Shiva is said to be mitahari.

44. The kundalini shakti lies above the kanda in eight coils. For the ignorant it is the form of bondage, but for the yogis it always grants liberation.

45. The yogi, who knows maha mudra, nabho mudra, and uddiyana, jalandhara and moola bandhas, is fit to attain liberation.

46. The heel should be pressing firmly against the genital region with pressure. One should contract (the perineum and) draw the apana vayu upward, which is known as moola bandha.

47. Apana (fuses) with prana, thus the urine and excreta become less. With regular practice of moola bandha, even an old man becomes young.

48, 49. Just as a great bird takes to flight after a long rest, similarly uddiyana is to be practised. Uddiyana is like a lion challenging the elephant of death. Drawing the abdomen below the navel towards the back is called paschimottana. Uddiyana is also practised by binding this region of the abdomen. Therefore, because of the binding or contracting it is called uddiyana bandha.

50, 51. That (is said to be) jalandhara bandha, which binds or prevents the water of the sky produced in the head from falling down (and which) destroys all troubles of the throat. By doing the practice of jalandhara bandha, along with the destruction of throat problems, the nectar does not fall into the fire, nor does the breath move in and out.

52. When the tongue is folded back and entered into the cavity of the head, and the sight is fixed in-between the eyebrows, that is khechari mudra.

53, 54, 55. Disease, death, and sleep do not trouble him who knows khechari mudra, nor hunger and thirst, nor swoon. One who knows khechari mudra does not suffer from disease, nor is he attached to karmas, nor bound by

304

anybody or anything. All the siddhas pay homage to khechari mudra by which one is able to rotate the consciousness in the cosmic space by moving the tongue into the cavity of the head.

56. The bindu is viewed as the original cause of the whole body. It is situated in the nerves and blood vessels and sustains the entire physical structure from the toes to the head.

57, 58. One who closes the cavity of the palate from above with khechari will not lose the bindu even in the embrace of a woman. As long as bindu is retained in the body, from where arises the fear of death? Bindu is not wasted as long as it is bound by nabho mudra.

59. If bindu falls down and merges in the fire (of manipura), even while burning, after being prevented (from dissipating further), it can be raised upward by the practice of yoni mudra because of its power.

60. That bindu is again divided into two types, paandara (white) and lohita (red). The white is called shukla and the red is called maharaja.

61. The red bindu, which is like a heap of vermilion, is situated in the place of the sun and the white bindu is situated in the place of the moon. The merger of both (bindus) is difficult.

62. The (shukla) bindu is Brahma and rajas is Shakti. Bindu is the moon and rajas is the sun. By uniting the two, the highest state is attained.

63. When rajas is moved by the force of vayu, it attains union with bindu, then the body becomes divine for all time to come.

64. Rajas is united with the sun and shukla with the moon. The one who knows the full merger of both, he is the knower of yoga.

65. The method taught for purification of the entire nadi structure governing the movement of the moon and the sun and absorption of the vital fluid is maha mudra.

66, 67. Press the chin into the throat cavity. Press the perineum firmly with the left foot for a long duration. Stretch the right leg in front on the ground and hold the (right) toes with both hands. Draw in the breath, filling up both parts of the abdomen completely. After holding the breath, it should be slowly exhaled. This mudra is very important for men and it is the destroyer of all diseases. Practise well through the moon and again through the sun. When the number of rounds becomes equal, then the mudra should be released.

68. By the power of this mudra, wholesome or unwholesome foods are digested and all tasteless things also become tasteful. Overeating does no harm and even poison is digested like nectar.

69. Tuberculosis, leprosy, fistula, indigestion and tumour are cured, and all possible future ailments prevented for those who practise maha mudra.

70. This maha mudra, which was mentioned earlier, is the bestower of great powers for men. It should be kept secret, with care, and not taught to anyone.

71. Sitting properly in padmasana, with the head and body straight, fix the attention firmly at the tip of the nose and continuously repeat the Aum mantra in a solitary place.

72. Vishva, the ruler of the conscious state, is always the enjoyer of the gross dimension also. Tejasa, the ruler of

the subconscious, enjoys the subtle dimension. And Prajna, the ruler of the unconscious, enjoys the blissful dimension. Sarvasakshi is the witness of all these and beyond them as well.

73. The Pranava resides in all living beings ever enjoying. It resides in all states also with the mouth downward, enjoying the world.

74. The 'A' letter corresponds to the waking state and is located in the eyes. The 'U' letter corresponds to the dream state and is located at the throat. The 'M' letter corresponds to the deep sleep state and is located in the heart.

75, 76a. The 'A' sound form, which is rajasic and red, has been called the consciousness of Brahma. Similarly, the 'U' sound form, which is sattwic and white, is called Vishnu. Like this, it has been said that the 'M' sound form, which is tamasic and black, is called Rudra.

76b, 77. From the Pranava emanate Brahma, Vishnu and Rudra. That Pranava originates from the supreme reality. Brahma merges in the 'A' sound form, Vishnu merges in the 'U' sound form.

78. Rudra merges in the 'M' sound. Then only the Pranava continues to illumine. In the realized ones (this Pranava) faces upward, (whereas) in the ignorant it faces downward.

79. Thus resides the Pranava. One who knows this is certainly realized or knowledgeable. In its anahata form (the Pranava) becomes an ascending (path) for the wise.

80. The Pranava flows like oil, constant and unbroken, like the sound of a very big bell. Thus its front portion is called Brahma.

81. That front portion is luminous and beyond speech. The wise can visualize this by subtle intelligence. He who knows that is the real knower.

82, 83. In the waking state Hamsa shines at the eyebrow centre. Of these (two syllables), the 'Sa' has been called khechari, and is certainly indicative of 'Twam'. The letter 'Ha' is of the form of the Supreme Lord, and is certainly indicative of 'Tat' (That). The person who contemplates on 'Sa', i.e. 'Twam', surely becomes identified with the 'Ha' letter, i.e. 'Tat'.

84. The individual soul is bound by the senses, but the pure soul is never so bound. The individual soul is born of attachment and self-realization is attained by freedom from attachment.

85. All the planes, Earth, Intermediate and Heaven, and all the deities, Sun, Moon and Fire, are established in the (three) letters, of that supreme light which is Aum.

86. Ichcha, the power of willing, Kriya, the power of action, and Jnana, the power of knowledge, as well as Brahmi, the power of creation, Vaishnavi, the power of maintenance, and Raudri, the power of destruction, are established in that supreme light which is Aum.

87. That supreme light is Aum. One should always repeat that verbally, should practise that regularly within the body, and should repeat that mentally.

88. Whether pure or impure, one who always repeats the Pranava remains untouched by sin, just as the lotus leaf (remains untouched) by water.

89. When the prana moves, the bindu also moves. When the prana remains steady, then the bindu is also steady. Thus

the yogi becomes steadfast and firm. Therefore, the prana should be controlled.

90. As long as the prana is retained in the body, the individual soul does not leave. The departure of that (force) is death. Therefore, the prana should be controlled.

91. As long as the prana is tied down in the body, the individual soul does not leave it. As long as the vision is fixed on the eyebrow centre, from where is the fear of death?

92. Even Brahma, fearing a short life span, became a practitioner of pranayama. Therefore, yogis and munis should also control the prana.

93. Hamsa (the exhaled breath) goes out for twenty-six anguls or finger-widths. Pranayama is to be practised through the left and right paths.

94. When all the nadis and chakras become free from accumulation of impurities, then only the yogi becomes capable of controlling the breath.

95. (Sitting) in baddhapadmasana, the yogi should inhale the breath through the left nostril, retain it for as long as possible, and exhale again through the right nostril.

96. At the time of pranayama one should meditate on the luminous disc of the moon, which is like the ocean of nectar and white like the milk of cows.

97. At the time of pranayama, the yogi should meditate in the heart on the prescribed zone of the Sun, which is blazing brightly. Having established this state, he should be happy.

98. The breath should be drawn in through the left nostril, retained and taken out through the right. Again, the

breath should be drawn in through the right and retained, then taken out through the left. By practising this method regularly, one gains control over both points of sun and moon, and the energy channels become purified within two months.

99. With full retention of the breath, there is activation of the fire and inner sound is heard. Good health is gained by purification of the nadis.

100. As long as prana remains in the body, apana should be retained, so that the quantity drawn in one breath remains and moves up and down in hridayakasha.

101, 102. The inhalation, retention and exhalation are the Pranava itself. Pranayama should be practised like this for a number of twelve rounds. Twelve rounds through the ida and pingala nadis unfastens the net of impurities. The yogis should know this always.

103. The inhalation should be practised to the count of twelve, retention to the count of sixteen and exhalation to the count of ten. This is called the Omkara pranayama.

104. About pranayama it has been said that the lowest level is twelve counts, the middle level is double that or twenty-four counts, and the highest level is triple or thirty-six counts.

105. The lowest level causes perspiration. The middle level results in trembling of the body. At the highest level stability is achieved. Therefore, the breath should be retained.

106. Retiring to a solitary place, the yogi should sit in baddhapadmasana, with the gaze fixed on the nose tip. Paying homage to the Guru, who is Shiva, he should practise pranayama properly.

107. Closing the nine gates properly and retaining the breath, intensify the concentration. Performing shaktichalini mudra correctly, take the divine element, kundalini, along with apana vayu and fire (samana vayu) to the (crown of the) head. By this method become absorbed in meditation on the Self. When steadiness and stillness (are achieved), only then he does not praise the company of the great ones.

108. In this way, pranayama becomes fire for the fuel of sin, and has always been regarded by the yogis as a great bridge for crossing the ocean of the world.

109. Diseases are destroyed by asana and sins by pranayama. By pratyahara, the yogi removes the impurities of the mind.

110. By concentration, steadiness of mind is acquired. In samadhi a wonderful state of consciousness (unfolds). The auspicious and inauspicious actions are given up and liberation is achieved.

111, 112. People who are well-versed in yoga have said that by twelve pranayamas, pratyahara results. Twelve pratyaharas result in the auspicious state of dharana. By twelve dharanas, dhyana results and by twelve dhyanas, samadhi is attained.

113. In samadhi, (there is) supreme, infinite illumination in all directions. Having seen this, neither karmas nor birth and death remain.

114. Sit in sambaddhvasana, with both feet pressing the medhra. Close the gates of the ears, eyes and nasal passages with the fingers. Drawing the breath in through the mouth, retain it in the region of the chest, along with the apana vayu. Then raise (the vital air) up to the head

and fix it there. Like this, the yogi gains the supreme element and experiences God in his mind.

115. When the prana rises into the sky, inner sounds of musical instruments are produced, like the bell and so on, and the perfection of inner sound is achieved.

116. By the practice of pranayama, all diseases are removed. By not practising pranayama, all diseases arise.

117. Various types of diseases like hiccups, bronchitis, asthma and afflictions of the head, ear and eye accrue when pranayama is not practised.

118. Just as the lion, elephant and tiger are brought under control slowly and steadily, similarly the prana should be controlled, otherwise it becomes destructive to the practitioner.

119. The breath should be inhaled slowly with awareness. The breath should be retained properly with awareness. The breath should be exhaled slowly and carefully. Thus perfection is attained.

120. Withdrawal of the senses, such as the eyes and so on, in a systematic way, from involvement with the sensory objects, that is called pratyahara.

121. Just as the sun begins to withdraw its heat and light in the third quarter of the day, the yogic adept, established in the third limb, should remove the impurities of the mind.

Thus ends the Upanishad.

Bibliography

Aiyar, N.K., *Thirty Minor Upanishads*, Akay Book Corp., New Delhi, 1887

Dasgupta, S.N., *History of Indian Philosophy*, Motilal Banarsidass, Delhi, 1990

Desai, S.G., *A Critical Study of the Later Upanisads*, Bharatiya Vidya Bhavan, Mumbai, 1996

Deussen, P., *The Philosophy of the Upanishads*, Munshiram Manoharlal, Delhi, 1979

Feurerstein, G., *Tantra: the Path of Ecstasy*, Shambala Publications, USA, 1998

Feurerstein, G., *Textbook of Yoga*, Rider and Co. London, 1975

Gherand Samhita, Kaivalyadham, SMYM Samiti, Lonavala, 1978

Johari, H., *Chakra*, Inner Traditions, Vermont, USA, 1992

Sastri, A.M., *The Yoga Upanisads*, Adyar Library and Research Centre; Madras, 1983

Brahmananda, Swami, *The Supreme Knowledge Revealed through Vidyas in the Upanishads,* Divine Life Society, Rishikesh, 1990

Saraswati, Swami Chidananda, *Philosophy and Practice of Yoga*, Divine Life Society, Rishikesh, 1991

Saraswati, Swami Muktibodhananda, *Hatha Yoga Pradipika: Light on Hatha Yoga,* Yoga Publications Trust, 2000

Saraswati, Swami Niranjanananda, *Dharana Darshan: Panoramic View of the Yogic, Tantric and Upanishadic Practices of Concentration and Visualization,* 2nd edn, Bihar Yoga Bharati, Munger, 1999

Saraswati, Swami Niranjanananda, *Prana Pranayama Prana Vidya,* Bihar School of Yoga, Munger, 1998

Saraswati, Swami Niranjanananda, *Yoga Darshan: Vision of the Yoga Upanishads,* Sri Panchdashnam Paramahamsa Alakhbara, Deoghar, 1994

Saraswati, Swami Satyananda, *A Systematic Course in the Ancient Tantric Techniques of Yoga and Kriya,* Bihar School of Yoga, Munger, 1981

Saraswati, Swami Satyananda, *Asana Pranayama Mudra Bandha,* Bihar School of Yoga, Munger, 1998

Saraswati, Swami Satyananda, *Kundalini Tantra,* Yoga Publications Trust, 1999

Saraswati, Swami Sivananda, *Kundalini Yoga,* Divine Life Society, Rishikesh, 1994

ABOUT THE AUTHOR

Swami Satyadharma

- Born in Danbury, Connecticut, USA., on 26th June 1946.
- From 1965–1975 she travelled extensively throughout the world in search of her spiritual path.
- In 1975 she was initiated into Poorna Sannyasa by Swami Satyananda and remained in India as a sannyasin disciple under his guidance.
- From 1976–1994 she compiled and edited *Yoga* magazine, and many major yoga publications such as the *Teachings of Swami Satyananda Vols. 1–5, Early Teachings of Swami Satyananda, Yoga Darshan, Sannyasa Darshan* and *Dharana Darshan.*
- From 1995 she has directed the Department of Undergraduate Studies at Bihar Yoga Bharati, and is a member of the Yoga Education Council at BYB.
- She is based in Munger and currently travels around the world, conducting lectures and seminars, and assisting in the development of Satyananda Yoga worldwide.

INTERNATIONAL YOGA FELLOWSHIP MOVEMENT (IYFM)

The IYFM is a charitable and philosophical movement founded by Swami Satyananda at Rajnandgaon in 1956 to disseminate the yogic tradition throughout the world. It forms the medium to convey the teachings of Swami Satyananda through its affiliated centres around the world. Swami Niranjanananda is the first Paramacharya of the International Yoga Fellowship Movement.

The IYFM provides guidance, systematized yoga training programs and sets teaching standards for all the affiliated yoga teachers, centres and ashrams. A Yoga Charter to consolidate and unify the humanitarian efforts of all sannyasin disciples, yoga teachers, spiritual seekers and well-wishers was introduced during the World Yoga Convention in 1993. Affiliation to this Yoga Charter enables the person to become a messenger of goodwill and peace in the world, through active involvement in various far-reaching yoga-related projects.

BIHAR SCHOOL OF YOGA (BSY)

The Bihar School of Yoga is a charitable and educational institution founded by Swami Satyananda at Munger in 1963, with the aim of imparting yogic training to all nationalities and to provide a focal point for a mass return to the ancient science of yoga. The Chief Patron of Bihar School of Yoga is Swami Niranjanananda. The original school, Sivanandashram, is the centre for the Munger locality. Ganga Darshan, the new school established in 1981, is situated on a historic hill with panoramic views of the river Ganges.

Yoga Health Management, Teacher Training, Sadhana, Kriya Yoga and other specialized courses are held throughout the year. BSY is also renowned for its sannyasa training and the initiation of female and foreign sannyasins.

BSY provides trained sannyasins and teachers for conducting yoga conventions, seminars and lectures tours around the world. It also contains a comprehensive research library and scientific research centre.

SIVANANDA MATH (SM)

Sivananda Math is a social and charitable institution founded by Swami Satyananda at Munger in 1984, in memory of his guru, Swami Sivananda Saraswati of Rishikesh. The Head Office is now situated at Rikhia in Deoghar district, Bihar. Swami Niranjanananda is the Chief Patron.

Sivananda Math aims to facilitate the growth of the weaker and underprivileged sections of society, especially rural communities. Its activities include: distribution of free scholarships, clothing, farm animals and food, the digging of tube-wells and construction of houses for the needy, assistance to farmers in ploughing and watering their fields. The Rikhia complex also houses a satellite dish system for providing global information to the villagers.

A medical clinic has been established for the provision of medical treatment, advice and education. Veterinary services are also provided. All services are provided free and universally to everyone, regardless of caste and creed.

YOGA RESEARCH FOUNDATION (YRF)

The Yoga Research Foundation is a scientific, research-oriented institution founded by Swami Satyananda at Munger in 1984. Swami Niranjanananda is the Chief Patron of the foundation.

YRF aims to provide an accurate assessment of the practices of different branches of yoga within a scientific framework, and to establish yoga as an essential science for the development of mankind. At present the foundation is working on projects in the areas of fundamental research and clinical research. It is also studying the effects of yoga on proficiency improvement in various social projects, e.g. army, prisoners, children. These projects are being carried out in affiliated centres worldwide.

YRF's future plans include literary, scriptural, medical and scientific investigations into other little-known aspects of yoga for physical health, mental well-being and spiritual upliftment.

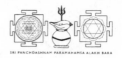

SRI PANCHDASHNAM PARAMAHAMSA ALAKH BARA (PPAB)

Sri Panchdashnam Paramahamsa Alakh Bara was established in 1990 by Swami Satyananda at Rikhia, Deoghar, Bihar. It is a charitable, educational and non-profit making institution aiming to uphold and propagate the highest tradition of sannyasa, namely vairagya (dispassion), tyaga (renunciation) and tapasya (austerity). It propounds the tapovan style of living adopted by the rishis and munis of the vedic era and is intended only for sannyasins, renunciates, ascetics, tapasvis and paramahamsas. The Alakh Bara does not conduct any activities such as yoga teaching or preaching of any religion or religious concepts. The guidelines set down for the Alakh Bara are based on the classical vedic tradition of sadhana, tapasya and swadhyaya, or atma chintan.

Swami Satyananda, who resides permanently at the Alakh Bara, has performed the Panchagni Vidya and other vedic sadhanas, thus paving the way for future paramahamsas to uphold their tradition.

BIHAR YOGA BHARATI (BYB)

Bihar Yoga Bharati was founded by Swami Niranjanananda in 1994 as an educational and charitable institution for advanced studies in yogic sciences. It is the culmination of the vision of Swami Sivananda and Swami Satyananda. BYB is the world's first government accredited university wholly devoted to teaching yoga. A comprehensive yogic education is imparted with provision to grant higher degrees in yogic studies such as MA, MSc, MPhil, DLitt, and PhD to the students. It offers a complete scientific and yogic education according to the needs of today, through the faculties of Yoga Philosophy, Yoga Psychology, Applied Yogic Science and Yogic Ecology.

Residential courses of four months to two years are conducted in a gurukul environment, so that along with yoga education, the spirit of seva (selfless service), samarpan (dedication) and karuna (compassion) for humankind is also imbibed by the students.

YOGA PUBLICATIONS TRUST (YPT)

Yoga Publications Trust (YPT) was established by Swami Niranjan-ananda in 2000. It is an organization devoted to the dissemination and promotion of yogic and allied knowledge – psychology (ancient and modern), ecology, medicine, vedic, upanishadic, tantric darshanas, philosophies (Eastern and Western), mysticism and spirituality – nationally and internationally through the distribution of books, magazines, audio and video cassettes and multimedia.

YPT is primarily concerned with publishing textbooks in the areas of yoga philosophy, psychology and applied yogic science, research materials, practice texts and the inspiring talks of eminent spiritual personalities and authors aimed at the upliftment of humanity by means of the eternal yogic knowledge, lifestyle and practice.